Music *by*
Laxmikant Pyarelal

Music *by*
Laxmikant Pyarelal

The Incredibly Melodious Journey

RAJIV VIJAYAKAR

RUPA

First published by
Rupa Publications India Pvt. Ltd 2021
7/16, Ansari Road, Daryaganj
New Delhi 110002

Sales Centres:

Allahabad Bengaluru Chennai
Hyderabad Jaipur Kathmandu
Kolkata Mumbai

Copyright © Rajiv Vijayakar 2021

The views and opinions expressed in this book are the author's own and the facts are as reported by him which have been verified to the extent possible, and the publishers are not in any way liable for the same.

All rights reserved.
No part of this publication may be reproduced, transmitted, or stored in a retrieval system, in any form or by any means, electronic, mechanical, photocopying, recording or otherwise, without the prior permission of the publisher.

ISBN: 978-93-5520-136-2

Second impression 2022

10 9 8 7 6 5 4 3 2

The moral right of the author has been asserted.

Printed by Parksons Graphics Pvt. Ltd.

This book is sold subject to the condition that it shall not, by way of trade or otherwise, be lent, resold, hired out, or otherwise circulated, without the publisher's prior consent, in any form of binding or cover other than that in which it is published.

*For Shree Khandoba, Shree Jogeshwari Mata,
Shree Shirdi Sai Baba, Shree Saraswati Mata
and my Guru,
Shree Dada Bhagwat*

TO MY FAMILY

*Nishika, Dr Neha, Rhea, Dr Dhirajkumar Khodke,
Neehar Vijayakar,
Ananya and Nitya Khodke*

CONTENTS

Introduction   ix

I
An Epic Saga Begins

1. Growing Up with Music   3
2. The Trials and Tribulations   12
3. Fast and Steady Wins the Race   19
4. Ascent to Big Time   27
5. The Superlative Deluge   34
6. Top Guns at Last   42
7. The Secret of a Spectacular Victory   48
8. The Historic Sweep Continues   55
9. The 1980s: The Decadent Decade   66
10. 1990–2004: When 'Packaging' Overruled 'Content'   75
11. A Hit... and Some Misses   81

II
The Rhythm of Laxmikant-Pyarelal

12. Knowing the Man behind the Music: Laxmikant   91
13. Knowing the Man behind the Music: Pyarelal   100
14. The Secret Sauce and the Camaraderie   104
15. Another Long-Lasting Relationship: Anand Bakshi   121
16. The Last Call...   125

III
Memories and Impressions

17. Their Singers		129
18. Their Lyricists		173
19. Their Stars		178
20. Their Filmmakers		187
21. Their Musicians		208
22. Their Recording Engineers		222
23. Family Priest, Friend, Financial Advisor—and Fan		224
24. Laxmikant-Pyarelal: Universal L-ong P-lay		227

Epilogue   247

Appendices   255

Bibliography   310

Acknowledgements   311

INTRODUCTION

To me, for a multitude of reasons, they will always remain *the* music directors. For the film industry and for millions of fans, Laxmikant Shantaram Kudalkar and Pyarelal Ramprasad Sharma will also be the most complete composers showbiz has seen, and perhaps will ever see. They were a heady combination of unique synergy and unmatched individual brilliance.

As a child, it was their music which resonated best amidst the songs from the plethora of legends that existed then. Today, when I look back, I realize that Laxmikant-Pyarelal were doing so many films and were delivering outstanding music, even though the quantum of songs was much larger than what their seniors were composing.

I was to realize only much later that the quantity, as conventionally believed, did not affect quality in their case. The reason for this will be clear before this book ends.

Sant Gyaneshwar, Harishchandra Taramati, Dosti, Mr X in Bombay, Pyar Kiye Jaa, Aaye Din Bahaar Ke, Aasra, Anita, Milan, Farz—these were the first L-P (as the duo is known) films I was exposed to on radio. The songs were accorded rave remarks by my parents, friends and relatives, who, of course, were not particularly familiar with either L-P or any other film composers.

As a pre-teen, I was exposed to everything, from Radio Ceylon's *Binaca Geetmala* and Vividh Bharati's *Manchahe Geet*, to the records my father bought and everything we watched on our movie outings. My parents were hardcore film buffs and as the only child, I went with them to the movies. I was also an ardent reader of the film magazines that were brought home—*Screen, Star & Style, Filmfare* and *Picturpost*.

But it was the credit-titles of L-P's films that interested me. I would eagerly scan the complete credit titles, trying to compare the cast and music people of every film I watched. I knew that the music credits came just before those of the producer and director.

Here too, despite the musical splendour that was uniformly being served by all the other composers around, I realized that whenever the three words, 'Music: Laxmikant-Pyarelal' came on, the songs would usually turn out to be 'nicer' (that's how we think as kids, simply and sans any hype) than the others.

Yes, to me the 1960s are, even now, the most hypnotic era of Hindi film music, the golden times when S.D. Burman, Roshan, C. Ramachandra, Naushad, O.P. Nayyar, Ravi, Chitragupta, Hemant Kumar, Salil Chowdhury, Madan Mohan and Usha Khanna were simultaneously going great guns, with Shankar-Jaikishan effortlessly settled at the top spot.

Two young entities, Kalyanji-Anandji and R.D. Burman, both a shade senior to Laxmikant-Pyarelal, had blazed in with their early successes, but the L-P duo was something special. The L-P wave was a clean sweep; rich, immensely variegated, utterly unshakeable and unbeatable. Their music had that unique spark that ignited some music-combustible flame within me, and I was just one in an ocean of film music lovers of all ages who felt the same way.

Powered by its all-pervasive appeal and range, the L-P juggernaut thundered on, thrusting aside all the great competition as if it were incidental. Post-1949, Shankar-Jaikishan (S-J) had overtaken all competition to remain solidly at the top after a passing threat by O.P. Nayyar, but now, their bastion began to crumble under the L-P avalanche.

L-P were to do the same with competing contemporaries for a long while after they 'officially' took on the top spot in 1969. A combination of chartbusters, hit films and prestigious assignments on hand made this unequivocally clear. It happened after a cavalcade of hit scores in films, big and small, across all kinds of genres and scales, where the music became a hit, even when a film nosedived at the box-office. The sheer number of big banners they signed and the status of the biggest filmmaking names that shifted to L-P reaffirmed this. The trade too declared them as the topmost composers.

In the 1970s came the R.D. Burman wave, beginning with *The Train*, a film that L-P had turned down since they already had 10 films on hand, which they thought were too many. A solid musical 'fight' was put up, and after *Daag* and *Bobby* in 1973, no one doubted that L-P had won it. A decade and more later came the Bappi Lahiri boom, but L-P seemed to contemptuously toss it aside.

During these decades, paradigm shifts had happened by way of the younger generation and newer technology. Most filmmakers and even lyricists and singers had been replaced by younger names.

In this profession, most people have to retire or organically stop getting work due to changing trends and content, but through the changing kaleidoscope, L-P strode on, unaffected. When they had opened their 'score' in 1963, a completely different army of associates (filmmakers, stars, lyricists, singers) had been ruling. When they shut shop, some of the names at the top in all these fields were those who had been just born when L-P had begun their magical and extraordinarily long innings!

I was observer to all these major professional battles—L-P's victory over S-J with all the films mentioned earlier, as well as with *Mere Lal, Jaal, Baharon Ki Manzil, Night in London, Wapas, Mere Hamdam Mere Dost, Aaya Sawan Jhoom Ke, Raja Aur Runk, Izzat, Intaqam, Aansoo Ban Gaye Phool, Patthar Ke Sanam* and more in rapid succession.

I also witnessed how L-P withstood the formidable avalanche of R.D. Burman chartbusters, charging ahead with timeless scores such as *Jeevan Mrityu, Sharafat, Humjoli, Khilona, Abhinetri, Jal Bin Machhli Nritya Bin Bijli, Aan Milo Sajna, Mehboob Ki Mehndi,*

Haathi Mere Saathi, Mera Gaon Mera Desh, Uphaar, Dushmun, Piya Ka Ghar, Shor, Raja Jani and more.

By the time we came into 1973–74, not even R.D. Burman's *Namak Haram, Aap Ki Kasam* and *Yaadon Ki Baraat* (his aces in this phase) could withstand the supremacy of *Daag, Bobby, Roti, Amir Garib, Imtihan* and *Roti Kapada Aur Makaan*. The Bappi Lahiri onslaught, in comparison, barely mattered. L-P's *Coolie, Hero, Pyar Jhukta Nahin, Meri Jung* and *Utsav* were enough to overrule it when it came in as a minor turbulence in 1983.

I saw how L-P never jettisoned Mohammed Rafi in the Kishore Kumar wave and yet did far more justice to Kishore's versatility than anyone else. In that crucial phase between Kishore's rapid ascent in 1970 to the time L-P were responsible for Rafi's supposed 'comeback' with Manmohan Desai's *Dharam-Veer, Amar Akbar Anthony* and *Chacha Bhatija,* along with Nasir Husain's *Hum Kisise Kum Naheen* with R.D. Burman, the duo doled out some of their finest-ever songs with both singers!

When the time came for me to finally meet the duo as a journalist, it was the early '90s and they were still market-leaders, although Nadeem-Sharavan and Anand-Milind had made it big at the expense of L-P contemporaries Kalyanji-Anandji and R.D. Burman, and juniors Rajesh Roshan and Bappi Lahiri. I had had experiences of multiple kinds—great, good, ho-hum and unpleasant—as a journalist with film celebs, and often wondered what kind of people my childhood idols, L-P, would be.

After all, as the late Manmohan Desai had stated in the '80s, they had even seen the times when they were 'numbers one to 10' and not merely Numero Unos. Enough reason indeed to have massively swollen heads! And in the 31 years that elapsed between 1963 and 1993, Laxmikant-Pyarelal had annexed a neat 250 songs out of 1,008 *Binaca Geetmala* toppers—an incredible score indeed, with the nearest second, Rahul Dev Burman, at 140. That left a little more than 600 songs divided among more than (at an estimate) two dozen other composers!

But the two of them came across as delights—absolutely lovely people sans ego or attitude. Friendly, down-to-earth extroverts (yes, Pyarelal too, contrary to popular perception), they sincerely appreciated my knowledge of their music in particular. Both of them shared a mischievous sense of humour that came up, sometimes at my expense, in the most unexpected moments.

My first interaction with Laxmikant was a memorable one. I had called him on his landline in 1990—mobiles were still some years away. His musician-cum-manager of sorts, whom I later came to know very well as Sudhir, told me he was busy with his sittings and would need about an hour to get free. I called after 90 minutes and Sudhir apologetically said, 'Laxmi-ji is still not free. Please leave your number.' I did so, knowing that in the industry, no one called back.

An hour later, my wife Nishika excitedly came to me and said, 'There's a call for you from Laxmikant!' The numero uno composer in Hindi films had actually returned my call, and when my wife asked who was speaking, had told her, 'I am Laxmikant.'

I told the maestro that I had called to ask his views on their favourite lyricist Asad Bhopali, who had just passed away and for whom I was writing a tribute. He called me the very next day to Mehboob Studios, where a recording for *Saudagar* was going on. In between rehearsals with his singers, Laxmikant gave me a clear and concise account of their association.

My first meeting on the same day with Pyarelal was unremarkable; he did not speak much. This was partly because he was busy at the recording console with recording engineer A.N. Tagore and because his partner, who interacted with the late lyricist more than him, had already spoken to me. But Pyarebhai, as I was to call him later like so many others, was cordial, polite and warm.

A year or so later, I was commissioned to write a *Junior G* featuring the duo. The sponsored supplement, a pocket-sized 32-

page booklet, was attached inside the prestigious and large-sized *G* magazine every month, and was a biography of a celebrity. Names like Ashok Kumar, Nutan and others had already been covered and this was to be the first *Junior G* on anyone behind the screen, as they usually focussed on stars. But Bhawana Somaaya, the editor, who had just returned from a two-month concert tour with the duo abroad, was highly impressed with them.

Once again, I called up Laxmikant's home and Sudhir asked me to come the same evening to the composer's bungalow—and a landmark in upscale Juhu—Parasmani, named after their first film. I sat in the waiting room, surrounded by people I recognized (along with a few unknown faces) but who did not know me then. Among them were Subhash Ghai, K.C. Bokadia and T. Rama Rao, all waiting their turn to be summoned inside for a 'music sitting' (where a song for them was readied).

When I was called out of turn, Sudhir had to assure the gaping filmmakers that I was a journalist and not a favoured director! I explained to Laxmikant what I was writing—a small book about their life and times. Laxmikant condensed their triumphant life journey in 10 minutes flat, which would not have been enough even for a 700-word article. In vain, I told him I needed many more details. And as L-P were so busy, he told Sudhir to give me a fresh appointment—a fortnight later.

That would never do, I thought! Deadlines were not indefinite! But I was saved by the tea he had ordered for me. Piping hot tea.

Laxmikant had courteously told me to drink my tea (which had not yet been served) before leaving. So I grabbed the opportunity to ask him about one of their many rare beauties in an early film, that was not very popular but was one of my favourite songs. A strange expression lit up his face, as if he was pleasantly surprised that I knew the song. He spoke about it and then the tea came.

I suddenly knew my way out. As the tea was very hot and I had to sip it, I employed the time in asking quickly about two more hit songs of those times that were barely available then. This was, thanks to the music company HMV's discriminatory marketing of old songs, which led to many gems from Indian composers being ignored or unavailable in the market. He answered my questions and by the time my tea was finished, he had called Sudhir again and asked him to give me an appointment within two days.

The composer then gave me Pyarelal's residential number and told me to call him the next morning. The reason was unknown to me then: he would later speak to Pyarelal and brief him that someone with a decent knowledge of their work was coming to meet him to write a small book about them! Surprisingly, over the few sittings I had with Pyarelal, he became more vocal and candid. So much so that a neat 25 per cent of whatever he told me then about their associates had to remain off-the-record—and that applies even now!

After some meetings, Pyarelal invited me to his twenty-fifth wedding anniversary party which was due in a few days and played me the new songs of Talat Aziz's *Dhun* on their fabulous music system. He also gifted me a music cassette of the film. Later, knowing that I had a decent collection of their songs, he requested me to record songs of my choice from their early films, which were not available on records or cassettes. Within a few days, I presented him with four TDK music cassettes of 90 minutes each—six hours of L-P music.

At Pyarelal's party, when I went to take Laxmikant's leave, the latter firmly told me that I had to come to his Silver Jubilee wedding party too, six days later. Yes, the two had even married six days apart!

As I kept interacting with them and got personal insights into their work as well, it became evident why L-P so easily became the L-ongest P-laying record in Hindi cinema, and vindicated my special love for them.

And so, it is now an honour to dole out overdue justice to these uncrowned monarchs of Hindi film music through this book. A lofty aim, but I hope and pray that I will be able to match up to and do justice to their colossal career filled with exceptional triumphs.

I
AN EPIC SAGA BEGINS

1

GROWING UP WITH MUSIC

No one could have foretold it then, but on Laxmi Poojan Day during Diwali of 1937 (2 November as per the Roman calendar), the Goddess decided to bestow exceptional wealth to the treasury of Hindi film music. A boy was born to Shantaram Kudalkar, a mill worker, in Mumbai. This lad was to fashion (with his partner) the course of film music and shape so many careers—of singers, lyricists, musicians, actors and filmmakers—across three generations. Because he was born on that auspicious day, he was named Laxmikant.

About three years later, on 3 September 1940 in Mumbai, his future partner Pyarelal was born in the house of Pt Ramprasad Sharma, a musician of immense knowledge and repute. Pyarelal was the eldest of six brothers and two sisters. Pt Ramprasad's flair, grasp and knowledge of both Indian and Western music and their notations, were soon to be elevated to another level by the boy.

Providence must have planned the union that was to happen about a decade later. Nothing else explains how they were the only young boys who were accomplished musicians and would play for leading composers. Nothing else explains how Pyarelal, later, inspired by Yehudi Menuhin, wanted to go abroad to make a career in Western music like his close friend Zubin Mehta. Instead, he was stopped and invited by Laxmikant to form a music duo with him.

Then there was Pyare-bhai's statement that he had once planned to form a duo with R.D. Burman, while, if the buzz was true, it was nothing less than the wish of Lata Mangeshkar herself that Laxmi-ji (as Laxmikant is still remembered) form a team with her own brother Hridaynath Mangeshkar!

However, the Supreme Power had decided that Hindi cinema would dazzle, for over three decades, with songs created by a matchless entity called Laxmikant-Pyarelal.

Struggle Time

Laxmikant lived in a chawl[1] in Mumbai's suburb of Vile Parle (East) and from childhood, the boy was quite an actor and loved singing, becoming a sort of entertainer whenever his father would call his friends over for a get-together. Laxmikant recalled that while his father was quite strict, his mother, a full-time hospital nurse, was a 'gem of a lady, tremendously courageous and with an inifinite capacity to love'. He had two siblings—a brother, Shashikant, and a sister.

Laxmikant's father then decided that the boy should learn music, and he began taking mandolin lessons from Balmukund Indorekar, brother of the famed exponent Narayanrao Indorekar. His father also had some contacts in the film industry and Laxmikant acted in at least five films—*Aankhen*,[2] *Shaadi Ki Raat* and some others—as a child artiste.

In 1947 or '48, Laxmikant fell ill with typhoid. He had almost recovered when he contracted double pneumonia. He was admitted to the Nair Municipal Hospital for about 12 days.

A mendicant had visited and told his mother to light a lamp. If the flame remained lit until the next morning, her son would recover and become a very famous man, he had said, 'with a parade of cars outside his home'.

---

[1] A lower middle-class multiroom residential block in Mumbai with common amenities.
[2] The 1950 Devendra Goel film that introduced composer Madan Mohan and also L-P's future friend and filmmaker Raj Khosla as a singer.

Laxmikant had vivid memories of his mother breaking open several ampoules of what he was later told were Coramine injections and pouring them down his throat. Laxmikant's wife Jaya remembered her mother-in-law saying that Laxmikant's heart had stopped beating for a few seconds! As Laxmikant put it, 'I would like to think that my mother pulled me out of near-death, but I was so weak that it was goodbye to acting. I continued my mandolin lessons and began studying Indian classical music.'

Laxmikant's father used to ensure that his son did riyaaz[3] for six to seven hours daily, from 3 to 6 p.m. after school and from 8:30 p.m. to 1:00 a.m., when his father was at work. He would lock Laxmikant and Shashikant in a room and ask his wife to ensure that she heard them practice throughout!

During this phase, Laxmikant developed a friendship with Jaywant Kulkarni,[4] a renowned Marathi singer, who would come and chat with him through the window grill. Kulkarni initiated Laxmikant into eating paan and this was the one addiction to which Laxmikant was enslaved till the end!

One day, Laxmikant met flautist Sumant Rai, who advised him that he should learn the violin instead of the mandolin if he wanted to turn to music as a career. He became the shagird[5] of composer duo Husnlal-Bhagatram and began commuting daily from the western suburb of Vile Parle to Mumbai's far-off central suburb of Chembur. The return journey cost two annas[6] by train and six annas by bus, as he had to use both means of transport.

But the duo never let him play for them or taught him directly. Laxmikant had to just sit, listen and observe. He also had to

---

[3]Vocal music exercise and practice of the notes.
[4]Jaywant Kulkarni ended up singing only once for L-P in *Coolie* (1983) for character actor Nilu Phule in the song 'Humko Isaq Hua Hai'.
[5]Musical disciple or protégé.
[6]In old Indian currency, 4 annas was 25 paise and 16 annas was 100 paise or a rupee.

attend their recordings at the oldest of Mumbai's three Famous Studios, at midtown Cadell Road.

On the other hand, Pyarelal's father, Pt Ramprasad Sharma, was an acclaimed master of both Indian and Western music and notation. A short-tempered man, he would become furious about the fact that in those days, only Goan Christians could play the mathematically-precise Western notations. Others would play instruments 'by ear' as they were trained in Indian music, in which notations depended on every exponent's varied lipi[7].

Pyarelal recalled that these musicians were scornfully termed as 'by-hearters' as they would play only after memorizing the songs by heart. His father had nothing against any community or region, but he did not understand why anyone should have a monopoly on Western music.

One day, Pt Ramprasad Sharma and Pyarelal were sitting with Parshuram (Amar Haldipur's[8] father) and other famous musicians like Narvekar and Gajananrao, in front of the Gandhi statue in the Kardar Studio premises.

'My father made a vow to teach Western notation to anyone with the slightest musical bent. He would forcibly catch hold of anyone, even roadside mendicants, and teach them, often tying up their feet with ropes so that he would come to know if anyone tried to run away at night!' remembered Pyarelal.

These people (and Pyarelal's father taught hundreds of them!) would have to stay in their house and would be fed too, and Pandit ji was soon looked upon as some kind of madman. But for him, it was a mission and money, already scarce, became scarcer. Pyarelal soon had to leave his night school as they could not afford his monthly fee of ₹3.

Pyarelal's entire family was musically inclined. His brother

---

[7]The way music is written in notation.

[8]Amar Haldipur, musician, composer and arranger, worked as L-P's assistant for decades.

Ganesh later became a music director in his own right, and another brother, Gorakh, became their chief assistant along with Laxmikant's brother Shashikant. Pyarelal was often made by his father to dress up neatly and sit in recording studio waiting-rooms, with instructions to rise and salute if a top music director walked past. He was already proficient by the age of 12, incidentally making his debut as a musician for a song in Bulo C. Rani's *Jogan*.

(*Though he uncharacteristically became a shade immodest, Pyarelal, much later, began to count himself along with Oscar Pereira, Michael Martin, Alexander D'Souza and Siloo Panthaki among the finest violinists of his generation.*)

Pyarelal then joined Ranjit Studios, where his duties were threefold—as a musician, as an 'extra' (a child junior artiste in a group of children on screen) and as violinist for the owner of this prestigious studio and banner (Ranjit Movietone), Chandulal Shah's pleasure!

The family lived in Ahmed Mansion, near the same Famous Studios where Laxmikant would come. That was the regular workplace also of Anil Biswas, and the now-legendary musician Louiz Banks would be there as well. Top filmmakers like D.D. Kashyap and P.N. Arora would shoot there. 'The mansion is still there, and we would pay its monthly rent of ₹13 late, every six months!' said Pyarelal.

And Famous Studios—a prophetic name indeed—is where Laxmikant and Pyarelal met.

And the Two Met…

Laxmikant was 10 years old and Pyarelal was seven when they first met as kids. The two would play bat-ball (the kiddie version of cricket) and *teen patthar*, a crude children's game with three stones. They would meet at lunch-time and slowly became friends. Pyarelal was working for C. Ramachandra—known as Annasaheb—and Chitragupta at the time, and knowing that his father's financial condition was not good, Annasaheb offered him a chance to go with him to Madras (now Chennai) to play for his film's song.

Pyarelal had to leave at very short notice. Laxmikant was a part of the contingent, as he was already working for the senior composer. The film was *Devata*, produced by Narayan Films and starring Gemini Ganesh and Anjali Devi. Vyjayanthimala played the vamp in it! That was the first film in which both of them played and the first time they saw big money—Pyarelal was paid ₹6,800 and so bought a gold ornament worth ₹1,200 for his father!

The friendship between the boys grew with time. Pyarelal remembered, 'We would go to the studio canteen and eat vada-pav or misal-pav, sharing whatever money we had in our pockets, usually eight annas or less. Laxmi was also doubling up as a child actor, like playing the childhood version of the hero, and being paid ₹10 per hour. He would help me get in for group or crowd scenes of children. Once, my brother Mahesh and I had to act dead, and we were so tired that by the time the shot was over, we had gone to sleep!'

Pyarelal remembers the day the actress Madhubala had recalled his scene with the legendary Om Prakash in *Rail Ka Dibba* (Shammi Kapoor's first released film). Carrying an umbrella in the scene, he got to speak a rude repartee to Om Prakash. Madhubala loved it and praised him when they met! The young musician's schedule was soon to be frenetic. He would wake up at 6 a.m., catch the 6:55 O-2 bus route to Colaba in Mumbai South and practice violin at the house of his famed musician guru Anthony Gonsalves[9] from 8 a.m. Pt Ramprasad had taught him the basics, but had wanted Gonsalves

---

[9]This Goan musician was immortalized in L-P's 1977 hit 'My Name is Anthony Gonsalves' in *Amar Akbar Anthony*, as filmmaker Manmohan Desai, at Pyarelal's request, changed Amitabh Bachchan's character's name from Anthony Fernandes to Anthony Gonsalves.

to refine his son's playing. Gonsalves was kind enough to let the young boy leave at 9 a.m. to reach the headquarters of the Bombay Symphony Orchestra or BSO (now called the Symphony Orchestra of India or SOI) nearby.

Pyarelal would leave from the BSO by 10 a.m., reach Ranjit Studios at 10:45 a.m. and, though that would be late, no one said anything to him. At 5 p.m., he would reach Cadell Road, and walk via the seashore to St. Michael's Church in Mahim, where he would attend school between 7 and 10 p.m. He remained a musician in the choir during church services even after quitting school.

In films, the two thus exploded the myth that only men above 35 could become good musicians, and they would often be made to sit on tall stools so that they were visible to the composers and their conductors.

And along with this came the phase when the duo became very close to the Mangeshkar family, even staying with them in their house 'for months' as Pyarelal put it. In Laxmikant's words, 'We were two souls, musically inclined. Gradually, our circle widened.'

There was Hridaynath (Mangeshkar) and his sister Usha, Laxmikant's brother Shashikant, Pyarelal's brothers Ganesh and Gorakh, Mayekar, who was a sitar player, and some others. The group began to do shows under the name of Surel Kala Kendra. It was then that Laxmikant and Pyarelal began to take long walks together, because that was when they composed tunes of their own. Both were in their teens then.

The Mangeshkar chapter had begun in the mid-'50s when Lata Mangeshkar had heard Laxmikant play the mandolin while she was performing at the Radio Club. She enquired about this boy whose playing was so beautiful, so polished, and on learning of his poor financial status, heeded his request to put in a word for him. This she did with Shankar-Jaikishan, Ghulam Mohammed, Jaidev (who also introduced Laxmikant to S.D. Burman) and some others.

Meanwhile, Pyarelal began to arrange music for C. Ramachandra, though according to him, his first break was in the 1958 *Phir Subah Hogi*, which was, incidentally, Khayyam's first independent film as a composer. And when Kalyanji-Anandji began their careers as independent composers, they employed Shankar-Jaikishan's arranger Sebastian, but Shankar-Jaikishan objected to this and Sebastian had to leave. Laxmikant had already joined them, and he suggested that Pyarelal be called in, as he was a master at arrangement. Together, therefore, they first worked with the senior duo in *Chandrasena* (1959), in which Kalyanji was billed as Kalyanji Virji Shah and Anandji as his assistant. Kalyanji liked to work with Laxmikant and Pyarelal, while Anandji preferred Jai Parte, according to Pyarelal. 'Kalyanji bhai loved us a lot. He would often take us home. We loved the phulkas made there and I would eat almost a dozen! He would also take us to the races,' he said.

Their joint tenure under Kalyanji-Anandji proved to be fruitful. Though technically their assistants, the two would handle and treat the film almost as their own. Sometimes, Kalyanji-Anandji would leave everything to the two of them.

The term 'assistant music director' is a term peculiar to Indian cinema. Abroad, apart from the composer, there are the musicians who actually play the music, while the arranger decides the notes, the type and the number of instruments. The conductor then conducts the orchestra. Here, an assistant may do one or more of these things and even rehearse a singer or compose a tune. The two youngsters would work unflaggingly for them.

In several Kalyanji-Anandji films, Laxmikant-Pyarelal were thus not just billed as assistants but as 'Associate Music Directors'—*Himalay Ki God Mein, Jab Jab Phool Khile* and *Juari* among them. Later, Pyarelal had even stated that if an emergency arose with Kalyanji-Anandji, he would leave his own recording but make sure their music arrangements were looked after.

Pyarelal recalled a long phase when, after working the full

day as musicians for others, they would work with the senior duo from 11 p.m. to 4 a.m., snatch two hours of sleep and then work the entire day again as musicians! One prominent song wherein Pyarelal played the solo violin was in Madan Mohan's 'Main Yeh Soch Kar' in *Haqeeqat*. Simultaneously, they would also arrange the music for dubbed Hindi versions of South Indian films and also do extensive work on the background music (BGM) of other films; S.D. Burman's *Ziddi* among them.

Between them, as musicians, they worked with almost every composer who mattered. These included Shankar-Jaikishan, Roshan, Ravi, Madan Mohan, O.P. Nayyar, Naushad, Chitragupta, Hemant Kumar, Usha Khanna and finally, R.D. Burman, for whom they arranged the music of his first two films that were produced by Mehmood—*Chhote Nawab* and *Bhoot Bangla*. The last film in which they played was Roshan's *Bahu Begum*, which released in 1967, four years after their debut as independent composers. 'Roshan saab was a strict man in such matters,' Laxmikant had quipped. 'And he did not know we were among the musicians!'

The composer stressed that they learnt from all the stalwarts not only what to do as musicians, but more importantly, what *not* to do as musicians and as people.

And this was probably the secret behind Laxmikant-Pyarelal becoming the darlings of all their musicians, from the Indian classical and Western luminaries who played for them, to the smallest names, as well as singers, lyricists, filmmakers and stars. As Pyarelal put it, 'I had a quick temper, but Laxmi would look after everything and never lose his equanimity.'

2

THE TRIALS AND TRIBULATIONS

The saga of Laxmikant-Pyarelal was a classic case of the tortoise struggling in the initial race. Their team was already formed in spirit—they just needed a break. They got it when K. Parvez[10] offered them a Chandrashekhar-Vijaya Choudhary film called *Tumse Pyar Ho Gaya*. They recorded four songs for the film before it got shelved.

'We approached K. Parvez, one of the directors we knew well and asked him for a film,' recollects Pyarelal. Even their first release, *Parasmani*, happened because they had approached producer-cinematographer Babubhai Mistry themselves. Laxmikant said that Mistry had been lucky for so many, talents (Aruna Irani also made her debut in *Parasmani*) he had introduced, including Kalyanji-Anandji. Mistry too was aware of their work.

Having worked with Shankar-Jaikishan, Laxmikant, already enamoured with Jaikishan's flamboyant and larger-than-life manner and dressing style, wanted Jaikishan's favourite Hasrat Jaipuri to be the songwriter. The first recording of their career was thus a Hasrat Jaipuri-written song rendered by Lata Mangeshkar and Subir Sen. Incidentally, Sen was to never record a song with them again. After this, Mangeshkar and Mukesh sang the second song. Word spread and Laxmikant stated in his *Junior G* interview,

---

[10]The late K. Parvez took on the name of Kalpataru in the 1980s and was a prolific director who worked till the late 1990s, doing several films with Laxmikant-Pyarelal. In 1977, he also introduced Laxmikant's son Hrishikesh a.k.a. Tinku as a child artiste in a film named *Tinku*.

'Hasrat saab requested us to set him free, as S-J were against his working for us. Our next two songs, both solos, and sung respectively by Mohammed Rafi and Asha Bhosle, were written by Qamar Jalalabadi saab, who was close to Kalyanji-Anandji.'

It is here that Pyarelal revealed his penchant for recording at the right studio and sticking to one venue. They always had what they called 'one temple of work'. For decades, it was Famous Studio at downtown Tardeo. Many years later, for certain personal reasons, they shifted to Mehboob Studios in Bandra, and till the end, they rarely recorded elsewhere. In the case that they did, it was only for practical reasons such as urgency.

As we proceed, we will see how Pyarelal was so particular about the equipment, technology and sound, especially in the case of two big films, one in the 1970s and the other in the 1990s. In the case of the latter, they even left the big (and now super-hit) film!

The fledgling duo took up three more films after *Tumse Pyar Ho Gaya*—*Chhaila Babu* (which was interminably delayed and got released only in 1967, and was also directed by K. Parvez), *Hum Tum Aur Woh*, *Piya Log Kya Kahenge* and one more untitled film whose details the duo does not remember. The last three films never got completed either! The title song of *Piya Log Kya Kahenge* was set to the tune that was used by them later in *Dosti*—the line 'Awaaz main na doonga' in the mukhda of 'Chahoonga Main Tujhe' in *Dosti.*

Laxmikant's footnote on this was that, though *Chhaila Babu* was delayed, it was the beginning of their association with the late Asad Bhopali, who became their favourite lyricist in their early years. The association became less frequent because of Bhopali's yen for alcohol, but they still worked with him off and on, until their last collaboration, which released after Bhopali's death— *Ranbhoomi* in 1991.

The First and Lasting Impression

All these trials and tribulations taught the young duo valuable and valid lessons. By the time cinematographer-director and special effects wizard Babubhai Mistry signed them for *Parasmani*, starring Mahipal and Geetanjali, the Laxmikant-Pyarelal list of dos and don'ts were clear, and put into practice immediately to shape their exceptional careers. *Parasmani*, produced under the Movieland banner, was released in 1963. The duo would go on to work in over 500 released films[11] until 2004, which saw their last release, the Akshay Kumar-Sridevi movie *Mere Biwi Ka Jawaab Nahin*.[12] The film came out six years after Laxmikant passed away. They ruled the music scene as undisputed leaders from 1969 to 1993—a full 25 years!

But we are racing ahead. In 1963, setting a blueprint later followed by early Bappi Lahiri (by default), Nadeem-Shravan (never acknowledged) and Himesh Reshammiya (who acknowledges it openly), Laxmikant-Pyarelal decided that the music should be the biggest star of all their films.

Lata Mangeshkar made that happen for them and has always remained special for them. Said Laxmikant emotionally, 'In those days, we would never conceive a song without her. And though she was expensive and we were nobodies, we never compromised. Often our small producers would allot us only ₹5,000 per song, and her fees alone would be ₹3,000! So what about the musicians and us? As we were making enough as musicians, Pyare and I would fork out ₹1,500 each just to be able to afford her fees.' The musicians were all friends and we would persuade them to work free for us or at least take lesser rates. The shoestring budgets

---

[11] The only Indian composer who has worked on more films than L-P is the South's Ilaiyaraaja whose score is around 1,000 films from 1976 till date, as of 2021. L-P also did some regional films.

[12] This movie was directed by Pankaj Parashar and finally completed by an unknown name.

could thus be amazingly stretched.'

Mohammed Rafi and Mukesh were well-known for being completely flexible in price or would even write off remunerations for the composer duo in their early films.

The other lesson that L-P had imbibed from Kalyanji-Anandji and Shankar-Jaikishan was the value of a large orchestra when a song warranted it. There too, the duo often spent from their own pockets, but saw to it that the composition did not suffer. The aim was simple: their music had to stand out.

And it did!

The music not only stood out but became a rage and drove *Parasmani* into re-runs. Lata Mangeshkar and Kamal Barot sang 'Hansta Hua Noorani Chehra', which became the No. 6 song of that year in the annual *Binaca Geetmala*, while from the 32 annual toppers, Rafi-Lata's 'Woh Jab Yaad Aaye' came in at No. 15. Mukesh was the only other singer in that film's album. Pyarelal distinctly remembered using 36 violins in the orchestra only because Naushad had 20 and Shankar-Jaikishan used 30! As he put it, 'We had a newcomer's silly, childish enthusiasm to outdo the top names. I remember that after the recording, Lata ji had complimented and blessed us.'

Incidentally, 'Hansta Hua Noorani Chehra' was filmed on two dancers—Nalini Chonkar and Jeevankala. The latter married the hugely successful screenwriter Ram Kelkar, who later was to script some of L-P's most successful musicals like *Piya Ka Ghar*, *Aasha*, *Hero*, *Ram Lakhan* and their last super-hit, *Khal Nayak*.

Laxmikant had been highly impressed by C. Ramachandra's 'Aplam Chaplam' from *Azaad*. Shankar-Jaikishan also had composed several popular all-female duets, so they decided that they had to match the record. On the whole, most of L-P's all-female duets did become hits. The other hit songs of this phenomenal musical included Rafi's 'Roshan Tumhi Se Duniya', Mukesh-Lata's 'Chori Chori Jo Tumse Mile' and Lata Mangeshkar's 'Ooi Maa Ooi Maa' and 'Mere Dil Mein Halki Si'.

In their very first film, we also got to know of a playful habit that Laxmikant later told me: modeling compositions on the styles of the existing composers. This was something they would do off and on for a long time! 'Woh Jab Yaad Aaye' was inspired by Roshan's style, while 'Chori Chori Jo Tumse Mile' was clearly along the lines of Shankar-Jaikishan and there was a hint of Chitragupta in 'Mere Dil Mein Halki Si'.

Best Feet Forward

Diamonds cannot be diamonds without passing through fire. Titans in any field of life too have to persevere through difficult struggles before reaching their zenith. And Laxmikant-Pyarelal's case was no different. Despite *Parasmani*, it was no cakewalk for the duo. Those were the peak days of Shankar-Jaikishan, O.P. Nayyar, S.D. Burman, Roshan, C. Ramachandra and Naushad besides Madan Mohan, Ravi, Salil Chowdhury, Chitragupta, Hemant Kumar and others. L-P were still nobodies but they had creativity and confidence on their side. 'Pyare and I had the talent, the dedication and the grit. In short, we had what it takes,' declared Laxmikant in his *Junior G* interview, with justifiable pride.

In their earliest songs, some influence of Shankar-Jaikishan might have been there, but the duo insisted that they never copied anyone. There was already such a thing as a Laxmikant-Pyarelal style. Lata Mangeshkar, Mohammed Rafi, Mukesh and Asha Bhosle had all seen their relentless hard work and resultant steady climb. They were all helpful and steady sources of encouragement. From their earliest days, L-P followed the S-J policy of taking on multiple assignments. And the result was that very soon, Lata began reserving a fixed number of days in a month for them![13]

Laxmikant also recalled going to producer and film baron S. Mukerji with 30 tunes and humbly asking for a film on the

---

[13] Lata Mangeshkar continued with this for years.

strength of their work as arrangers for his Usha Khanna films, *Aao Pyar Karen* and *Hum Hindustani*. 'He gave us a lecture, and told us that Shankar-Jaikishan were at the top and two dozen composers ranked next. "You are No. 26!" he said. "Do you think you can face the competition?" We told him very confidently that we would be No. 1 within five years!¹⁴ But he never called us.'¹⁵

In 1982, however, S. Mukerji presented his son Shubir's film *Teesri Aankh* with L-P's music.

And since merit is always recognized and hard work always rewarded, L-P were never short of work. But the struggle now was only to *get* big films. *Harishchandra Taramati*, a mythological, was their only other release in 1963. Their only film with lyricist Pradeep, it was marked by evergreens like 'Jagat Ki Roshni Ke Liye', their first solo with Hemant Kumar, which ranks among his all-time bests, and Lata Mangeshkar's raag-rich 'Meghwa Gagan Beech Jhanke' and 'Main Ek Nanha Sa'. The film was produced and directed by B.K. Adarsh, who edited and published the leading trade weekly *Trade Guide*.

The film began their association with the other two Mangeshkar sisters—Asha Bhosle and Usha Mangeshkar—with the dance number 'Yeh Jawani Phir Nahin Aani'. It also featured their first song with Mahendra Kapoor, 'Yeh Jeevan Kya Jeevan Hai', which was featured only in the film and not on its LP (Long-

---

[14] In 1969, it was confirmed that Laxmikant-Pyarelal, by dint of all parameters like track-record, signing of big banner and big director films, and their clout as composers, were numero uno and had ended the 19-year reign of Shankar-Jaikishan.

[15] L-P went on to do films with S. Mukerji's brother Subodh Mukerji—(who worked on *Shagird* as producer, *Abhinetri* as producer-director and *Teesri Aankh* as director, which S. Mukerji presented), son Shomu Mukerji (*Chhaila Babu* directed by S. Mukerji's star son Joy Mukerji and *Fiffty Fiffty*) and had been signed for the aborted *Dehati* that was to be directed by Joy for his other brother Deb Mukerji. The film was to star Shammi Kapoor, Jeetendra and Joy Mukerji. Deb is director Ayan Mukerji's father.

Play or 33-1/3 rpm) record. Mohammed Rafi ('Dharm Ki Khatir Bik Gaya Raja') and Kavi Pradeep himself ('Toot Gayi Hai Mala') rendered litanies in the background. Lata also had the pathos-laden 'Main Teri Abhagan Maa Hoon'.

In the following decisive year, 1964, L-P were to work on a personal record of five films. In these musically-successful movies, they were to begin some of their most memorable associations—with lyricist Anand Bakshi, singers Kishore Kumar and Manna Dey and with director Satyen Bose. They were also to build on the BGM and other work they had done as musicians for distributor Tarachand Barjatya by starting a memorable association with his prestigious production banner, Rajshri Productions.

3

FAST AND STEADY WINS THE RACE

Laxmikant-Pyarelal could not have possibly known in 1964 that their last release would be all of four decades later! At the time, L-P continued to score big and the 1964 aces, led by *Dosti*, went on to include the devotional films *Sant Gyaneshwar* and *Sati Savitri*, the sci-fi movie *Mr X in Bombay* and the stunt film (as B-grade actioners were termed then) *Aaya Toofan*.

'We put in our best in every film we got,' said Laxmikant. Asad Bhopali wrote all the songs except the title track for *Aaya Toofan*, which was written by another huge talent who was working with them again after *Parasmani*, Farukh Kaiser. Kaiser was close to the film's director Mohammed Hussain, then famous for stunt films.

The highlight of the score was Lata's 'Hum Pyar Kiye Jayenge', which was modeled audio-visually as a stunt film version of 'Jab Pyar Kiya To Darna Kya' from *Mughal-E-Azam*. Mischievously, the duo not only fashioned the composition along Naushad's lines but also used his tenor for the choral accompaniment

The other film, in which Asad Bhopali contributed just one song, 'Allah Kare Tu Bhi Aa Jaaye', was *Mr X in Bombay*. The rest were written—in a first collaboration—by Anand Bakshi.

'We were searching for someone with whom we could form an excellent and lasting team,' said Laxmikant during his *Junior G* interview. 'For *Mr X in Bombay*, we took Anand Bakshi, with whom we had worked under Kalyanji-Anandji. His mega-talent and terrific tuning with us can be gauged by that first score!' According to Laxmikant, not only did Bakshi have an instinct for words and a deep sense of melody, but he could also sing. More vitally, his pen had the power that only simplicity could provide. L-P knew then that they had found their counter to the great lyricists who had formed teams with great composers. The film marked another legendary start—their relationship with Kishore Kumar. Bakshi and Kishore both had their start with one of the greatest songs of the four together, the immortal 'Mere Mehboob Qayamat Hogi'. The song, as per Anand Bakshi's immaculately-maintained diary, was recorded on 28 July 1963.

Here, Pyarelal added a vital footnote: 'We wanted to give something different by way of style to Kishore da, different from what he had been singing for Dada (Burman) and others. We fashioned the song accordingly.'

Kishore Kumar was blown by the song and even made his domestic staff hear it as soon as it was recorded, by taping it! His son Amit Kumar not only listed it as one of his top 12 Kishore Kumar numbers of all time, but also revealed that his father too ranked it very high.

The other Bakshi songs in the film were no less. The all-hit score of this film (which is otherwise said to have done only average business) included timeless classics like Kishore-Lata's 'Khubsoorat Haseena' (filmed with the actor-singer and Kum Kum in a jalopy flying over Bombay, as Mumbai was known then), Kishore's 'Chali Re Chali Re Gori' and 'Ruk Ja Rokta Hai Yeh Deewana' and Lata's 'Julmi Hamare Sanwariya Ho Ram'.

Sant Gyaneshwar and *Sati Savitri* were L-P's firm answer to close friend and well-wisher R.D. Burman, who had warned them against scoring music for mythologicals and devotionals after *Harishchandra Taramati*. He had told them, 'Tum log S.N. Tripathi[16] ban jaaoge (You will become another S.N. Tripathi).' And Laxmikant had replied, with characteristic confidence, 'Don't worry, we will rise up even with such films!' L-P were to do *Naag*

---

[16]A hugely respected, prolific and illustrious composer-actor-director-lyricist who was, however, always slotted in mythological and devotional films.

Mandir in 1966, but if they did not score more mythological and devotionals afterwards, it was only because they began to get bigger setups.

Sant Gyaneshwar was produced by Ramraj Nahata, B.K. Adarsh's younger brother, and also a trade analyst, and is remembered largely for the classic rendered separately by Mukesh and Lata Mangeshkar, 'Jyot Se Jyot Jagaate Chalo'. And Lata's 'Ek Do Teen Char Bhaiya Bano Hoshiyar' (for a child artise), 'Main To Chhail Chhabili Naar' (a lavani—this remains L-P's only composition in that Marathi folk dance genre), the plaintive 'Mere Laadlo' and the magnificent 'Bahut Din Beete' proved how she was their ubiquitous choice for every kind of song. It was in this year that the duo began their magnificent and double-barrelled association with Manna Dey—with the thoroughbred classical number 'Jaago Re Prabhat Aaya' and that scintillating perennial 'Tum Gagan Ke Chandrama Ho' (with Lata) for their other triumphant album, *Sati Savitri*. For 'Jaago Re Prabhat Aaya', Laxmikant wanted to work with the renowned classical singer Ustad Amir Khan, who was ready, but wanted to spend a few months on the sittings. And the duo hastily opted for Manna Dey!

These two small films had lyrics by the gentle giant Bharat Vyas, known for his mastery at writing for ethnic subjects. *Sati Savitri* also features the timeless Lata song 'Jeevan Dor Tumhi Sang Bandhi' apart from the frisky Lata-Usha-Kamal Barot number 'Itni Jaldi Kya Hai Gori' and the haunting 'Kabhi To Miloge Jeevan Saathi'. Both 'Jeevan Dor Tumhi Sang Bandhi' and 'Kabhi To Miloge Jeevan Saathi' were set in Raag Kalavati. Pyarelal admitted that they always wanted to score a Kalavati composition with Lata because they had loved Pt Ravi Shanker's song for her, 'Haaye Re Woh Din Kyun Na Aaye' from *Anuradha* and had been musicians on it. 'But when we had composed "Meghwa Gagan Beech Jhaanke" in *Harishchandra Taramati* in Kalavati, we had employed a Madhyam(Ma), which happens to be a forbidden note in this raag. Similarly, "Bandhan Toote Na Saawariya" from *Mom*

Ki Gudia was based on Raag Puriya Dhanashree, but in that, we placed a Shuddh Rishabh instead of the prescribed Komal Rishabh note. Laxmi employed this raag also in "Meri Saanson Ko Jo Mehka Rahi Hai" in *Badaltey Rishtey*,' Pyarelal adds.[17] In 'Suno Sajana' (*Aaye Din Bahaar Ke* in 1966), L-P again did away with the convention of following the Nishaad (Ni) with the landing note of Shadja (Sa). The composer noted that Lata Mangeshkar was always appreciative of such innovations. 'She made it clear to us that in popular music, what sounds good to the ear is more important than just rigidly following the prescribed norms of a raag,' smiled Pyarelal.

That their effort was rewarded is an understatement: Lata has declared that 'Jeevan Dor Tumhi Sang Bandhi' ranks among her 10 finest songs of all time. This song has another (as we shall see in the book) sparkling story that dates forward to the year 2002! In fact, both Laxmikant and Pyarelal name it among their all-time personal favourites from their own work.

But L-P's crowning glory in 1964 was *Dosti*, with an all-hit score that won them the Filmfare Best Music award, in the face of scores like Shankar-Jaikishan's *Sangam* and Madan Mohan's *Woh Kaun Thi?* Interestingly, both the 'RKs' who directed these respective films—Raj Kapoor and Raj Khosla—were to later work extensively with L-P. *Dosti*, the story of a young blind man who is an ace singer and his friend, was L-P's smash beginning with Satyen Bose, a rewarding association for long, and also with producer Tarachand Barjatya. It was also their first film with the man who went on to write the greatest number of songs for them after Anand Bakshi—Majrooh Sultanpuri.

Sanjay Khan, then known as just Sanjay, made his debut in the melodrama but had no song of his own. The all-hit Rafi-fest was led by 'Chahoonga Main Tujhe' (which won not only Mohammed Rafi but also Majrooh Filmfare awards), 'Teri Dosti

---

[17]Interview of Pyarelal with Dr Shekhar.

Mera Pyar', 'Raahi Manwa Dukh Ki Chinta', 'Jaanewalon Zaraa' and 'Mera To Jo Bhi Kadam Hai'. Lata contributed the delightful 'Gudiya Humse Roothi Rahogi', the twinkle-toed number that was yet another addition to L-P's list of superb children's songs of all hues, which had begun with *Harishchandra Taramati* and *Sant Gyaneshwar*. This is a genre they came to master and dominate for years, with several classics like 'Maa Mujhe Apne Aanchal' (*Chhota Bhai*), 'Mere Soone Jeevan Ka Aasra' (*Aasra*), 'Ek Gagan Ka Raja' (*Darpan*), 'Sui Ja Tara' (*Mastana*), 'Mother Mary' (*Bachpan*), 'Yashoda Ka Nandlala' (*Sanjog*) and 'Kaushalya Main Teri' (*Eeshwar*) among others.

It is common knowledge that 'Chahoonga Main Tujhe' was almost scrapped or considered as a possible female song (one can only wonder how). And how L-P got *Dosti* was a tale by itself. Barjatya had just produced *Aarti*, which had a fabulous score composed by Roshan. Naturally, Roshan was approached and was shown the Bengali original on which *Dosti* was based. Legend has it that Roshan turned down this 'story of two beggars', as he saw it, and an incensed Barjatya approached L-P, the youngsters who had been arranging songs for the dubbed films that he distributed.

Majrooh had revealed to me that he was sceptical of the new composers who had come in, and had wanted to leave the film too after Roshan's exit. Luckily, he mentioned this to the late composer Chitragupta (the duo Anand-Milind's father) during a song sitting with him. Chitragupta rid him of his wrong impression, stating emphatically that the two young boys were immensely talented—they had worked with him as musicians—and that Majrooh should not even think of quitting the film. The rest is history.

In the following year, 1965, L-P scored for five films, and two of them once again featured Kishore Kumar—*Shreemaan Funtoosh* and *Hum Sab Ustad Hain*. There were also two more films (after *Aaya Toofan*) featuring Dara Singh, *Boxer* and *Lootera*. Admittedly, L-P were facing all the legends who were, at the time, composing and scoring at their best, like Ravi's *Waqt*, *Kaajal* and *Khandaan*, Shankar-Jaikishan's *Arzoo*, *Janwar* and *Gumnaam*, Chitragupta's *Oonche Log*, S.D. Burman's *Teen Devian* and *Guide*, O.P. Nayyar's *Mere Sanam*, Prem Dhawan's *Shaheed* and two films of Kalyanji-Anandji featuring L-P as assistants—*Jab Jab Phool Khile* and *Himalay Ki God Mein*. They were all prestigious, but the big-ticket film was where L-P's career had not yet reached.

More than 55 years later, the songs specially cherished from the Kishore Kumar films are Lata-Kishore's 'Sultana Sultana Tu Na Ghabrana' and Kishore's 'Yeh Dard Bhara Afsana' from *Shreemaan Funtoosh* and Kishore's 'Pyar Baant-Te Chalo'[18] and Kishore's and Lata's versions of 'Ajnabi Tum Jaane Pehchane Se Lagte Ho' from *Hum Sab Ustad Hain*. However, almost all the other songs were popular on radio (a major index of popular evaluation in those times), including the duo's first-ever Kishore-Asha duet, 'Kya Teri Zulfein Hain' in *Hum Sab Ustad Hain*. While lyricist Bakshi worked on the first film, Asad Bhopali had done the latter.

These two scores seemed to be fashioned in the *Mr X in Bombay* template wherein L-P maintained their own distinct touch alongside Kishore's singing style. Kishore was losing ground as a hero in that phase, and the hit songs helped him to an extent as a star.

With 'Ajnabi Tum Jaane Pehchane Se Lagte Ho', the subtle nuances in the happy Lata version, especially the variation in the '*jaane pehchaane se lagte ho*' portion of the mukhda, seemed to underscore L-P's nascent mastery at such two-version songs (something done with distinction earlier in 'Jyot Se Jyot' from *Sant Gyaneshwar* with its versions sung by Lata Mangeshkar and Mukesh). The composition's appeal lay also in the orchestral difference between the upbeat Lata version and the melancholic avatar of Kishore's.

---

[18]Pyarelal once revealed in an interview that the prelude of the 'Pyar Baant-Te Chalo' was heavily based on Rod Goodwin's theme music for the black-and-white Miss Marple films—which can be called L-P's first 'lift'!

Boxer was another example of how L-P never gave short shrift to even small films. The stunt film featured Dara Singh with Mumtaz, the actress with whom L-P would go on to cherish a long association, with films like *Roti, Prem Kahani, Lafange* and *Nagin*, the last four films she starred in at her peak, and her signature tune 'Bindiya Chamkegi' from the 1969 *Do Raaste*.

Each of the five songs from *Boxer* was exotic and astoundingly distinct from the rest. This also was the first of many L-P films that featured only female singers, such as *Baharon Ki Manzil, Sharafat, Kucche Dhaage* and the six-singer *Thief of Baghdad*. This fact is especially significant in current times when we have so many film soundtracks without a female voice. Their ace that year was the timeless score for *Lootera*, the first of their 11 films for producer Rajkumar Kohli—an association that went on till 1990—and here again there was no male singer!

When we mention *Lootera* as an all-female score, we do not mean that the hero had no lip-synched song. Dara Singh and another male artiste enacted 'Patli Kamar Nazuk Umar' but they were dressed as women for the scene. The song was thus sung by Shamshad Begum, singing playback for Dara Singh, and Kamal Barot, for the other male actor. L-P here followed Kalyanji-Anandji, who had used Shamshad's heavy vocals for Shammi Kapoor in drag in the 1963 *Bluffmaster*. O.P. Nayyar completed this 'drag' trilogy of the 1960s with his chartbusting 1968 song 'Kajra Mohabbatwala' from *Kismet*, in which Shamshad sang for Biswajeet.[19]

Recalled Kohli, 'Both Laxmi and Pyare were such good human beings. When you worked with them, *mazaa hi alag tha* (the

---

[19] Laxmikant-Pyarelal were billed as 'Assistant Music Directors' in *Bluffmaster*. Both *Chhalia* (1961) and *Bluffmaster* (1963) were directed by Manmohan Desai, and were their first two associations with the director with whom they would achieve a streak of nine jubilee hits between 1974 and 1983. *Chhalia* was also when they were first noticed by Raj Kapoor.

enjoyment was unique). They were not just great composers but very nice and homely people. Most of the time, I did not even think of working with others, and every song in *Lootera* was a hit!' *Lootera*'s evergreen stature came from six diverse songs by Lata Mangeshkar, including the hugely popular 'Raat Se Kaho Ruke Zaraa',[20] 'Neend Nigahon Se Kho Jaati Hai', 'Kisi Ko Pataa Na Chale Baat Ka' and the unusual 'Sanam Raah Bhoole', 'O Dilwalo' and 'Mujhe Dekhiye Main Koi Dastaan Hoon'.

Though musically meritorious, this was the last year in which L-P spent in the 'small film' zone. 1966 would mark the beginning of their big innings. These five films graphically underscored L-P's flair for versatile music and also the L-P maxim that their songs would be the biggest stars of these modest films.

---

[20]The song could be called L-P's first rework of a complete mukhda. It was 'taken' from 'Misirlou', a folk song from the Eastern Mediterranean region, with origins in the Ottoman Empire. The original writer of the folk song is not even known, but it was known to Arabic, Greek and Jewish musicians by the 1920s. The earliest known recording of the song is from 1927, with multiple international versions of the song later. Pyarelal remembers defending the tune as a Laxmikant original when Shammi Kapoor had cast doubts on its originality, only to be told later by his partner that he had taken it from a folk tune from abroad! And Pyarelal apologized to the star, who had also begun to notice their work.

4

ASCENT TO BIG TIME

*L*et us rewind to Laxmikant's firm belief that hard work would always pay. Laxmikant was a musician on the BGM of Shankar-Jaikishan's *Ayee Milan Ki Bela* when its big-name producer J. Om Prakash (Hrithik Roshan's late maternal grandfather) approached Laxmikant and promised him work for Prakash's next film, *Aaye Din Bahaar Ke*. Om-ji, as he was known, had worked with the team of Shankar-Jaikishan-Hasrat-Shailendra in *Aas Ka Panchhi* and *Ayee Milan Ki Bela* and Laxmikant had this to say, 'It was a momentous occasion for us, as the big banner Filmyug was the first of S-J's banners to come to us. We put everything into this one chance and vindicated Om-ji's trust in us.' And when, in an excited first reaction, Laxmikant asked the filmmaker, 'Can we announce that we are doing your film?' The filmmaker gently told him to wait until the background score was ready. In an interview, he had told me that he was irritated by S-J's habit of asking for higher remuneration every time a film was a hit and that he saw in L-P the same potential for the future.

There was one hiccup after the announcement was made: L-P had a sitting again with Hasrat Jaipuri for this new film before S-J came to know and objected to his working there. And so, Anand Bakshi came in. *Aaye Din Bahaar Ke* (1966), with its all-hit soundtrack, created havoc when it was released, and signalled the beginning of an association with the filmmaker that, despite some turbulence in the '70s, lasted until 1988's *Agnee*. It was also the first of over 60 of L-P's films with emerging star Dharmendra (including four of his home productions and a significant recreation in a fifth) and a long association with both leading lady Asha Parekh and director Raghunath Jhalani. In 1996, Asha Parekh was to make her debut as a director in L-P's last musical ace, *Bhairavi*, but she opted out due to creative differences with the producers and never directed any film.

The hit parade of *Aaye Din Bahaar Ke* included all-time classics like 'Suno Sajana', 'Meri Dushmun Tu Meri Dosti Ko Tarse', 'Yeh Kali Jab Talak Phool', 'Khat Likh De Saawariya Ke Naam', 'Khudaya Khair' and 'Ae Kaash Kisi Deewane Ko', L-P's first Lata-Asha duet. 'Suno Sajana' remains a cult favourite with connoisseurs. As recently as in 2008, when the song was being performed on stage at Pt Hariprasad Chaurasia's seventieth birthday celebrations, two girls sitting in front of me, the elder of whom must have been not more than 12 years old, sang the entire lyrics in sync with the singer.

So happy was J. Om Prakash with L-P's music and professionalism, that he introduced them to other members of United Producers, a consortium that jointly presented films of all its members. Among the United Producers were Mohan Kumar, Subodh Mukerji, Mohan Segal, Shakti Samanta, G.P. Sippy and others. The first three signed them, and G.P. Sippy (who later produced their 1989 film *Bhrastachar*) offered them *Raaz*. 'We had to refuse *Raaz* as we had too much work!' smiled Laxmikant. 'The film, which was Rajesh Khanna's and Babita's first release, went to Kalyanji-Anandji and both the film and its music were hits.'

One by one, not just S-J loyalists Mohan Kumar and Subodh Mukerji, but even the likes of L.V. Prasad (who was influenced by Tarachand Barjatya) also shifted to L-P and began to form durable associations with the duo. Laxmikant clarified that they had the highest regard for Shankar-Jaikishan. 'Our industry has never seen and probably will never see composers of their range, calibre and originality,' he said. But L-P had to prove that they were good too! They wanted to show that they could match S-J with equally good music. Here, Laxmikant also admitted that they started the trend of undercutting. 'It was simple logic: if you are paying 10 rupees for something and we give you the same quality for two rupees, will you spend more?' Laxmikant asked me. 'We simply wanted the best banners and filmmakers.' And this is where Laxmikant had stressed that they were in a position to give equally excellent music. 'We were compromising on our price, not on our work, composing original music with our distinctive stamp. Besides, in this industry, you have to keep yourself in the limelight. We had to keep coming out with films, otherwise we could not hope to survive in a field where two of every three films flop!'

And while saving money is always welcome for a filmmaker, false economy can be counter-productive, and so it was to L-P's eternal credit that all the banners that moved away from S-J, continued to work with L-P forming long-lasting relationships and even returning to them after doing films with other composers.

By 1969, L-P had given such a consistent stream of hit scores and melodious songs that for the first time in almost two decades, there was an answer, an alternative and a strong challenge to the supremacy of S-J. L-P were declared numero uno by the film trade in 1969 on the strength of their consistency of great music, come hit movie or flop, and their signing with big banners and films with major directors. In the 1966–9 period, L-P still did nine small films too, but their music remained of high calibre. And while they won their second Filmfare award for the L.V. Prasad hit *Milan*, they also got their first Sur-Singar Samsad award for the Mohammed Rafi gem, 'Painjaniya Chhanke Ram' from the small film *Wapas* (1969), produced and directed by their *Dosti* director Satyen Bose. This was a prestigious honour from an organization that celebrated Indian classical music, and had instituted a special annual award for the Best Classical Film Song of any year! These awards continued till the late 1980s, and L-P won it again for *Ram Lakhan* in 1989.

But we are racing ahead again. Let us examine the 1966–9 era in detail.

No Room for Complacency

L-P's love for experimentation with both musical notes and singers was a habit they kept up from the very first day. They experimented with Lata, as their long-standing muse, probably more than with anyone else. *Mere Lal*, the eight-song score (which included five solos by Lata) for Satyen Bose,[21] saw Lata zoom to ethereal heights with the unique 'Badal Roya Naina Roye' and hit a popular high with 'Payal Ki Jhankar Raste Raste'. The film was a modest production starring Dev Kumar and Indrani Mukherjee. Never composers to be bogged down by the branding and image of singers who had been well-entrenched in the industry for almost 20 years, L-P gave Mukesh, often associated with the sad song genre, the frothy 'Jab Tak Yeh Sansar Nachaye' in *Mere Lal*.

A personal observation of critical importance: Gradually, and seemingly primarily with *Dosti*, the two had also learnt the fine art of making the most impactful sad songs. I firmly believe that a good sad song, while touching the core of the listener's heart with its musical and lyrical content, should never depress its listener or viewer. Instead, such a song should, simultaneously and paradoxically, invoke admiration for it. No L-P sad song can be found guilty of this aberrational quality that ails so many litanies of every hue from many other composers.

The other 1966 releases were the ensemble cast laugh-riot *Pyar Kiye Jaa*, the Nutan melodrama *Chhota Bhai* and AVM's *Laadla* (these were their first three films made in Madras), the biggie *Aasra*, Mala Sinha-Sanjay Khan's *Dillagi*, and the modest-budgeted *Daku Mangal Singh*, *Naag Mandir* and *Sau Saal Baad*. Each film did well musically, though only *Pyar Kiye Jaa*, *Chhota Bhai* and *Aasra* did commercially well. Among the evergreens were 'Mere Soone Jeevan Ka Aasra Hai Tu', 'Daiyya Re Daiyya',

---

[21]Satyen Bose was one of the four Bengali directors who worked extensively with them, the others being Dulal Guha, Asit Sen and Samir Ganguly.

'Neend Kabhi Rehti Thi', 'Shokhiyaan Nazar Mein Hai' (*Aasra*) and almost the entire score of *Pyar Kiye Jaa*, considered one of Hindi cinema's best comedies. Songs like 'Kisne Pukara Mujhe', 'Gore Haathon Par Na Zulm Karo', 'O Meri Maina', 'Din Jawaani Ke Chaar', 'Dil Humne De Diya', 'Phool Ban Jaoonga' and 'Kehne Ki Nahin Baat' were all popular. Kishore Kumar was again the hero, though Shashi Kapoor and Mehmood were also prominent figures.

Chhota Bhai was a classic melodrama. By the time it came out, as we have seen, L-P had acquired a mastery over children's songs as well, thanks to Lata Mangeshkar's ever-present support. And so, Lata came in to sing the two songs filmed on the protagonist, played by child actor Mahesh Kothare, 'Na To Hum Darte Hain' and the classic heart-wrencher 'Maa Mujhe Apne Aanchal Mein Chhupa Le'. However, the ace in this score was 'Bhagwan Ne Apne Jaisa' filmed on Nutan. This devotional song towered in its potent amalgam of philosophical lyrics and deep melody, wondering how, if God had made human beings to resemble him, had they learnt to lie and commit sins ('*Bhagwan ne apne jaisa har ek insaan banaya / Yeh jhooth kidhar se aaye yeh paap kahan se aaya*'). This song exemplifies, in a superlative way, the individual mastery and combined synergy of Anand Bakshi's words and Laxmikant-Pyarelal's potent compositions. It served as a perfect illustration of what lyricist Hasrat Jaipuri told me in 1990 for a *Mid-Day* interview, 'If we [Shankar-Jaikishan and Hasrat Jaipuri] lost the RK banner with *Bobby*, I am happy that we lost to the only other great composer-lyricist team in Hindi cinema—Laxmi-Pyare and Anand Bakshi!'

L-P also composed what was their earliest blend of two tunes in one: the robustly earthy 'Baaje Baaje Mirdang' with its alternative inner melody 'Jao Jao Ghanashyam' in *Chhota Bhai*.

The smaller films were no less: *Naag Mandir* had the two-version (Lata and Mahendra Kapoor) haunting piece 'Mere Sanam Sun Mera Gham' and Rafi's superb 'Khamosh Zindagi Ko Awaaz

De Rahe Ho'; *Daku Mangal Singh* had the exceptional Lata hit 'Ek To Yeh Bahaar'; while *Sau Saal Baad* must rank among their best work in that year. *Sau Saal Baad* had beauties like Lata's reverberating triumph, 'Yeh Raat Bhi Ja Rahi Hai', exquisitely structured and orchestrated; Manna Dey-Lata Mangeshkar's classical masterpiece 'Ek Ritu Aaye Ek Ritu Jaaye' and Rafi's ultra-melodious 'Na Jaiyo Radhe Chhedenge Shyam'. Manna-Lata's 'Ab Ke Baras Yeh Bahaar' was another lovely semi-classical tune, strikingly different from the raag-based songs we were used to hearing in those times.

The eight-track *Dillagi* saw Rafi-Asha's unusually rhythmic 'Ab Jeene Ka Mausam Aaya', Lata's 'Kya Kahoon Aaj Kya Baat Hai' and the surefire hit, Lata-Mukesh's 'Hum Jeelenge Bin Tumhare'. Then there was the super-hit Mala Sinha-enacted number 'Kabutar Kabutar', her only song sung by Usha Mangeshkar.

Laxmikant once admitted that he had made the song to tease filmmaker O.P. Ralhan[22] whose nickname was 'kabutar' (pigeon) among insiders. But the exotic one was Rafi's 'Tauba Yeh Nazaare'. At this juncture, let us notice that Sanjay Khan had made his debut with *Dosti*, in which no song had been lip-synced by him. And so *Dillagi* began his tryst with the music duo, with predominantly Rafi numbers in seven more films (*Milan Ki Raat, Madhavi, Intaqam, Shart, Woh Din Yaad Karo, Haseenon Ka Devta* and *Duniya Ka Mela*) that had a certain similarity in tenor while still sounding totally different. Their last film together, *Kala Dhanda Goray Log* (1986) again had no song filmed on him. Interestingly, the film was also based on Khan's own story and was directed by him, with Rafi clones Shabbir Kumar and Mohammed Aziz as the only male voices!

---

[22]O.P. Ralhan had launched *Samson & Delilah* in the '70s starring Dharmendra and Hema Malini, in 70mm with L-P, which never took off. In the mid-'90s, Ralhan had launched *Dosh* with the recording of a song by them, but that film too was shelved.

Dillagi and *Mere Lal* quickly established the *Dosti* team of L-P and Majrooh Sultanpuri as one to reckon with, especially since there was nothing common in these three scores. For years, L-P and Majrooh were to remain a reputed and distinguished combination. *Laadla* was L-P's second film with lyricist and writing whiz Rajendra Krishan after *Pyar Kiye Jaa*. Even in a comparatively lesser score, they still managed two outstanding Lata numbers of contrasting hues: 'Meri Dua Le Ja Re' and 'Dil Ae Dil Teri Manzil'. Majrooh and Rajendra Krishan were now L-P's second and third backups respectively, after Bakshi.

The message now was very loud and clear: regardless of genre and setup, Laxmikant-Pyarelal were here to stay, and no one could ignore their chartbusting melodies. A new music duo was connecting with a new India, almost two decades after Independence, and pan-Indian melodies were given a fresh, innovative and vibrant treatment. There was more to come, for among other things, L-P were determined to mould the singing greats in their own way.

5

THE SUPERLATIVE DELUGE

In 1967, Laxmikant-Pyarelal once again chalked up 10 films as in 1966, but there was a cardinal difference: Except *Chhailla Baboo* (the first of their signed films to be finally completed) and the unreleased *Duniya Nachegi*, the remaining eight were big-setup movies. L-P had finally made the grade.

Having done Mala Sinha-Biswajeet's musical hit *Aasra*, they went on to work on two more films—*Jaal* and *Night in London*, both crime dramas, with the pair scoring extraordinary songs in both, though neither film garnered success. Those were the happy times when the film and its music had separate fortunes, and however bad or disastrous a film was, its songs would be noticed if they had merit. Suffice to say, these two films, as well as *Anita* and *Taqdeer* (both flops), and the three blockbusters *Milan*, *Shagird* and *Farz* each had multiple smash hit songs, and no song on those soundtracks was unpopular.

It was in this phase that the battle between S-J and L-P began.

L.V. Prasad's *Milan* was their monumental feat that year. L-P not only annexed their second Filmfare award but also topped the only and very popular radio countdown show *Binaca Geetmala* with the Mukesh-Lata duet 'Sawan Ka Mahina', which still draws applause whenever performed in any corner of the world. Chartbusters like 'Hum Tum Yug Yug Se', 'Bol Gori Bol', 'Mubarak Ho Sabko' and 'Tohe Saawariya' were the rage, not just heard on radio but also at functions and processions of all kinds, celebrations and parties, restaurants with piped music, jukeboxes and performed by orchestras—in short, just about everywhere.

Said Nitin Mukesh in my interview in the 1990s: 'Despite a huge hit like *Sangam* in 1964, my father had faced an inexplicable lull for two years when he barely got to record a new song. But after *Milan* and until his death in 1976, there was never a low in his career.' Needless to add, Mukesh never forgot this debt to L-P, as we shall see.

But Mukesh never fully knew what he owed L-P. After the phenomenal performance of *Dosti*, Tarachand Barjatya (as *Milan*'s financier) wanted an encore with Rafi as the only male singer, but the duo had thought of composing this score with Mukesh as the voice of the earthy village boatman hero who is reincarnated in *Milan*. Fortunately, in those days, interference from financiers was limited. L-P composed the songs with Mukesh and 'Mubarak Ho Sabko' was the first song to be created and recorded.

The young composers, still not in a strong enough position to overrule the powerful influence of Barjatya, quietly recorded the song in the morning. Mukesh sensed that something was wrong during the recording, but the composers reassured him. After Mukesh left, Barjatya and L.V. Prasad arrived and asked to hear the song Rafi had recorded! Hesistantly, Laxmikant told them that they had recorded with someone else. Laxmikant was able to convince Barjatya that a simple soul like the film's boatman hero, uneducated and rural, needed the innocence of Mukesh's voice. He requested them to hear the song, and promised that if they still wanted Rafi, they would scrap it. That did not happen.

L-P, as new composers, had a tough call in *Milan*. They had to at least match the two musical magnum opuses based on lovers reincarnated—Khemchand Prakash's 1949 film *Mahal* and Salil Chowdhury's 1958 *Madhumati*. And, as their future director K. Vishwanath revealed, they had to match the original Telugu film *Mooga Manasulu*'s score by K.V. Madadevan as well!

Farz began their almost 75-film and 30-year association with Jeetendra, who had signed a James Bond-like action drama to earn money for his sister's marriage—the actor had then released only his debut movie *Geet Gaya Pattharon Ne*, which had done well. 'Many actors had rejected *Farz*, but the filmmakers wanted only 35 days from me,' explained the actor, who thus took it on. Jeetendra and his new composers met the filmmakers based in South India in Mumbai at Famous Studios, where they had been summoned to watch the Telugu original, *Goodachari 116*, by producer Dhoondy and director Raveekant Nagaich. Krishna, then the top South hero, who is contemporary star Mahesh Babu's father, was the lead. Laxmikant drummed out 'Hum To Tere Aashiq Hain' and two more super-hit tunes on the actor's second-hand Fiat car while they drove back to the suburbs.

Jeetendra believes that when someone's destiny starts working, there is no limit. The actor feels that destiny works when there is talent, and talent works when there is passion for work. As he put it with a laugh, 'I hit it off from day one with Laxmikant-Pyarelal, and though one top composer tried to get close to me in the early 1970s, I was very comfortable with them. Their music was amazing even in my own production and biggest flop *Deedaar-E-Yaar*, which almost wiped me out in the '80s!'

Jeetendra acquired the lasting image of 'Jumping Jack' with *Farz*. Recently, when the actor met Pyarelal at a function, and he had to speak on the maestros, he had said, 'I have a four-storeyed house, and I want to tell everyone that out of those four floors, two are because of the contribution of Laxmikant and Pyarelal to my career!' The songs of *Farz* included the birthday perennial, Rafi's 'Baar Baar Din Yeh Aaye', a song so endemic that no one can dream of re-creating it in these times. Lata's 'Dekho Dekho Ji', Rafi-Suman Kalyanpur's 'Tumse Ae Haseena' and Rafi's 'Mast Baharon Ka Main Aashiq' all slalomed to the top along with Lata-Mukesh's 'Hum To Tere Aashiq Hain', which initially led the charts.

The third blockbuster was Subodh Mukerji's *Shagird*, L-P's second foray into Shankar-Jaikishan terrain. It was their earliest triumph vis-à-vis the man who had mocked them—S. Mukerji—

for Subodh was his younger brother who had also made many musical hits.

In 1967, for a while, the mini-saree worn by Saira Banu became a sensation, and the song 'Dil Vil Pyar Vyar' sung by Lata had a great deal to do with it. The introductory lines in this song had been sung by Rafi but did not make it to the record. The song topped the *Binaca Geetmala* 1968 annual programme—their second in a row after *Milan*, because the film was a late 1967 release and made most of its countdown run in the following year.

Rafi's appearance for two lines in this song within the movie was a sign of the deep affection and respect this monumental singer had for the duo. Such gestures by singers have often been seen in L-P's songs later. Amit Kumar rendered a line for Amitabh Bachchan that went '*Akbar tera naam nahin hai*' in the Rafi-rendered super-hit qawwali number 'Parda Hai Parda' filmed on Rishi Kapoor in *Amar Akbar Anthony*. In the final audio, it is only Rafi. Anup Jalota sang just two introductory lines—because had coincidentally walked in to meet the duo at their recording of 'Solah Baras Ki Bali Umar', their *Ek Duuje Ke Liye* Lata Mangeshkar classic. A barely-known fact is that Mahendra Kapoor and Manna Dey have sung a few lines in the beautiful 'Mere Man Baaja Mirdang' from the 1985 *Utsav*, though they are placed within the choral lines of the Suresh Wadkar-Anuradha Paudwal duet that picked up a Filmfare award for the latter! All these examples highlight the high and affectionate esteem both veteran and young singers had for the music duo.

Jaya, Laxmikant's wife, and Pyarelal share an interesting tidbit about 'Dil Vil Pyar Vyar'. 'We had a troublesome new Marathi maid who would constantly neglect important duties. When she was reprimanded, she would go "Aiyya!"' recalled Jaya with a laugh. And Pyarelal added, 'We were recording "Woh Hai Zara Khafa Khafa" for *Shagird*. And Laxmikant came in much later than usual. He said that the delay was because of this new maid who, when talking to his mother, would keep exclaiming, "Aiyya!"

(the Marathi equivalent of the exclamations 'Gosh!' or 'My God!')' Laxmikant confessed that he enjoyed their spats, and gave his partner an idea for the next song!

Pyarelal chuckled as he recollected that Laxmikant started singing the now-famous '*Aiyya! Dil vil pyar vyar main kya jaanoo re*', stating that this was the next song we could record for another situation in the same film! The words were Laxmikant's own, spontaneously born, and when he made lyricist Majrooh hear them, the writer had mock-reprimanded, '*Laxmi, tu mujhe kaam karne dega ki nahin?* (Will you let me do *my* work or not?)' That word was interpolated at intervals in the song and proved to be the highlight. And that's how the biggest chartbuster from the film was born. 'Bade Miya Deewane', 'Udte Pawan Ke Sang Chaloongi', 'Duniya Pagal Hai' and 'Kanha Kanha Aan Padi Main' formed the rest of the hit-fest by Lata, Rafi and Manna Dey. I.S. Johar's exclamation '*Yahi to maloom nahin hai*' in the first song by Rafi became another highlight. L-P and Majrooh had delivered another sixer.

The next musical milestone, in terms of release, preceded *Milan*, *Farz* and *Shagird*: Raj Khosla's *Anita*, planned as the last of a trilogy of his Sadhana suspense aces, *Woh Kaun Thi?* and *Mera Saaya*. Unlike those two thrillers, *Anita* flopped and again, unlike them, the chartbuster music was scored by L-P, not Madan Mohan, though the lyricist in both was the underrated Raja Mehdi Ali Khan. Said Khosla for an interview with *Mid-Day* in 1990, 'After I worked with L-P, I did not need anyone else!' The last of the nine films they did with Khosla, *Mera Dost Mera Dushman*, came in 1984. Khosla had signed L-P for a new suspense thriller just before his death in 1991.

Khosla had described their emotional bond thus: He had hit a very rough patch in the 1980s with finance no longer forthcoming after consecutive flops. 'When I planned my comeback film in 1988, they were at the very top, and I did not want to exploit our friendship by requesting them to reduce the price they commanded. So I signed Kamaal Makhdoom, a poor music teacher, to score music for *Naqab* with Rishi Kapoor and Farha, which released in 1989. But on Diwali day in 1990, I rang up Laxmi to tell him that we would be working together on my next. And Laxmi-ji told me, "You have given me the best possible birthday gift."'

Sadly, the filmmaker passed away while the film was being scripted.

Anita rocked the charts with its milestone perennials like Mukesh's 'Tum Bin Jeevan Kaise Beeta' and 'Gore Gore Chand Se Mukh Par', Lata's 'Kaise Karoon Prem Ki Main Baat', 'Saamne Mere Saawariya', 'Hai Nazar Ka Ishara' (with Usha Mangeshkar) and that unique masterpiece, 'Karib Aa Yeh Nazar'. Anand Bakshi wrote 'Hai Nazar Ka Ishara' after Khan passed away, while 'Gore Gore Chand Se Mukh Par' was a classic ghazal penned by Arzoo Lucknowi, who had migrated to Pakistan and had passed away there in 1951.

Taqdeer, L-P's Rajshri follow-up to *Dosti*, as well as *Jaal* and *Night in London* (their first film shot abroad) all featured impressive music. Like all of L-P's songs that year, the music spread like wildfire around the country, heard in every nook and cranny. Sulakshana Pandit, later a top star and also a singer, made her debut as child singer with 'Saat Samandar Paar Se' alongside Lata Mangeshkar, Meena Patki and Ila Desai. The other big hits were 'Jab Jab Bahaar Aayi' (in three versions), 'Kaise Koi Jaane Bhala' and 'Mujhe Bhool Jaana Agar Ho Sake'. Mohammed Rafi was the major male singer.

Jaal and *Night in London* also were hit-fests: In the former, Laxmikant playfully employed the Madan Mohan style for Lata's 'Meri Zindagi Ke Chirag Ko', written by that senior composer's favourite lyricist Raja Mehdi Ali Khan. The other songs that also hit the pop parade were 'Dhadka Hai Dil Mein', 'Rokna Hai Agar' (both solos by Lata), Lata-Rafi's 'Mizaj-e-Garami Dua Hai Aapki' and Rafi's 'Akela Hoon Main Humsafar Dhoondta Hoon'. *Night in*

London had the all-time favourite 'Nazar Na Lag Jaaye' by Rafi, who also sang 'Bahosh-O-Hawaas Main Diwana', the Lata duets 'Baag Mein Phool Kisne Churaye Hain' and the title song. The Lata-Mahendra Kapoor duet 'Sun Ae Bahaar-E-Husn' was also very popular. And for the unique cabaret number by Lata, whose refrain was 'Jameela', L-P took a note out of O.P. Nayyar's book—Lata enunciated this word differently each time, similar to what Rafi had done in the lines *'Taarif karoon kya usski'* in that composer's 'Kashmir Ki Kali', where he had sung each 'Taarif' differently! Recalled Pyarelal, 'We even travelled to London to get a feel of the city, which helped us in setting the music for "Nazar Na Lag Jaaye" and the title song, which was a duet by Rafi and Lata.'

The film *Chhailla Baboo* is best known for the Rafi stunner 'Tere Pyar Ne Mujhe Gham Diya'. Salim Khan,[23] the legendary writer and father of Salman Khan, enacted 'Kyoon Jhuki Jhuki Hai Palkein', with Mukesh as his voice in the Lata duet.

In this film, L-P also used Mukesh as the voice for comedian Rajendranath in 'Raahi Hoon Albela', while recording the very catchy 'Dekho Ji Behke Na Chaal' with C. Ramachandra, whom they adored and admired as a senior singer-composer, and Asha Bhosle. About their bond with the senior legend, Laxmikant had this to say during his *Junior G* interview, 'In those days, the Filmfare awards were declared in the newspapers. On the day it was announced that *Dosti* had won us the award, Anna (C. Ramachandra) came to our house early in the morning, and pounded on our door, shouting, "*Uthaa gaadhvaano, tumhala award milala aahe!* (Get up, donkeys, you have won an award!)"'

---

[23]Laxmikant-Pyarelal composed for Salim Khan's first film as writer, *Do Bhai*, and in 1971 for his first collaboration with Javed as a writer, *Haathi Mere Saathi*. In 1986, L-P also scored Salim Khan's first independent film after his split with Javed—*Naam*. Destiny indeed is strange: for when Salman Khan started out, his debut film (though no song was lip-synched by him) was L-P's *Biwi Ho To Aisi*. And *Chhaila Baboo* was L-P's first signed film to see completion.

The Superlative Deluge

Among their other releases in the decisive year that was 1967, *Milan Ki Raat* saw another musical winner in its roaring Rafi hit 'Aankh Milaye Na Muskurayae Na'. But in this rather average score, the zinger was Asha's 'Doom Tara', a heady display of coquetry that has few equals. However, *Duniya Nachegi* remains a bit of a conundrum. As an actor, Kishore Kumar's grasp on the market was so low by then that the music was released, but the film never got a pan-Indian release. However, it did have a couple of remarkable songs. With this film, L-P joined the list of composers, led by Shankar-Jaikishan and O.P. Nayyar, who had used other playback voices for Kishore on screen. They employed Manna Dey as his voice in 'Jo Main Hota Hawaa Ka Jhonka', a delightful duet with Asha that remains the duo's only song written by the then-struggling Yogesh. Kishore's own 'Nahin Nahin Javoonga' was a crazy trip for the boisterous star-singer.

In such a solid deluge, the competition had to start drowning. And the L-P flood never receded for a long, long time.

6

TOP GUNS AT LAST

For those who lived through those times, the S-J versus L-P battle was perhaps the most magnificent one ever fought in the annals of Hindi film music, with only outstanding songs as weapons. 1968 and 1969 saw S-J fighting valiantly to retain their supremacy, with their own split and Lata Mangeshkar refusing to record for Shankar[24] becoming added liabilities. One must also concede that Jaikishan's spirit had been heavily affected after he and his partner separated, despite the fact that they had always composed songs separately even when together. *Brahmachari, Shikar, An Evening in Paris, Jhuk Gaya Aasmaan, Mere Huzoor, Yakeen* and *Prince* were their strongest scores in these two years among other films that had individual super-hit numbers, some examples being 'Likhe Jo Khat Tujhe' (*Kanyadaan*), 'Seekha Nahin Sabak' (*Sapnon Ka Saudagar*) and 'Dooriyaan Nazdeekiyan Ban Gayi' (*Duniya*).

But with L-P unleashing a far greater number of films that also included, for starters, musical humdingers like *Baharon Ki Manzil, Patthar Ke Sanam, Mere Hamdum Mere Dost, Raja Aur Runk, Izzat, Do Raaste, Sadhu Aur Shaitan, Sajan, Aya Sawan Jhoom*

---

[24]Lata Mangeshkar was furious with both Raj Kapoor and Shankar for making her sing '*Main kya karoon Ram mujhe buddha mil gaya*' from *Sangam*. It is said that Shankar promoting Sharda as singer also had an additional role. Jaikishan continued to record with Lata till his demise in 1971. While Raj Kapoor brought in L-P for *Bobby* to be able to record with her again, Shankar made his peace with her only with *Sanyasi* (1975).

Ke, Jeene Ki Raah (which won them their third Filmfare trophy), *Dharti Kahe Pukar Ke, Anjaana, Jigri Dost* and *Intaqam*, one could even say that there was no real battle—for L-P's army of great melodies was far greater. Quantitatively as well as qualitatively, S-J were completely outclassed. As trade analyst Vinod Mirani put it, 'I find it truly remarkable that the incredible success story went on for three decades through paradigm changes in trends, tastes and lifestyles, and without the kind of media-hype, marketing and promotion seen now. All that was there in their time was the radio. And their only weapon was their tune and the melody in it. L-P were not all about one or two hit songs per film. The entire album would be a hit!'

In these two years, this was true of all the scores above. And as Naushad had stated in the 1990s in front of the duo, 'We all did 60 or 70 films in our entire career. And these youngsters have done almost 500 films. *Yeh hum logon ke bas ki baat nahin thi* (This was something beyond our capacities)!'

And this wasn't all. There were lesser popular scores too, like *Pyasi Sham, Aansoo Ban Gaye Phool, Meri Bhabhi, Shart, Wapas, Madhavi, Satyakam* and the last of their initial lot of small films, *Mera Dost* and *Spy in Rome*.

To mention the hits from each of the first lot of aces above would simply occupy too much space, as they are all well-known songs to this day. A mention of the mix of the biggest hits and best songs should serve the purpose here, though I grant that the 'best' can have a subjective interpretation. Happily, most of these songs fall in the former category as well: 'Mehboob Mere' and 'Koi Nahin Hai' besides the title-track from *Patthar Ke Sanam*; 'Na Ja Kahin Ab Na Ja', 'Chhalkaye Jaam', 'Hui Sham Unnka Khayaal' and 'Chalo Sajana' (*Mere Hamdam Mere Dost*); 'Mera Naam Hai Chameli' and 'Phirkiwali' (*Raja Aur Runk*); 'Kya Miliye Aise Logon Se', 'Jaagi Badan Mein Jwala' and 'Yeh Dil Tum Bin' (*Izzat*); 'Bindiya Chamkegi', 'Yeh Reshmi Zulfen', 'Chhup Gaye Saare Nazarein', 'Apni Apni Biwi' and 'Khizaan Ke Phool' (*Do

Raaste); 'Resham Ki Dori' and 'Sajan Sajan' (*Sajan*) and 'Maanjhi Chal O Maanjhi Chal', 'Rama Duhai', 'Yeh Shama To Jali' and 'Badraa Chhaye' (*Aaya Sawan Jhoom Ke*) were among the best. It is interesting to know that for 'Ae Dushmun-E-Jaan' from *Patthar Ke Sanam* sung by Asha Bhosle, the duo found inspiration while on a trip to Lebanon. They had met Fairouz, the famous Arabic singer, and her husband and his brother who composed her songs. L-P liked her guttural way of singing so much that they got Asha to do the same in the way she intoned 'Ahaa' after the word 'Allah'.

And there were many more hits: 'Aap Mujhe Acche Lagne Lage' won Lata the last of the Filmfare awards she accepted, and there were also 'Ek Banjara Gaaye', 'Badi Mastani Hai' and 'Aa Mere Humjoli Aa' in *Jeene Ki Raah*; 'Je Hum Tum Chori Se', 'Khushi Ki Woh Raat Aa Gayi' and 'Ja Re Kaare Badra' (*Dharti Kahe Pukar Ke*); 'Ke Jaan Chali Jaaye', 'Woh Kaun Hai' and 'Rimjhim Ke Geet' (*Anjaana*); 'Raat Suhani Jaag Rahi Hai' and 'Phool Hai Baharon Ka' (*Jigri Dost*); the timeless cabaret 'Aa Jaan-E-Jaan', 'Geet Tere Saaz Ka' and 'Kaise Rahoon Chup' (which topped the *Binaca Geetmala* in 1969 in their hat-trick) and 'Jo Unnki Tamanna Hai' (*Intaqam*) among several others.

Few songs of L-P have shown their mastery over Western music as much as 'Aaja Re Piya Khilne Lage' (*Baharon Ki Manzil*) with its piquant structure, and this score was noteworthy for the fact that all its four songs were sung by Lata Mangeshkar, and yet were of totally diverse shades! The evergreen was 'Nigahen Kyoon Bhatakti Hai', but they composed another children's song in the saccharine 'Janam Din Aaya' and went the Madan Mohan way again after *Jaal* with the brilliant 'Yeh Daaman Ab Na Chhutega'. According to Pyarelal, this was done on Lata Mangeshkar's request.

There are two films of import here—*Anjaana* and *Dharti Kahe Pukar Ke*. About *Anjaana*, hit writer-filmmaker Mohan Kumar said, 'Rajendra Kumar was losing out commercially thanks to multiple flops. I decided to rejuvenate his career with a young heroine, Babita, and a fresh music team—Laxmikant-Pyarelal and Anand Bakshi. *Anjaana* became his first musical hit after multiple flops.'

The other important film was *Dharti Kahe Pukar Ke*, memorable for one more reason. Shailendra, who the late Hasrat Jaipuri remembers as the dada (in this case, the man who called the shots) of their quartet with S-J, was a close friend of the film's producer Deenanath Shastri, who was also Dharmendra's secretary then. As per the lyricist's son, Dinesh Shailendra, the master poet had expressed a wish to work with the upcoming boys Laxmikant and Pyarelal and was signed for this film. But the lyricist passed away a few days before the muhurat. His health had begun failing after he produced the monumental flop *Teesri Kasam*, and he died before even a sitting could take place. Shailendra thus remains the only major lyricist from this era with whom L-P never worked.

As we have mentioned, the hit-fest was not restricted at all to the all-hit scores: *Pyasi Sham* had that unique gem by Rafi, 'Awara Maanjhi', topping the list. *Aansoo Ban Gaye Phool* had the exquisite Asha delight for Helen, 'Meherbaan Mehboob' (which must be one of the most soothing seduction numbers in film music history and oozed sensuality) besides the hit Kishore-Asha duet 'Jaane Kaisa Hai Mera Diwana'. Kishore was the sole male singer in this Ashok Kumar home production officially produced by their brother Anoop Kumar. Thus, this film is the first home production of any big star with L-P's music, another area in which they were to soon reign supreme.

The lullaby was another genre in which L-P had proved their mettle after *Aasra* with 'Mere Soone Jeevan Ka Aasra' and *Milan* with 'Ram Kare' and their third quasi-masterpiece in *Meri Bhabhi* 'Soya Mera Pyar'. This film's other Lata stunner that was on charts was 'Pawan Jhakora Sang Mere Gaaye'.

Shart had the popular Rafi track 'Ae Haseena Nazneena' and Lata's 'Tu Kaun Hai', but the one that grabbed attention was Suman

Kalyanpur's intensely melodious 'Aaj Raat Jaadoo Sa'. *Wapas* saw the super-hit sparklers 'Ek Tera Saath', 'Aayi Baharon Ki Shaam' and 'Painjaniya Chhanke Ram'—the latter song we have already mentioned.

Madhavi had the superb Lata devotional 'Sham Savere Adharon Pe Mere' and the sweet Lata-Asha duet 'Nandkishore Nandgopal' and *Mera Dost* had the sonorous 'Tumhi Se Hui Hai Shuru' by Rafi. *Spy in Rome*, their weakest score since they started out, was salvaged, however, by the exquisitely orchestrated Rafi solo 'Rome Ki Waadiyon Se'.

Behind *Sadhu Aur Shaitan* (a home production of Mehmood) is a small and unconfirmed story: Mehmood had launched R.D. Burman's career and done three films as a producer with him. Burman was also close to L-P and they had arranged two of those films, *Chhote Nawab* and *Bhoot Bungla*. This had brought L-P close to Mehmood as well. It is said that when *Padosan* (now a cult film) was first released, it entailed losses for its distributors, and in those days the convention was that the producer's next film should compensate them. A small-budget film was thus conceived: a crime thriller with loads of emotions and humour (total comedies were not really known to work at the box-office then) and many guest appearances by stars like Dilip Kumar and Mumtaz among others. It is possible that the distributors insisted on the more saleable L-P, as one source told me, and their combination with Rafi.

So, Kishore Kumar, who was one of the pivotal actors in *Padosan*, ended up starring in this new film too, but not having a single song either for himself or anyone else—making the film a unique one in his long career. From the four songs here, the two fun Rafi solos 'Kabhi Aage Kabhi Peeche' and 'Mehbooba Mehbooba Bana Do Mujhe Dulha' filmed on Mehmood were hits. The film too did well and Mehmood was out of the red. As a filmmaker, Mehmood returned to R.D. Burman, but the Mehmood-L-P friendship and professional association continued with other films like *Humjoli* (starring Mehmood in a triple role) and *Mastana* (in which Mehmood played the eponymous hero) besides many other films.

Satyakam (produced by Dharmendra's brother-in-law S.J.S. Punchhe) has been openly declared by Phalke laureate and ace director Hrishikesh Mukherjee as his finest film ever. From its mere three songs, Lata's 'Do Din Ki Zindagi' and 'Abhi Kya Sunoge' are now thought of as classics, and Kaifi Azmi's third hard-hitting song, 'Aadmi Hai Kya', was unique in the fact that three major singers sang it together—Mukesh (for Dharmendra), Mahendra Kapoor and Kishore Kumar. The dual structure of the song stood out with the boisterous Mahendra-Kishore portions (filmed on supporting artistes Asrani and Robi Ghosh) and the sobriety of Mukesh's lines. This proved unequivocally, if proof was still needed, that L-P were unparalleled at composing for a situation and for characters. To put it in a paradoxical nutshell, they were masters at being slaves to a film's situation.

The 1960s had ended with Laxmikant-Pyarelal upstaging Shankar-Jaikishan, an iconic duo that had ruled for 20 years. After 53 films in seven years, L-P did not know it then, but their rule at the top was going to be a very long one.

7

THE SECRET OF
A SPECTACULAR VICTORY

'Laxmikant often stated that they became music directors because they wanted their songs to be played on the *Binaca Geetmala*!' recalls radio legend and *Binaca Geetmala* host Ameen Sayani. And L-P achieved, within six years, what other giant composers could never do in 20—steal a march over market leaders Shankar-Jaikishan.

Around the end of the 1960s, the first big name to sign L-P was V. Shantaram, for his dance musical, *Jal Bin Machhli Nritya Bin Bijli*, also Indian cinema's *first* soundtrack in Stereophonic Sound. They also signed two films with Bengali whizkid Asit Sen—*Sharafat* and *Maa Aur Mamta*—and one with producer Premji (*Mastana*). H.S. Rawail signed them for *Mehboob Ki Mehndi* as well.

Maa Aur Mamta was produced by M.M. Malhotra and Baldev Pushkarna. These two producers, individually and together, never worked with any other composer all the way to their last film in 1996—*Paapi Devataa*. The list included seven films, of which *Aakhri Dao* and *Chacha Bhatija* did good business, but most films had good to great music, especially *Roop Tera Mastana*. The industry and everyone had observed the duo from close quarters, and the simple common explanation, 'They worked very hard' was not entirely enough. In addition, one has to look at other factors.

And one prominent one was the social era of those times. A keen observer notes the point that in those times, a lot of middle-class and educated people looked down upon Hindi cinema. I personally recall, as a child, the huge prejudices, bordering even on contempt that some relatives, friends and their families had against movies as well as film folk. Some of my own close relatives even lambasted Hindi cinema and its music as 'cheap' and never looked beyond Marathi semi-classical and classical music. In fact, in many households, even in North India, listening to a Hindi song on radio was forbidden! Television had yet to come in, except for a two-hour broadcast in New Delhi.

Songs serenading girls, mujras, cabaret numbers and many other kinds of lyrics were looked down upon despite their content of rich verse and raags. The prominent western influences brought in by some leading composers added to the 'negativity' of opinion.

There was a sharp compartmentalization: those who listened to Western classical or traditional Indian music of all hues never liked Hindi film music, and vice-versa. Thus, there was a sharp divide: there were those who loved Hindi film music and Hindi cinema, and those who loathed it. Add the fact that gramophone records were expensive (for those times) and the general condescension towards film people, especially actors and actresses, and it all added to films being, almost, 'forbidden fruit'.

L-P's music broke this barrier.

Also, barring films of a few composers like Shankar-Jaikishan and O.P. Nayyar, and occasional soundtracks from others, there was no craving to buy the entire LP (Long-Playing) record, because very few complete scores of other composers were worth keeping for posterity. This is where L-P scored success: soundtrack after soundtrack (over 20 until 1969) was deemed worthy of treasuring as complete albums. That made the expensive L-P record worth its price. Suddenly, there was a plethora of music that everyone seemed to like, and detractors of the genre did not mind them and gradually started liking and humming these songs. The simple compositions (and 'simple' is the most difficult to make) oozed Indianness and melody, the strong raags were the solid base, and the folk elements connected deep at the core of even urban Indians, while striking a natural resonance in smaller towns and rural areas. The nation, almost en masse, found the songs hummable. The opposition melted and new followers came in. In short, here was pan-Indian music for, perhaps, the first time in a long while. For all of S-J's versatility, O.P. Nayyar's popular appeal, C. Ramachandra's mastery, and Naushad's and S.D. Burman's elite mix of classicism and folk, the sustained power of L-P, which could go into any zone with melodious ease, was seemingly born to eliminate the competition. When the duo came in, it was with the vital armamentarium of knowing the best and worst qualities of all the leading composers they had assisted, and the two youngsters knew what they should do as composers and what they should not. And such 'dos' and 'donts' were even more important for them as people.

Laxmikant himself recalled experiencing or watching the tempers of some of his seniors and their humiliating behaviour towards assistants, musicians, singers and other associates. Pyarelal admitted that while he was inclined to be temperamental and hot-headed, his partner was the balm that soothed not only him but everyone else around. Said Amar Haldipur, who worked with them for 33 years as a musician: 'Laxmi-ji would just put his arm around an irate filmmaker's shoulder and the result would be magical.' They had learnt swiftly from the errors of others around them. L-P had found a soulmate in lyricist Anand Bakshi, yet they knew the importance of working with every writer to enrich their repertoire.

And so, almost every lyricist worked with them, even if for only one film, like Pradeep (*Harishchandra Taramati*), Neeraj (two songs in the unreleased 1986 film *Uddhaar*) and Qamar Jalalabadi (*Kachcha Chor*). A few worked on only one song, like Shakeel Badayuni (in that superlative L-P-meets-Naushad lullaby 'Mere Dil Aaj Tu Maayoos' from *Jurm Aur Saza*), Yogesh (as mentioned in *Duniya Nachegi*) or Prem Dhawan ('Kal Raat Ek Sapna Dekha' recorded by Lata and Rafi for the shelved *Hum Tum Aur Woh*—their first recorded but unreleased song with the male singer).

The same applied to singers, though the composers' natural affinity for the top singers led them to use those voices more. Like Kishore in 'Mere Mehboob Qayamat Hogi', L-P also steadfastly refused to be cowed down by the singers' pre-existing styles and made Lata, Rafi and Mukesh blaze new trails like Kishore. The same was done to greater or lesser extents with Manna Dey, Mahendra Kapoor and Asha Bhosle. Economically, the fact that most of their scores were well-rounded albums also made their music good value-for-money, and this extended to the era of cassettes in the 1990s. A veteran salesman at Mumbai's then prime music outlet, Rhythm House, requesting anonymity, stated to me in 2003, that there were less than a handful of composers whose soundtracks continued to sell for decades and this exclusive list was led by the duo.

The duo had a precious mantra which they held on to rigidly to the end: that a filmmaker's brief and song situation were supreme and ruled their creativity. There was not even the faintest desire to 'show off what we could do' in any song or score, as Laxmikant once candidly expressed to me. Citing the example of the deceptively simple 'Main Shaayar To Nahin' in *Bobby*, Laxmikant said in an interview with me, 'A convent-school boy, who has lived in a boarding school for long, comes home. With such a background, this rich Punjabi boy can hardly be a master of Hindi as a language. So when he falls in love at first sight and wants to express his feelings, he uses simple words in a simple tune.' He had added, matter-of-factly, 'This was not the place to show off our classical expertise or where Bakshi ji could write a ghazal rich in Urdu or Hindi. Raj (Kapoor) saab understood this, but in all honesty, many of our seniors would have done precisely that! A song should never be at the expense of the film, but to fit its story and characters.'

Laxmikant's hardcore businesslike approach, minus

compromise on quality, turned S-J's gambit back on the veteran duo. The senior duo would also go to top filmmakers expressing their wish to work with them, using this technique to get big names on their list. But to L-P's credit, in over 90 per cent of the cases, the filmmakers did not move away from them for a long time, even to more economic composers or newcomers. 'We became a habit,' summed up the smiling Laxmikant, without the faintest hint of arrogance. As Laxmikant's wife Jaya said with wry pride, 'I never remember getting a proper vacation with L[25] in over 30 years of marriage. His life was for music. Once we went with him for a brief vacation, and even there, he excused himself to discuss music on the phone with a producer!'

In the mid-1990s, there was once one of those power failures that would affect the entire city. At Mehboob Studios in Bandra, around 4 in the afternoon, the recording was cancelled and Laxmikant, who would come around that time, had been called and told not to drive down. I remember driving in from town for a routine visit to their recordings, unaware of the power failure, and found Pyarelal to be missing. The musicians waiting below the first-floor recording studio told me that he had not gone home though.

After searching for him everywhere, including in the studio canteen and other rooms, I decided to peek into the recording engineer's room. It was in pitch darkness as that area and the recording hall had no windows and the airconditioning too was obviously off. To my amazement, as soon as I opened the door, I heard the tinkle of a piano from inside the recording hall. I opened the door of the hall (which could accommodate over 150 musicians and dozens of chorus singers) and saw a glow in the darkness. Oblivious of the lack of fresh air and light, Pyare-bhai was sitting on a piano, writing and playing music in the wan

---

[25]Mrs Jaya Laxmikant always addressed and referred to her husband by this pet name: 'L'

light of just one candle!

As Padma Vibhushan flautist Pt Hariparasad Chaurasia, who had worked with them for most of their long and prolific career, told me, 'Their temperament showed how their parents had brought them up. There was a lot to learn from both of them, and they understood what film music should be. They came armed with their elders' aashirwad (blessings), prepared to do endless hard work, and to learn so much that eventually, everyone else could learn so much from them.'

Almost 55 years later, Pandit ji is still wonder-struck at their quick progress and triumph. 'When I had composed music for an Odia film in the early 1960s, they had been among my musicians, and I found them very sureele (musically perfect),' he recalled. 'When they were signed for *Parasmani*, they invited me to play the flute, and I saw another image. Laxmikant made such hummable songs for any situation and Pyarelal gave it an *alag roop* (unique form) because of his arrangements: what that man can do is beyond understanding!'

He went on, 'And they came in, with a small film, amidst so many diggajh (stalwart) composers. And all of them had no choice but to watch these youngsters zoom past! *Kehna nahin chahiye, par aisi acchi jodi nahin dekhi.* (Maybe I should not say it, but I never saw a team like them.) Waah!'

I remember a huge off-handed compliment Pandit ji had paid L-P on stage during a show to commemorate his seventieth birthday, in 2008 in Mumbai. The mega-event was held by the music label Music Today, and Pandit ji had talked about his experiences as a musician with every composer from the 1950s to the millennium. When it came to Laxmikant-Pyarelal, he simply said, '*Bhagwan ne inke saath bahut badi nainsaafi ki hai.* (God has been very unjust to them.)' After a dramatic pause, he had added, '*Inko aisa hunar diya hai jo kisiko nahin diya!* (He has given them talent of the level He never bestowed on anyone else!)'

I gently reminded the living legend of this incident when we met for this book in 2019. He looked at me, made an expressive gesture with his hands and said, '*To sahi to baat hai* (Should I not say something that is correct)! *Hum din ko kya din nahin kahenge* (Should I not call a morning a morning)?' That remark, then heard by a couple of thousand people in the auditorium (and remembered maybe by only a few of them), is now audio-recorded with me for posterity.

And so, all the legends who lost out to L-P did not need to really feel upset. If they did fall behind, it was to this extraordinary calibre of creators in those turnaround years for Hindi film music.

8

THE HISTORIC SWEEP CONTINUES

The 1970s began scintillatingly for them, though one senior critic scoffed at them, asking, 'And what standards can you expect from L-P when they did so many films?' But L-P, as said earlier, never found quantity a problem. *Abhinetri, Khilona, Sharafat, Jeevan Mrityu, Mastana, Suhana Safar, Maa Aur Mamta, Humjoli* (Jeetendra's home production), *Bachpan, Darpan* and *Aan Milo Sajana* were their multiple highs in 1970, with iconic songs leading their charts like 'Jhilmil Sitaron Ka Aangan Hoga' (*Jeevan Mrityu*), 'Accha To Hum Chalte Hain' (*Aan Milo Sajana*), 'Sa Re Ga Ma Pa' (*Abhinetri*), and 'Khilona Jaan Kar' (*Khilona*).

For good measure, they had also done an Indo-Iranian co-production, *Subah-O-Sham*, featuring Sanjeev Kumar, Waheeda Rehman and a top Iranian actor, Fardeen, way back in 1972.

From here on, my detailing of individual years and even decades will be far less detailed. And here are the reasons.

The first and foremost reason is that after 1969, L-P had nothing left to prove, other than the fact that quantity never really affected their quality as their passion and hard work never reduced. If L-P completed their first seven years in the 1960s with 53 films, thus averaging almost eight films a year, their 1970s tally was an incredible 166, their average over double of that figure!

And giving L-P consistent support in such prolific output were all the singing greats of those times, apart from the master poets.

Let it be remembered that these 166 films meant about 850 songs as well as those films' background scores, which the duo never left to assistants, and which sometimes took weeks to compose if the producer or director was fastidious enough! Here, we also do not consider songs recorded for films that never took off or were aborted midway.

Among such films was *Rajmata*, their first Hindi-Marathi bilingual. Launched soon after their 1978 tour-de-force, *Satyam Shivam Sundaram*, the film, based on Chhatrapati Shivaji's mother, Jijabai, was to be directed by Padmanabh, Raj Khosla's former assistant. It was to be produced by an organization dedicated to the legacy of Jijabai, the Rajmata Jijau Pratisthan.

A song, written by Pt Narendra Sharma, who had staged a comeback with *Satyam Shivam Sundaram*, was recorded by Lata Mangeshkar for the film in which Nutan was to play the title-role. Sharma's son Paritosh had said that song was 'incredible', but there is no access to it as of now.

Yes, to seemingly contradict what we said earlier, there was a perceptible fall in quality. But there were cogent reasons for that. The most important one was the dubious practice of 'sittings' that came in during the early 1970s. We do not know why this happened, though in light of how things began to fare even worse from the 1990s, a very possible reason was the emergence of the first music company to rival the monopoly of HMV (now Saregama)—the German giant Polydor (now Universal Music). This may have set the first of several unsavoury business practices into motion.

Polydor, whose first album with L-P was *Bachpan* (1970), even issued cover-versions of popular HMV scores, but they did it after HMV started this dubious practice with the new company's first hits!

So what were these 'sittings'? Well, music directors were made to display their 'wares', that is, the tunes they had in stock or could compose on-spot. Very often, the choice of the song by a director (as perfect for the situation) would be overruled for perceived 'economic' reasons by not just the music company executives but even the distributors and just about anyone else, producer and star included.

Another reason, seemingly far-fetched yet very real, was the significant reduction in competition. Laxmikant did once tell me that most of their inspiration came from other composers, all of whom, he said, 'kept us on our toes'. The mid-1970s also saw the fall of S-J (barring a *Lal Patthar* and *Sanyasi*, as Shankar just could not match up commercially after Jaikishan's death).

'It was Kalyanji-Anandji, R.D. Burman and Dada (S.D. Burman) who kept alive our competitive spirit,' the composer told me. And S.D. Burman passed away in 1975.

The decline or exit of music directors as varied as Ravi, Chitragupta, O.P. Nayyar, Hemant Kumar, Salil Chowdhury and Naushad and the 1975 deaths of Madan Mohan (and Vasant Desai) added to this. Then in 1976, Mukesh also passed away, ironically after recording his last song for L-P in *Satyam Shivam Sundaram*. After the recording, he left for the airport for a U.S. concert tour, from which he never returned.

There is also, unconfirmed and almost in the category of gossip, one more reason. As someone very close to the two, who would not like to be named, told me, 'Lata Mangeshkar gave an interview in 1975, stating that music was now "finished" as Jaikishan, Madan Mohan and Dada Burman had all gone. At a time when she was recording half her film songs for L-P alone, and sometimes two or three songs in a day, this reached the ears of Pyarelal, who was furious! Until then, Pyarelal did have a hand in shaping many compositions, but after that, he refused to have anything to do with the tunes and concentrated on the orchestration for a while till he cooled down.'

As Laxmikant had told me at least twice, 'Pyare would not only compose great tunes but also tweak my tune here and there, and turn my 25-paise composition into one worth a rupee!'

Those who swear by L-P's vintage sound and songs will notice a sharp divide after 1975. 'That's when L-P became absolutely commercial,' explained an associate. 'Of course, work had increased tremendously as well, and many distributors had begun to insist on them for different reasons, all leading to the same goal—L-P! They thus chose to divide their work: Laxmikant began to look after making the tunes and sittings with the filmmakers, and Pyarelal concentrated on the orchestration and recordings.'

Thus, smaller banners or filmmakers needed the market boost from their music, while the big-name banners and filmmakers could do even better with L-P's name, clout and music, and those who had given flops with other music directors believed that they could turn their luck around with L-P. 'Signing L-P increased the look and viability of a film,' recalled trade analyst Taran Adarsh, son of B.K. Adarsh.

Add loyal filmmakers who themselves wanted to repeat the duo, and we see why they did so many films. Laxmikant could never say 'No' to anyone, and for him, price was never the issue. All he wanted was work, which was something he could not do without.

An interesting example here is revealed by filmmaker Ravi Tandon, who is actress Raveena Tandon's father: Tandon had wanted to sign a top composer for his own first production, *Anhonee*, a suspense thriller with Sanjeev Kumar, and had gone to meet him. 'At that time, he virtually took my interview, asking me how I would be managing my finances, what would happen if the film got stuck midway, and so on,' Tandon told me.

But when Tandon met Laxmikant, all he said with a smile was, 'Don't worry about the budget. You look after the making of the film. We will look after its music.' He won the filmmaker's heart.

That *Anhonee* had the all-timer 'Hungama Ho Gaya' (re-created in the 2014 *Queen*) and hit songs like 'Buddhu Pad Gaya Palle', 'Main To Ek Paagal' and 'Balma Hamaro Motorcar Leke Aayo Re' speaks volumes for the composers' approach. L-P went on to do six more films with Tandon, including the musically rich *Majboor* (1974), *Apne Rang Hazaar* (1975) and *Jawaab* (1985).

Towards the late '70s, L-P shifted from Famous Tardeo to

Mehboob Studios in Bandra, a stone's throw from Pyarelal's house and much closer for Laxmikant as well. Pyarelal, who never worked from home, would reach the studio around 10 a.m. and would be there until the recording concluded, any time between 6 p.m. and midnight! Robin Chatterjee, with whom L-P had worked earlier as musicians in films like Kalyanji-Anandji's *Jab Jab Phool Khile*, was the sound recordist in this studio, followed by Vasant Mudaliar and finally A.N. Tagore.

Their music thus acquired a big sound from the late 1970s, as the sound at Mehboob was recorded on the audio part of a 35mm film tape. Pyarelal extracted the best from the maximum musicians, which included renowned names even from classical music.

Even out-of-work musicians and composers would be respectfully asked to come into the orchestra, which became known as a langar—the term for a Sikh community tradition where a free meal is served to visitors without distinction of economic status or ethnicity.

Their singers also had to be full-throated for their voices to command attention over the large orchestra. Legendary recordist Hitendra Ghosh of Rajkamal Studios, who worked on the final mix of completed films, had this to say, 'The lyrics must be heard prominently among the 16 tracks of the song. I have had problems convincing some of the composers on this. But then there have been composers like Kalyanji-Anandji, Laxmikant-Pyarelal, Nadeem-Shravan, A.R. Rahman and Himesh Reshammiya, who made sure that the words were heightened and clearly heard.'

1971 and 1972 were years in which, after *The Train*, R.D. Burman came in like a cyclone, leaving everyone demoralized except good friends L-P and K-A. After Jaikishan's death, Pancham, as he was known, was also signed by S-J's loyal producers G.P. Sippy and Bhappi Sonie.

L-P too were affected a tad by the R.D. wave. Raj Khosla

produced *Do Chor* with him. After his brother's *Humjoli* with them, Jeetendra's next home production *Parichay* too went to R.D. Burman because of writer-director Gulzar, and so did Dharmendra's *Samadhi* after his uncle's *Satyakam* with L-P's music. J. Om Prakash too went with R.D. as his writer, Sachin Bhaumick, had promised Pancham a break if he ever turned director, which he did with *Raja Rani*. And Ravee Nagaich, who had directed *The Train*, preferred R.D. for *Pyar Ki Kahani* and *Mere Jeevan Saathi* (after L-P's tepid *Haseenon Ka Devta* with him in 1971). The Chennai-based banner of Olympic Pictures that had produced L-P's *Chhota Bhai* and *Devi* switched to R.D. with *Apna Desh*. R.D. had also been signed by RK Films for *Dharam Karam* on the same day that L-P were signed for *Bobby*. And Yash Chopra directed *Joshila* with R.D. for good friend and business partner Gulshan Rai even as his own production, *Daag* with L-P, was already being made.

But L-P preferred to count their blessings instead. Morale held high with their new conquests, they decided that just being true to what they were was the best competition they could give their friend and everyone else. The only change they made was in giving the 'in' voice—good friend and admirer Kishore Kumar—a larger share of their songs.

And once again, they came up with dream songs for Kumar—the mujra-qawwali blend 'Sacchai Chhup Nahin Sakti' in *Dushmun* (that went on to be a cult favourite), the ghazal-like 'Mere Dewanepan Ki Bhi' in *Mehboob Ki Mehndi*, the soft ghazal 'Mere Dil Mein Aaj Kya Hai' in *Daag* and qawwalis like 'Haal Kya Hai' (*Anokhi Ada*), 'Tu Mere Pyaale Mein' and 'Kahin Janaab Ko' (*Amir Garib*) and 'Hamein Kya Garaz' (*Anari*).

Last, but in no way the least, they came up with the Easter song 'My Name Is Anthony Gonsalves' (*Amar Akbar Anthony*), the disco numbers recorded in the late '70s for *Karz* and paved the way for composers to consider Kishore for Punjabi folk-based songs with 'Ab Chahe Maa Roothe Ya Baba' (*Daag*).

By 1973, with R.D. becoming repetitive and quite stale despite some iconic output, L-P had got a decisive upper hand, and by 1975, despite mega-hit films from R.D. like *Deewaar* and *Sholay*, the battle was over.

Here is a lowdown of the career-decisive films of both in these five decisive years:

1971

L-P: *Aan Milo Sajana, Jal Bin Machhli Nritya Bin Bijli, Mehboob Ki Mehndi, Haathi Mere Saathi, Mera Gaon Mera Desh* and *Aap Aye Bahaar Ayee*

R.D. Burman: *Mela, Caravan, Kati Patang* and *Buddha Mil Gaya*

1972

L-P: *Uphaar, Dushmun, Shor, Raja Jani, Ek Nazar* and *Roop Tera Mastana*

R.D. Burman: *Hare Rama Hare Krishna, Amar Prem, Mere Jeevan Saathi, Jawani Diwani, Raampur Ka Lakshman, Parichay, Samadhi, Do Chor* and *Seeta Aur Geeta*

1973

L-P: *Bobby, Daag, Loafer, Anhonee, Kucche Dhaage, Jwar Bhata* and *Anokhi Ada*

R.D. Burman: *Yaadon Ki Baraat, Namak Haraam, Anamika, Aa Gale Lag Jaa* and *Joshila*

1974

L-P: *Roti Kapada Aur Makaan, Manchali, Dosi, Imtihan, Amir Garib, Roti, Majboor, Paise Ki Gudiya* and *Bidaai*

R.D. Burman: *Aap Ki Kasam, Manoranjan* and *Heera Panna*

1975

L-P: *Dulhan, Pratiggya, Prem Kahani, Ponga Pandit* and *Aakraman*
R.D. Burman: *Sholay, Aandhi* and *Khel Khel Mein*

In this phase, Kalyanji-Anandji also were tough competition indeed, scoring aces like *Johny Mera Naam, Safar, Saccha Jhutha, Geet* and *Gopi* in 1970, *Purab Aur Pacchim, Paras* and *Maryada* in 1971, *Victoria No. 203, Apradh* and *Joroo Ka Gulam* in 1972, *Zanjeer, Blackmail, Banarasi Babu, Samjhauta* and *Kahani Kismat Ki* in 1973, *Kora Kagaz* and *Haath Ki Safai* in 1974 and *Dharmatma* in 1975. But L-P effortlessly dominated the music scene.

In 1973, Manmohan Desai and Rajesh Khanna had signed L-P for *Roti Kapada Aur Makaan*. Life would never be the same again for Desai or L-P and they forged an unbroken, very rewarding partnership till 1983. By 1976, the effects on music of the action and crime dramas that had become trendy thanks to Amitabh Bachchan and Salim-Javed were being felt, besides all the factors mentioned earlier in this chapter.

1976 saw L-P serve up strong melody in *Nagin, Charas, Jaaneman* (for which Dev Anand preferred them after *Amir Garib* though director Chetan Anand wanted Madan Mohan!) and *Dus Numbri* (ghost-directed by Manoj Kumar). In 1977, they ruled the box-office and charts with *Amar Akbar Anthony* and *Dharam-Veer* and brought Mohammed Rafi back in the commercial reckoning, besides scoring high in *Chacha Bhatija* (also Rafi-based) and *Parvarish*. Desai and L-P thus managed four of the top five hits of the year, leaving the third position for R.D. Burman and Nasir Husain with *Hum Kisise Kum Naheen*. The last film also had a major hand in Rafi's comeback.

Rajesh Khanna, at this point, had a temporary personal fallout with R.D. Burman (as per Shakti Samanta's statement to me) and this made him sign L-P for *Anurodh*, another masterpiece of a 1977 score. Khanna's home production *Aashiq Hoon Baharon Ka*,

Chhaila Babu, and the fleetingly very-popular-on-radio potboilers *Dildaar* and *Chhota Baap* also did well musically.

In 1978 and 1979, a determined L-P went melody-wards again with a vengeance, with Raj Kapoor's long-cherished dream project, *Satyam Shivam Sundaram* and the musical opus *Sargam* that began their 10-year association with the legendary South director K. Vishwanath. *Apnapan, Badaltey Rishtey, Main Tulsi Tere Aangan Ki, Jaani Dushmun, Suhaag* and their first film with Subhash Ghai, *Gautam Govinda*, also happened in this phase.

In 1978, they were also signed for *Dostana*, which launched the banner of Dharma Productions, as well as *Karz*, the first production of Subhash Ghai, though officially produced by Jagjit Khorana and Akhtar Farooqui, both Ghai's close relatives (Subhash Ghai's wife Mukta, who previously went by the name of Rehana, was Akhtar Farooqui's daughter. This was thus, the launch of the now-famous banner of Mukta Films, which later became Mukta Arts, and was named after Ghai's wife.

Surinder Kapoor, Boney and Anil Kapoor's father, had also shifted to L-P after doing films with different composers. After he worked with L-P in *Ponga Pandit* (1975), he stuck to them all the way to *Prem* (1996) in a total of seven films. By now, home productions of actors were a part and parcel of their careers. (see Appendix)

In their entire career, Laxmikant-Pyarelal have 'presented' only two films, industry speak for financing or co-financing a project. It is possible that Laxmikant co-financed *Tinku* (1977), directed by K. Parvez again, which starred Master Hrishikesh, Laxmikant's son, in the title-role—Tinku was also his pet name. Three stars very close to them by now—Dharmendra, Rajesh Khanna and Hema Malini—helped out with cameos. The other L-P presentation was *Zalim*, launched in the '70s but released in 1980 with Vinod Khanna in the lead.

The 1970s ended with L-P set for unique glories in the 1980s. They had crossed all frontiers of acceptance, popularity and stardom and had even signed incredibly big films that did not go beyond announcement or at best a few reels of shooting (see Appendix).

By now, they had also become rulers in what can be termed 'signature tunes' in Hindi cinema—the first songs that come to mind with any star's name, be it Mumtaz ('Bindiya Chamkegi' in *Do Raaste*), Saira Banu ('Dil Vil Pyar Vyar' in *Shagird*), Sunil Dutt ('Sawan Ka Mahina' in *Milan*) or Raakhee ('Jhilmil Sitaron Ka' in *Jeevan Mrityu*).

There were many more: Dharmendra ('Main Jat Yamla' in *Pratiggya* superceding all older songs), Babita ('Sheeshi Bhari Gulab Ki' in *Jeet*), Sanjeev Kumar (*Khilona*'s title song), Jeetendra ('Mast Baharon Ka Main Aashiq' in *Farz*), Rishi Kapoor (the songs of *Bobby*, *Amar Akbar Anthony* and *Sargam*, to which *Karz* would be added in 1980), Dimple Kapadia ('Hum Tum' in *Bobby*), Jaya Prada ('Dafliwale' in *Sargam*) and Laxmikant's sister-in-law Bindu ('Hungama Ho Gaya' in *Anhonee*). There would be more to come in the 1980s and 1990s.

They won three more Filmfare awards—for *Jeene Ki Raah* (1969), which they received in 1970, and for *Amar Akbar Anthony* (1977), *Satyam Shivam Sundaram* (1978) and going on to a hat-trick with *Sargam* (1979, for which they won in 1980).

In the days when Silver, Gold and Platinum Discs (for extraordinary sales of music) were genuine rather than gimmicks, they won Hindi cinema's first ever sales disc—the Silver for *Haathi Mere Saathi*, the Gold for *Bobby* and the first-ever pre-release (of the film) Gold Disc, followed by the Platinum Disc for *Satyam Shivam Sundaram*.

Haathi Mere Saathi won them (along with Anand Bakshi, Mohammed Rafi and the filmmakers) a unique award—for promoting the welfare of animals with the hard-hitting Rafi song 'Nafrat Ki Duniya'. This award was given by the Society for Prevention of Cruelty to Animals (SPCA).

Shailendra Singh and Narendra Chanchal (*Bobby*), Kavita

Krishnamurthi as a dubbing artiste (with *Chacha Bhatija*) and lyricist Anand Bakshi himself (*Mom Ki Gudia, Charas*) were introduced by them as singers.

L-P probably had no idea then that they were set to enter their busiest—and in some ways—most unusual decade with the 1980s. Mukesh was gone, and they would also lose their favourite male singer, Mohammed Rafi, seven months into 1980. The 1980s would be their most turbulent decade. But once again, they would continue to rule the charts as their contemporaries fizzled out and juniors were unable to go past them.

In short, despite many setbacks, L-P would turn up tops by the end of this decade again.

9

THE 1980s: THE DECADENT DECADE

The 1980s posed an altogether different challenge for Laxmikant-Pyarelal. By late 1987, Kishore Kumar also was gone. During the 1980s, L-P were selective in their use of Kishore though they continued to give him some of their finest songs, like the classic from a flop film, 'Prem Ka Rog Lagaa' (*Do Premee*), the ghazal 'Sarakti Jaaye Hai' (*Deedaar-E-Yaar*) and 'Zindagi Ki Yehi Reet Hai' and 'Kaate Nahin Kat-Te' (*Mr India*)—besides the hits of *Karz, Judaai, Dostana, Ram Balram, Naseeb, Avtaar* and many more. There was a significant shift in their music. By 1982, the last of the Rafi triumphs (*Naseeb, Hum Paanch, Aas Paas, Khuda Kasam, Rajput, Deedaar-E-Yaar* and some others)[26] were out, and L-P went on a spree to discover soundalikes of Mohammed Rafi, beginning with the late Manmohan Desai's directions to find someone 'like Rafi' for *Coolie*, because he did not want Kishore then!

The first was Shabbir Kumar, then based in Gujarat as an orchestra singer of Rafi songs. Playback singer Anwar was already around, but used to act difficult with everyone, despite L-P giving him superlative solos like 'Mohabbat Ab Tijarat' (*Arpan*) and 'Mere Khayaalon Ke Rehguzar Se' (*Yeh Ishq Nahin Aasaan*) besides 'Zindagi Imtihan Leti Hai' in *Naseeb*, and 'Yeh Pyar Tha Ya Kuch Aur Tha' in *Prem Rog*, all in the 1981–84 phase. Shabbir's throw was excellent, but the weightier songs, composition-wise, needed

---

[26]Two delayed films with Rafi's songs—*Madadgaar and Mera Karam Mera Dharam*—were released in 1987.

a more trained singer and soon, L-P picked up Anu Malik's and Manmohan Desai's (who had left them by then) re-discovery Mohammed Aziz,[27] who could be trusted with challenging, high-pitched and varied songs like 'Duniya Mein Kitna Gham Hai' and 'Sharafat Ali Ko Sharafat Ne Maara' (*Amrit*—with an ensemble led by Mahendra Kapoor), 'Aye Watan Tere Liye' (*Karma*) and many others.

So obsessed did they become with Munna (as Aziz came to be known) that in that single defining year of 1986, he sang in 16 out of their 22 releases. He became their main or only male singer in films as varied as *Karma*, *Naam*, *Amrit*, *Aakhree Raasta* and *Nagina*, singing everything from qawwali to patriotic, happy, sad, romantic and naughty numbers. In that year alone, he sang under them for artists as diverse as Dilip Kumar, Shammi Kapoor, Amitabh Bachchan, Rishi Kapoor, Jeetendra, Rajesh Khanna, Anil Kapoor, Govinda and Kumar Gaurav, besides other heroes and character artistes!

The Mukesh section was easier: not only did L-P give the Mukesh-like Manhar Udhas (who had been around since 1969) a major breakthrough with *Hero* in 1983 but they also began to use him frequently, especially for Subhash Ghai and Jackie Shroff films. Nitin Mukesh too began to get the cream of Manoj Kumar (*Kranti*, *Santosh*) and of Mukesh-heavy scores like *Eeshwar*, besides many other notable songs like 'So Gaya Yeh Jahaan' in *Tezaab*. On the female side, the duo had already begun to encourage Anuradha Paudwal and Kavita Krishnamurthi Subramaniam. Alka Yagnik too featured in their songs increasingly, starting from 1982. With Lata Mangeshkar frequently going abroad for tours, and

---

[27] The late Mohammed Aziz had made his debut in an obscure Bengali film *Jyoti* and its dubbed Hindi version *Amber* in 1983 under Sapan-Jagmohan. Word spread within studios and diehard Rafi fan, Manmohan Desai, and Anu Malik hunted out the struggler for *Mard* (1985), Desai's first film in 11 years without L-P's music.

the quantum of films that L-P had, Kavita as well as the other two began to record with them more often. Naturally, filmmakers saw little point in waiting for Lata and spending the extra money for dubbing artistes, when Kavita and occasional dubbing artiste Anuradha Paudwal were doing a great job at singing them.

It is thus supremely interesting to observe that L-P ruled the 1980s with a minimum share of the surviving saleable greats, Lata, Asha and Kishore, while their competition, which included Kalyanji-Anandji and R.D. Burman and new forces Rajesh Roshan and Bappi Lahiri could not match the duo, despite having all the three big names with them! And so, rapidly, L-P learnt another valuable lesson faster than anyone else—that they could not now afford to be dependent on any singer. The L-P scores from 1981 thus showed a remarkable variety in singers. Apart from Shabbir and Aziz in so many films, and of course Kishore in later films like *Swarag Se Sunder, Mr India* and others, they composed scores that could be said to belong to so many diverse voices.

S.P. Balasubramaniam may have dominated *Ek Duuje Ke Liye* because of its theme, but he also dominated *Ek Hi Bhool, Zara Si Zindagi* and *Andhaa Kaanoon*. I have already mentioned Shabbir, Mohammed. Aziz, Nitin Mukesh and Manhar: but there were also Suresh Wadkar (*Prem Rog, Utsav*), Sukhwinder Singh (*Yateem*), Amit Kumar (*Tezaab*) and Pankaj Udhas (*Jawaab*). Last, but emphatically not the least, were Pt Rajan Misra and Pt Sajan Misra in *Sur-Sangam*.

Post 1983, the Lata Mangeshkar-dominated scores naturally declined (with exceptions like *Pyar Jhukta Nahin, Nache Mayuri, Ghulami* and *Utsav*). The Asha scores were never of great significance in the L-P records of the 1980s as, at the time, they tended to employ her vocals whenever the music was not very demanding, such as her songs in *Meri Awaaz Suno, Farz Aur Kaanoon, Baghawat* and more, with wonderful exceptions like *Judaai, Ram Balram, Do Premee, Deedaar-E-Yaar* and a few more. Perhaps the most sparkling case of L-P bypassing both the Mangeshkars (one or both of whom had ruled the L-P female duet space) was 'Thare Vaste Re Dhola', that magnificent dazzler from *Batwara* (1989). Here, their three young favourites Anuradha Paudwal, Kavita Krishnamurthi and Alka Yagnik, sang for Dimple Kapadia, Amrita Singh and Poonam Dhillon in a big-ticket movie.

Another stunning number in the same film was 'Jo Main Aisa Jaanti' from Anuradha Paudwal and Kavita Krishnamurthi. The film had come and gone (it was a major flop) and the music had been barely heard (despite its exceptional calibre) thanks to the music company Venus' ham-handed marketing. But when I had met Kavita for the first time in 1991, she was shocked that I had never heard either that soundtrack or L-P's *Yateem* (also on Venus) the same year. She stressed that I should listen to them, and by a happy chance, I found a combination cassette of the two films in a music shop.

The compositions, orchestration and big sound were to die for, especially in 'Thare Vaste Re Dhola', in which every word, phrase and sentence was tailored to the distinct vocal textures and strengths of the three singers. The three singers had already collaborated on another peppy and pacy L-P track seven years before in *Jeevan Dhaara*, but the song, 'Jaldi Se Aa Mere Pardesi Babu' did not hit it big and was a straight and simple composition. Apart from the big sound, the shrewd Laxmikant sensed that despite the increased quantum of work, their compositions had to have an edge, as the contributions of the master-singers had reduced in L-P's music. And so, L-P's music veered even more towards semi-classical and *raag-daari* besides folk, to maintain that edge over the rest.

And did they succeed!

By now, with most major producer-directors already in their bag, L-P caught the attention of the newer and upcoming breed of directors—N. Chandra, Mukul S. Anand, Mahesh Bhatt, J.P. Dutta, Eesmayeel Shroff, Pankuj Parashar, Anil Sharma, Shekhar Kapur and Tinnu Anand among them. Ramesh Sippy had to shift to them because of commercial compulsions—his favourite R.D. Burman was going through a flop run and distributors had lost money on his *Shaan* and *Saagar*. Though there was no real rapport with L-P, the director told me that he saw no problem with their music in *Bhrastachar*. And the duo's fruitful associations with Subhash Ghai and K. Vishwanath continued.

New actors like Anil Kapoor openly opted for them and they also struck a rapport with Jackie Shroff and Madhuri Dixit. There was a significant jump in quantity (189 films between 1980 and 1989!). They also opted for fruitful if not-so-frequent liaisons with lyricists Hasan Kamal, old-time associate Farukh Kaiser and a resurgent S.H. Bihari. And with this last-mentioned O.P. Nayyar favourite, they did the maximum work within a short while (more than 12 films) after Bihari's grandslam comeback with them in *Pyar Jhukta Nahin* (1985) until his untimely demise in 1987.

This was also the decade when Raj Kapoor, Manoj Kumar and Manmohan Desai left them despite the music of *Prem Rog*, *Kranti* and *Coolie*. Anyone else would have been destabilized, especially since L-P's favourite singers too were no longer around. But the doughty Laxmi-Pyare, who had given these last hit scores for the three filmmakers with young singers like Suresh Wadkar, Nitin Mukesh and Shabbir Kumar respectively dominating, preferred to look at their new conquests and the variety that had opened up before them. And as Laxmikant had told me in the mid-1990s, 'We took great satisfaction from the fact that none of these banners went to other major names around. When Man ji signed a young Anu Malik, he said that we were still all the numbers from one to 10 for him!'

Pyarelal added that while their professional association stopped, their personal relationships remained intact. They would still be a part of all Raj Kapoor celebrations and remained in touch with Manoj Kumar, who introduced a new duo, Uttam-Jagdish (*Painter Babu*). Raj Kapoor opted for Ravindra Jain in

Ram Teri Ganga Maili.

In the 1990s, all three of the above banners were to return to them. Manoj Kumar signed them for *Jai Hind—The Pride*. Manmohan Desai announced *Dum Dum Diga Diga* with Anil Kapoor, Salman Khan and Madhuri Dixit, but died weeks after this announcement in 1994. His son Ketan Desai modified the script and gave us *Deewana Mastana* with Anil Kapoor, Govinda and Juhi Chawla. Raj Kapoor was no more, but his sons Randhir, Rishi and Rajiv Kapoor launched *Prem Granth* with L-P. Randhir was always involved in his father's films since *Satyam Shivam Sundaram*, and Rajiv made his directorial debut with *Prem Granth*. 'Working with us became a habit for everyone,' repeated Laxmikant with a smile when I went to meet him after this happened. 'They would miss us and the way we worked.'[28]

But L-P had old loyalists like J. Om Prakash, Mohan Kumar, Mohan Segal, Rajkumar Kohli, L.V. Prasad, K. Vishwanath, T. Rama Rao and others staunchly by their side as well, besides the new names mentioned above. And in the 1980s, they may not have been as consistent, but the highs, as seen below, were musically enriching, many even spectacular, with the majority of these scores being in films that were also successful at the box-office.

1980: *Karz, Aasha, Dostana, Judaai, Ram Balram* and *Do Premee*

1981: *Kranti, Hum Paanch, Krodhi, Ladies Tailor, Aas Paas, Naseeb, Pyaasa Sawan* and *Ek Duuje Ke Liye*

1982: *Prem Rog, Deedaar-E-Yaar, Rajput, Insaan* and *Ghazab*

1983: *Hero, Coolie, Andhaa Kaanoon, Woh 7 Din* and *Arpan*

1984: *Yeh Ishq Nahin Aasaan*

1985: *Utsav, Sur-Sangam, Sanjog, Meri Jung, Ghulami, Pyar Jhukta*

---

[28]During a 1995 interview for *Mid-Day*.

Nahin, *Do Dilon Ki Dastan* and *Jawaab*

1986: *Karma*, *Naam*, *Nagina*, *Amrit*, *Nache Mayuri* and *Love '86*

1987: *Mr India*, *Insaaf* and *Sindoor*

1988: *Tezaab*, *Dayavan* and *Janam Janam*

1989: *Ram Lakhan*, *Eeshwar*, *Chaalbaaz*, *Yateem*, *Batwara* and *Bees Saal Baad*

Fifty-two films out of 189 may not be much, but L-P's track-record in the degenerate decade for films was eons better than anyone else's, which is what finally mattered in that commercial era of music labels driven by individuals who edged past traditional corporate music labels like HMV. The fact that there was no competition that could inspire and motivate them was more of a reason for the decrease in their work. For one, their rivals, as we may call them for want of a better term, did barely distinguished work. Two, the arrival of the *Himmatwala* era marked the downfall of the lyrics, and the disco era did not help. L-P too had to compose several disco tracks for filmmakers, but fell short of the quality of *Karz*. The phase also spawned the non-film ghazal boom by the mid-'80s, as listeners again showed preference for meaningful lyrics and traditional music.

Over the next few years, L-P too ended up using the big stars of this new non-film field—Pankaj Udhas and later, Talat Aziz and Jagjit Singh.

Add turbulent political scenarios in the country, the arrival of the video era (where for many years, the middle- and upper-class audiences started to watch new films at home, even on pirated video cassettes) and we found distributors demanding the lowest common denomninator in film content. With cassettes ruling over records, audio piracy also boomed and the music industry also suffered a setback as they had to make musicassettes cheap—I have a double cassette of L-P's *Coolie* and *Woh 7 Din* that cost ₹15, as against one of *Hero* alone, earlier in 1983, that had cost ₹40.

L-P took all this head-on, giving their all to the filmmakers and subjects that mattered. Yes, they did partially let go of quality at times but the rule in their music room never changed: each filmmaker was called in the sequence he had arrived, with no favours to big or loyal names.

Krodhi (1981) had its background score composed by Kalyanji-Anandji because Ghai had a passing rift with L-P at that time—K-A obliged, but charged a token more than what their one-time protégés had charged Ghai for the five lovely songs they had made!

In the 1980s, L-P began the practice of doing only songs and not the BGM for some films, out of either budgetary reason or time constraints. The producers' demand for using stock music for a background score out of 'economic' compulsions was also anathema for Pyarelal. S.P. Balasubramaniam (*Hum Paanch*, *Nache Mayuri*), Enoch Daniels (*Gehrayee*, in which L-P's only contribution was the sole song in the film, 'Rishte Bas Rishte Hote Hain' rendered by Kishore Kumar) and Sapan-Jagmohan (*Insaan*) were the earliest names to score BGM for their movies. This was followed by many others from the 1980s to the 1990s, like Louiz Banks solo and with Sunil Kaushik, Viju Shah, Pyarelal's brother Naresh Sharma and some others. Salil Chowdhury, as late as 1991, composed the BGM for their *Khilaaf*!

At this point, a trivia: ace composer M.M. Keeravani (known in Hindi films as M.M. Kreem), and a great admirer of L-P, has scored the BGM for *Neti Siddhartha* (1990), the first Telugu film for which L-P scored the songs!

Despite all these factors, many of L-P's other most exquisite songs came in this decade. Among those in films outside the above list were 'Shabnam Ka Yeh Qatra Hai' (*Sharaara*), 'Sadiyan Beet Gayi' (*Triveni*) and 'Mora Roop Rang' (*Qatl*) all sung by Lata, 'Yoon Lagne Lagi' (*Santosh*—Lata with Nitin Mukesh) and Kavita's 'Surmai Andhera Hai' (*Pati Parmeshwar*). And not to mince words, Hindi cinema has never seen a purer classical—and original—score in that genre than *Sur-Sangam*, or the pristine melody of *Utsav*, the period film based on the ancient play *Mricchakatika*. That L-P could score such albums amidst working on potboilers like *Yadon Ki Kasam* or *Zakhmee Sher* and even compose a pure ghazal that was 'Sabak Jinko Wafaa Ka Yaad Hoga' (*Jawaab*) speaks volumes for their unparalleled versatility and tenacity.

Although *Utsav* was high up in popularity and Universal used the *Jawaab* song till the end of the CD era in their Pankaj Udhas ghazal compilations, the people, except for the connoisseurs, rejected *Sur-Sangam*. Very simply, just like his friend R.D. Burman, Laxmikant just said on the failure of *Sur-Sargam*'s music: 'We humbly accept the people's verdict.' For creators at that level, this remains a massively exemplary attitude compared to some upstarts (whose identities can be intelligently guessed!) from the millennium.

L-ongevity for P-osterity: this is how we could describe the magic of L-P. And their middle name was 'Humility'.

10

1990–2004: WHEN 'PACKAGING' OVERRULED 'CONTENT'

*F*irst things first: L-P had no film release after 1999 until their last remaining release, *Mere Biwi Ka Jawaab Nahin*, was released in 2004. The delayed Akshay Kumar-Sridevi film finally released even minus a director's credit-line, and had one song newly recorded for the opening credit titles, 'Taaron Ki Chhaon Mein', composed by Shyam-Surender. By release time, Shyam, the senior and Maharashtrian half of the '90s duo, had passed away.

By 1990, L-P had seen an unalloyed reign for over 20 years, and they entered their third decade at the top, after the '70s and '80s. However, every aaroha (ascent of the musical notes) must have an avroha (descent), and for L-P it began in the early '90s. Once again, other factors came in, some that they could have avoided, like the overwork—they did 67 films in the first four years! Yet again, the calibre of some scores remained outstanding, but the increasing rarity of excellence now stood out. For example, there was nothing extraordinary in 1990 despite 20 films, and the audio release of a twenty-first film, *Hum* (which released in 1991) was their only saving grace. There was a partial creative resurgence in 1991 with *Hum*, *Saudagar*, *Narsimha*, *Prahaar* and *Dhun*. 1992 saw one of their most accomplished scores in Amitabh Bachchan's home production, *Khuda Gawah*, as well as the brilliant *Heer Ranjha* and the audio release of *Roop Ki Rani Choron Ka Raja*. The latter two films' disastrous fate at the box-office, in 1992 and 1993 respectively, however, undid their superb music completely.

From the 1980s, we had come into an era when a film's fate also decided how the music fared, because how much it was promoted was also decided by the music labels. Unsold cassettes would be bought back by the music company and re-recorded with new music! This was an era driven by music companies with individuals at the helm, who authoritatively decided what music would reach the ears of the people. However, even the corporate HMV (now reborn after an Indian takeover as Saregama) began to follow a brazen commercial line to survive the unscrupulous competition. As an example, after massive pre-release hype for *Dhun*, including huge hoardings and print ads, the label gave up on the superlative music as soon as they found the completed film embroiled in dispute (it never released). Commercially, the music had done brilliantly in the initial stages. And we have already mentioned the fate of the music of both Venus's *Yateem* and *Batwara* earlier.

Moreover, with the exception of *Saudagar, Dhun, Prahaar, Khuda Gawah* and *Roop Ki Rani Choron Ka Raja*, none of the other scores really matched the quantum of musical excellence L-P were always known for. In 1995, came another disaster in *Prem*, whose music would have made a huge impact with a better singer than Nalin Dave, because its lyrics, compositions and even orchestration were all brilliant. Dave's entry into the film as one of the many singers who would hang around Laxmikant's music room to get work, proved a disastrous error of judgement by Laxmikant and the film's team, as admitted by director Satish Kaushik and producer Boney Kapoor. The fact remained that this was the decade when both the legends went wrong, both individually and together, and when we add natural aspects like exhausted creative juices and a paradigm shift in musical orientation and preferences, we see how L-P were nearing the end of the road, over three decades after they started out.

In another error of judgement, L-P sidelined better voices that had come in and made a mark. Yes, L-P never liked to jettison people with whom they formed a bond. For example, both Rafi and the duo would have suffered heavily had they sidelined him like so many composers did in the Kishore wave between 1970 and 1976. For composers like them, who had set trends with fresh voices in the 1980s, it was quite strange that they did not hold much truck with new and accomplished singers like Kumar Sanu and Abhijeet. For in the 1980s, other composers had employed singers whom L-P had introduced or mentored.

Once these singers made a mark, L-P's refusal to work with them—Abhijeet's career-first released song was actually with L-P in 'Prem Doot Aaya' from *Mujhe Insaaf Chahiye* (1983)—seemed to border on obduracy. The only exception was their work with Udit Narayan with *Prem Deewane, Narsimha, Bhairavi, Aashik Aawara* and the stunning but unsung 'Kya Tumhe Pataa Hai Ae Gulshan' (*Dil Hai Betaab*). But the duo was also caught between the devil and the deep sea, as the forces against them continued to increase: the music barons continued to back the new composers. As colleague and supposed rival Bappi Lahiri succinctly said a decade later, 'The music companies conspired to keep L-P and me sitting at home without work.'[29]

Shafi Inamdar, actor and stage stalwart, who turned director with the delightful 1995 Rishi Kapoor-Nana Patekar film *Hum Dono*, candidly told me, 'When we planned the film in 1993, I was keen on L-P for my debut movie. My producer, Ravi Malhotra, had always worked with R.D. Burman and would have loved to wait for him even though he was very unwell. But we were given three new options to choose if we wanted the music label to buy our music.' Yes, the tables had turned then and leading companies like T-Series, Tips and Venus, among others, were paying filmmakers and buying music rights, rather than the time-honoured practice

---

[29]During an interview with the author for *Screen*.

the world over of giving royalties later. With money flowing in, no producer opposed this practice despite the creative flipsides. Currency notes now had to take precedence over musical notes! A major and unavoidable factor that L-P did not envisage soon enough was the emergence of A.R. Rahman, though Pyarelal insists that it was he who made some of their filmmakers listen to this fresh, young talent when the Hindi (dubbed) album of *Roja* came out. Rahman's music made listeners pay a greater attention to sound, that is, the packaging of a song more than its content (lyrical, musical and vocal calibre) in the techno-savvy 1990s. Alongside, the technological upgrading of home and personal music systems, the onslaught of CDs and digital sound replacing analogue sound and the upgrading in recording techniques all contributed.

Ironically, the first individual CD of a Hindi film score had been L-P's Ram Lakhan in 1989!

And so, while on a commercial yardstick, it was the hype around Nadeem-Shravan and the support they had of music companies that placed L-P on a commercially lower rung than No. 1 for the first time in 25 years, it was Rahman's different strokes that unsettled them for good. *Aashiqui* had made all the difference, and *Saajan* (which L-P left after recording half a song with S.P. Balasubramaniam!) further consolidated N-S's success after 10 years of struggle and small films. Music barons also got an ego- and business-boost after introducing or mentoring new talents among composers, and some names were doing very well, like Anand-Milind, Raamlaxman and others.

History repeats itself. Rahman had made the same sudden impact on everyone that L-P had made when they arrived in 1963. Like L-P, he too was a disrupter. But there was a difference. Rahman's work in Hindi cinema, accompanied by media-hype and the arrival of the Internet, was more about catering to a niche, young audience, and about sound and technology than lasting power. L-P's songs on the other hand, as Shreya Ghoshal pointed out, were geared to be friendly for the singer's vocal flow and their master-lyricists helped out vitally. Rahman, not familiar with Hindi for quite a while, opted for words that were written to fit to his metres. L-P considered a song situation as sacrosanct, while Rahman often took the situation tangentially and his composition was sometimes at variance with the mood of the film and the lyrics. And for L-P, packaging followed content and did not take precedence. It was a different era of declining audience patience, heightened pace and also degeneration—if not complete apathy—in the people's aesthetic sense of poetry, diction and singing calibre.

And L-P no longer fitted in.

Their last music scores (*Prem, Bhairavi, Rajkumar, Jai Hind— The Pride*) or specific songs (in *Chauraha, Dilbar, Mohabbat Ki Arzoo, Prem Granth, Tejaswini, Deewana Mastana*) continued to have their classic touches, but they just could not match up to the 'young' competition, as the 'digital-savvy' generation overtly preferred the newer, more youthful cadences. Ironically, here is where Laxmikant-Pyarelal had their last flirtation with another composer's style—in the song 'Na Meri Zubaan Pe' from *Bedardi*. The stunner of a song was a clear adaptation of the Nadeem-Shravan style, sung by the younger duo's favourites Kumar Sanu and Alka Yagnik, with L-P's refined touch. Ironically, the song was removed from the final cut and hero Ajay Devgn does not even remember it! Given L-P's tendency to use separate singers for two heroes, we will not even be surprised to know that the song was intended for Naseeruddin Shah in the film, as Vinod Rathod was Ajay's voice in all the songs.

L-P's adieu in Laxmikant's lifetime came with the audio release in 1998, on Plus Music, of loyal producer K.D. Shorey's (Ranvir Shorey's father) *Maha Yuddh*, which launched his elder son Lokesh Shorey. This was a little after another slightly delayed release, *Barsaat Ki Raat*, on Venus. However, Manoj Kumar's *Jai Hind—The Pride*, which was released in 1999 though the audio came out in 1997, was L-P's last *complete* score.

Another film, *Yunhi Chup Chup*, produced and directed by Salauddin Parvez, was never released, but the audio came out in 2000, and besides L-P's four songs sung by Alka Yagnik, Kavita Krishnamurthi Subramaniam and Vinod Rathod, the score was completed by singer Bhupinder Singh as composer after Laxmikant's death.

And Venus also marketed the music of *Mere Biwi Ka Jawaab Nahin* (2004). In L-P's entire career, this was but the fourth such example of someone sharing the music credits with them: a *Nache Mayuri* (1986) song, 'Pag Padam', was composed by S.P. Balasubramaniam as a part of his background score for their film (as repeated in the Hindi version after the film's original, *Mayuri*), and in *Kshatriya* (1993), a single song was composed (and written) by Rafiq Sagar.

Musically, the L-P era had ended after 41 years. But Pyarelal continues to make music.

More vitally, their songs live on forever.

11

A HIT... AND SOME MISSES

The Story of *Bobby* and *Ghayal*

In 1971, Manoj Kumar switched to Laxmikant-Pyarelal for the music of *Shor* and B.R. Chopra signed them for *Dastaan*. Yash Chopra too broke away from BR Films and launched his still au courant banner, Yash Raj Films, in 1971, with L-P's *Daag*. And in 1972, in what can be called their biggest coup then, Raj Kapoor signed them for *Bobby*. Here, hangs an interesting tale.

As per Rishi Kapoor's statement to me, his father had a whimsical idea when Randhir Kapoor decided to sign R.D. Burman for his film *Dharam Karam*. He thought that his younger son should be launched in a film with music by R.D. Burman's father, S.D. Burman! It was Mukesh who suggested to Raj Kapoor that Laxmikant-Pyarelal would be his best bets. And Raj Kapoor sent him to L-P, who were recording for *Piya Ka Ghar* at Famous, Tardeo,

Pyarelal remembers Laxmikant refusing the offer even as he spontaneously did the same! 'We did not even exchange looks as he was in a different part of the hall,' recalls the maestro. 'We did not need to do so. Our only thought was that Jaikishan ji had just passed away and Shankar ji was alone. But Mukesh ji told us that if we turned down the film, it would go to Kalyanji-Anandji, S.D. Burman or anyone else but not to Shankar ji. And Laxmi immediately said that we would do the film.'

'At our first sitting with Raj ji, he brought us a song situation and a tune as well, which was his own, with lyrics written for it by his friend Vitthalbhai Patel: "*Woh kehte hain humse abhi umra nahin hai pyar ki*", Pyarelal said. 'Laxmi told him we do not work like that. We told him we would make something of our own for the situation, along with Bakshi ji, who has also been signed. And at the next sitting, we gave him 'Main Shaayar To Nahin', and he loved it!'

Raj Kapoor and L-P finally approved Shailendra Singh as the singer, and the filmmaker requested L-P to record their songs at the newly-opened studio, Navrang Cine Centre, in which he had a partnership share. The song was duly hyped in the media and recorded. Since L-P had brought together Raj Kapoor and Lata Mangeshkar after a rift of almost a decade, she was also present along with Mukesh and many others. However, after the final recording, both the composers felt that the song recording was not upto the mark, and the shortcoming lay in the studio's sound setup and not with the recording engineer. They both approached Raj Kapoor and told them about their reservations—what was lacking and why it could not be rectified. And so the song was recorded afresh a few days later at Famous Studios. Subsequently, every song of *Bobby* and later *Satyam Shivam Sundaram* were recorded only at Famous.

This is, perhaps, the right place to zoom ahead for a bit and talk about another such instance. Here was where Pyarelal's fastidiousness about technical perfection led to their losing a prestigious film that released in 1990—Dharmendra's *Ghayal*! Naturally, the duo was the first choice for the film as Sunny was going through a lean pre-*Tridev* phase when the film was announced and Dharmendra was very fond of L-P too. (Filmmakers and stars lean phases always turned to L-P for saving or rejuvenating their careers! Besides, L-P had done a superlative job in Sunny's *Yateem*, a Dharmendra home production). But Dharmendra had also started his own studio, Sunny Super Sound, and he wanted that the first recording there be done by Laxmikant-

Pyarelal, that too for his debut official production. However, when Pyarelal went to the studio, he did not find it acoustically up to their mark. Very politely, he told Dharmendra that he would not be able to work there unless certain changes were made. And the film went to Bappi Lahiri.

Films in Which Laxmikant-Pyarelal Were Replaced

Laxmikant-Pyarelal did not do some films they had been offered or signed on for diverse reasons, and other music directors took them up. In four prominent cases, the films they could not (or did not) take up, proved to be career-breakthroughs for the composers who came in their place, so we will start off with them.

Ravee Nagaich's *The Train* (1970)—R.D. Burman

Rajendra Kumar, who ghost-produced the film, wanted L-P (after the songs they had made for him in *Anjaana*), for this film starring Nanda with a yet-unproved newcomer Rajesh Khanna: *Aradhana* had not happened until then. Director Ravee Nagaich was also a L-P aficionado (*Farz, Jigri Dost*).

But at that point, L-P had 10 films on hand and they felt it was too much work! The film went to R.D. Burman and signalled his major breakthrough. After that film, R.D. went on a signing spree, something he could not achieve earlier despite the genius of his early scores, led by *Teesri Manzil* and *Padosan*.

Yash Chopra's *Kabhi Kabhie* (1976)—Khayyam

After the musical excellence of *Daag*, Yash Chopra repeated L-P for his production, *Gardish*, which was to star Amitabh Bachchan and Parveen Babi and was to be directed by Chopra's editor Pran Mehra. The film was soon dropped and the multi-star *Kabhi Kabhie* was announced. L-P had a sitting with Chopra and team but there was no consensus on a song. Sahir pulled a few strings and suggested the then out-of-work Khayyam for the film. Khayyam's successful phase as a composer began with this film, though he had been around and had given some hits since 1948.

Bhisham Kohli's *Chalte Chalte* (1976)—Bappi Lahiri

The news item and poster of the film (in leading periodicals led by *Screen*) showed that L-P had signed this small-budget musical when they had the cream of big films. However, for whatever reasons, soon it was Bappi Lahiri who was announced as the composer. And though the film did not do well, the music was a rage and Lahiri's career took off.

Lawrence D'Souza's *Saajan* (1991)—Nadeem-Shravan

The poster says it all. Half a song (we were in the piecemeal era of dubbing and recording already!) was even recorded by L-P with S.P. Balasubramaniam. Suddenly, the film changed hands and went to Nadeem-Shravan, who got their career-consolidating musical blockbuster after *Aashiqui*.

G.P. Sippy's *Raaz* (1966)—Kalyanji-Anandji

Once again, they turned down a film as they thought they were too busy already. Kalyanji-Anandji, L-P's mentors, took up this G.P. Sippy film and scored hit music. This was Rajesh Khanna's debut film and Babita's first release.

K. Shankar's *Sacchai* (1970)—Shankar-Jaikishan

Various views are there about why L-P did not take up the film but hero Shammi Kapoor did confirm to me that the duo had turned down the movie when it was offered to them.

V. Shantaram's *Pinjra* (1974)—Ram Kadam

The Hindi version of the V. Shantaram's 1972 Marathi blockbuster saw L-P being signed after their work for him in *Jal Bin Machhli Nritya Bin Bijli*. However, the composers watched the original and felt that the Hindi version would not work pan-India. They left the film and Ram Kadam, composer of the original, came in. Kiran Shantaram, however, claimed that his father did not go to them as they were very busy. Both the film and its music proved to be non-starters.

J. Om Prakash's *Aap Ki Kasam* (1974)—R.D. Burman

After his third super-hit with L-P, *Aan Milo Sajana*, J. Om Prakash decided to go back to Shankar-Jaikishan for *Aankhon Aankhon Mein* for one film. His writer Sachin Bhaumick also came up with *Raja Rani*, which he wanted to direct. He told his producer that he had promised R.D. Burman his first film as a director. After this, Gulzar came in to direct the producer's *Aandhi*, again with R.D. Burman.

All this hurt Laxmikant, and so when J. Om Prakash went to them again for his directorial debut *Aap Ki Kasam*, he turned him down! After this film, in the filmmaker's words, he explained things to L-P and they 'patched' up with *Aakraman*, going on to do eight more films together until 1988.

H.S. Rawail's *Laila Majnu* (1976)—Madan Mohan and Jaidev

This film was announced with L-P and Sahir, and the director was H.S. Rawail, for whom the duo had scored the excellent *Mehboob Ki Mehndi*. However, due to certain differences with the producers, L-P left and Madan Mohan came in. He recorded six songs and passed away and Jaidev came in to complete the film. Rawail did *Deedaar-E-Yaar* with L-P later.

Prakash Mehra's *Khalifa* (1976)— R.D. Burman

The film was first announced with L-P and would have been also their first film with lyricist Gulshan Bawra, whose name was also announced for this Randhir Kapoor-Rekha film. L-P never worked with Mehra finally.

Premji's *Meeraa* (1979)—Pt Ravi Shankar

Loyal producer Premji and writer-director Gulzar opted for L-P in this Hema Malini-Vinod Khanna film on the legendary poet-saint. At that time, Lata Mangeshkar was already recording a Hindi Meera Bhajan album with brother Hridaynath Mangeshkar and she refused to sing for the film, knowing that her album would face formidable opposition from the L-P film soundtrack (non-film albums had very little scope then).

L-P in turn could not imagine composing such a score without her and quit. Pt Ravi Shanker stepped in and singer Vani Jairam was chosen. The film and its music did not connect.

Ramesh Sippy's *Shakti* (1982)—R.D. Burman

Here again, no one knows why they were replaced. But at that time, producers Mushir-Riaz had announced three films, including Vijay Anand's *Rajput* (1982) with L-P and Shakti Samanta's *Aar Paar*, which got shelved, and had music by R.D. Burman. It is possible that R.D. was shifted into *Shakti*, as he had always been associated with Ramesh Sippy.

Indra Kumar's *Beta* (1992)—Anand-Milind

This Indra Kumar film, featuring Anil Kapoor and Madhuri Dixit (now Nene), was originally to be done by Laxmikant-Pyarelal and Javed Akhtar after their hit pairing with Kapoor and Dixit in *Tezaab*. Suddenly they were replaced by Anand-Milind and Sameer.

Kirti Kumar's *Radha Ka Sangam* (1992)—Anu Malik

The musical Govinda home production was announced in a full-page *Screen* ad with Laxmikant-Pyarelal as composers. But soon, Anu Malik came in.

II

THE RHYTHM OF LAXMIKANT-PYARELAL

12

KNOWING THE MAN BEHIND THE MUSIC: LAXMIKANT

*B*ehind every successful man is not just a woman but his own personality. And the story of Laxmikant-Pyarelal can only be understood when we know the bond both shared that led to their incredible saga of unequalled success. Jaya Laxmikant, the composer's wife and Rajeshwari, their daughter, together shed light on Laxmikant when we met up for the book. Jaya remembered the time Laxmikant-Pyarelal brought about the Raj Kapoor-Lata Mangeshkar patch-up with *Bobby* simply by telling her, '*Didi, aap ko yeh film karni hai* (You have to do this film).'

On another occasion, Jaya recalled taking a walk in their compound and hearing her husband sing 'Satyam Shivam Sundaram' at 3.30 p.m., two hours before Raj Kapoor was due, as the windows were open because the power supply had been interrupted. 'My husband had kept the song ready!' she said. Another memory is of Laxmikant taking her to watch *Maro Charitra*, the original of *Ek Duuje Ke Liye*. 'I was impressed with the Telugu film's music,' recalled Jaya. 'So, while returning, I asked my husband, "Do you think you can match that score?" In response, all he said was that I was too simple! And then he never made me listen to any song they made for the film. One day, during our Ganpati immersion, when he would always play his latest songs for us, he put on the music. When I told him these were such lovely songs, he smiled and said, "They are from *Ek Duuje Ke Liye*."'

A fond memory Rajeshwari has is of her father taking off to Khandala for three days with Anand Bakshi and T. Rama Rao, director of *Judaai*, to finalize the tunes, as they wanted the songs very fast. She recalls howling when he left in the morning. 'My mother consoled me, saying that he would come back in a few days!' recalled Rajeshwari. 'And at 2 in the night, there was a loud honking outside the gate and the watchman said, "*Saab aa gaye!* (Sir has come back!)" Daddy had actually given them five tunes within a single day, just for me! And of course, all five songs became hits.'

Rajeshwari remembered with fascination how people in the theatres would throw coins at the screen when L-P chartbusters came on. The late veteran producer N.N. Sippy had told them that an incredible one crore rupees in coins—in the 1970s—was ultimately collected from movie halls where *Sargam* was playing because of 'Dafliwale'!

Recently, actress Jaya Prada revealed that this song was going to be removed from the film because of the film's length and as its situation was not really important for the story. But Sippy kept it only because they had already shot it in Kashmir.

J. Om Prakash had also let on that the ushers and staff of movie-halls earned big money from 'Sheesha Ho Ya Dil Ho' (*Aasha*). And in the case of 'Ek Do Teen Char' (*Tezaab*), the shower of money was so much that the coins would hit the heads of the people sitting in front! *Khal Nayak* also set a record. A song for it was done in a record three hours on 7 January 1993 as Mumbai was witnessing communal riots and tension that day. The musicians were in a hurry to reach home and they completed the song very fast. *Khal Nayak* also remains the first and only film soundtrack where the audiocassettes were sold in the black market—in Kolkata, the music sold at a premium rate! Good Knight, the mosquito repellent brand, sponsored the cassettes. The high in music sales even came under the scanner of the Income-Tax department, which carried out raids at the offices of Subhash

Ghai and two distributors—Tolu Bajaj and Bharat—besides that of the music label Tips!

For Laxmikant, Jaya remembered, his music room was his sanctum sanctorum. Even when he had fever, he had to go and sit there for a short while, composing something. The bathroom was another location where inspiration would come and he would demand that someone bring his tape recorder so that he could record a tune that had just come to him. 'He went straight to his music room even after our wedding!' Jaya laughed. 'I began to cry and called up my sister Bindu and she consoled me. We had no honeymoon, and on most days, Laxmi-ji would return late at night. But I would never have dinner without him even if he was back at 2 a.m. from a recording.'

Pt Shivkumar Sharma and Pt Hariprasad Chaurasia had gifted Laxmikant's son Hrishikesh a toy organ on his first birthday, and when his father was toying with it, the classic tune of 'Ek Pyar Ka Naghma Hai' (*Shor*) was born from that toy instrument!

'My husband had seen such terrible times and this made him want to live life king-size,' explained Jaya. 'My mother-in-law told me that, at the age of 13, he would even play the mandolin in Mumbai's suburban trains and the commuters would give him 25 paise, eight annas or sometimes a rupee. He thus understood financial constraints and would never turn down any producer in distress.'

While commuting to work, a young Laxmikant would pass a beautiful bungalow called Purnima on the main road in Mumbai's Vile Parle area, and he told his mother that he wanted to build a bungalow like that. She told him, 'First get out of this slum and at least take a room on rent!' And a few years before he passed away, Laxmikant told his wife, 'I have so much that four generations can live in comfort.'

The first house Laxmikant bought was in Parle (East), and he refused to leave the place as long as his mother was alive, even though they had bought a plot at Juhu, which was being developed. After she passed away, they went to stay in a rented flat at Khar, in which J. Om Prakash used to stay. That apartment too proved very lucky for both the filmmaker and his composer. And how they bought Parasmani, their bungalow, is a story in itself. Laxmikant would always give his earnings to his mother, but after he got married, he would also give some cash to his wife. And Jaya had a small aluminum bag of the kind children carried to school in those days, and would save whatever she could, from ₹10 upwards.

The plot belonged to producer Gaffarbhai Nadiadwala, who wanted to sell it only to Gujaratis. It cost ₹1,75,000 and of that, one lakh was to be paid in cash. Jaya had collected that sum in her bag! Nadiadwala was also told that she was a Gujarati who never even consumed water until her daily pooja was over, and so her name came first in the agreement with Laxmikant's name next, because he was a Maharashtrian. And after that, Laxmikant left everything about the designing and construction of the bungalow to her, and for a significant part of that phase, Jaya was even pregnant.

Said Jaya: 'I remember my husband and Pyarelal having the muhurat (launch with prayers and a pooja) of eight films on one Dassera, and 48 films on hand on paper! Pyarelal asked my husband how they would manage, and he coolly replied, '*Ho jaayega* (We will manage). I can compose a complete score in 10 days!' However, after that the film associations imposed a ceiling of six films on stars and composers, and between the two of them, L-P could only do 12 films.'

Among L-P's singers, Mukesh's family and Jaya's family were extremely close even before they got married. Jaya met Mohammed Rafi a few times, but never did she meet Kishore Kumar and Manna Dey. Jaya would be away from their music, except for people who came home or for parties and dinner. But Rajeshwari recalled Kishore Kumar as someone who wrote the lyrics with a thick felt-pen on a chart-sized paper to memorize.

Terming Laxmikant an 'amazing father', Rajeshwari said that when there were recordings, he would barely get to see his children on weekdays. They would go to sleep before he came home. He would come and kiss them though Jaya would tell him not to disturb the two. 'So he made a rule that we would sleep with him on weekends!' recalled Rajeshwari with a laugh.

Rajeshwari has fond memories of her father recording her songs when she was a kid. 'He called me to Mehboob Studios on a Friday afternoon as I had no school on Saturdays. The song, 'Gaadi Aati Hai', was with Kanal, Pyare uncle's daughter, and a singer called Kamlesh Awasthi for *Tripti*, a film that got delayed a lot and was finally titled *Oonch Neech Beech*. I was in class three. Daddy was very keen that I learn music and he even got Iqbal Gill, known as Chhote Iqbal, to train me, as he had also trained Nitin Mukesh, Shailendra Singh and Anuradha Paudwal.' She remembers her father being quite a strict taskmaster. 'For the *Ek Hi Bhool* hit 'Hey Raju Hey Daddy', the rehearsals went on till 11 p.m.,' she recalls.'The next morning, however, he had changed the tune a bit and I had to bunk school to rehearse it again! But at the recording, my legendary co-singer S.P. Balasubramaniam made me very comfortable and said, "Just follow me."'

Rajeshwari stressed that this missing out on school was a one-off case: for otherwise, her father laid great stress on something he could never really acquire himself—education. When *Star & Style*, a well-known magazine then, did a story on how industry kids were faring in schools, her principal and teachers at Jamnabai Narsee High School told them that the brightest student among the film fraternity's kids was Laxmikant's daughter Rajeshwari. Rajeshwari was even presented as an example to her classmates, and her handwriting was shown to other children's parents. Her father, who did not even know the name of her school properly, was thrilled at all this. Later, Laxmikant was even more delighted when Rajeshwari won the Aga Khan Scholarship at Mithibai College.

Dr Priti Galvankar, Jaya's sister, said, 'Laxmi-ji had one grouse: he was only educated till class six or nine. So, he loved to be in the company of educated people, like my late husband Dr Dilip Galvankar, a urologist who also liked to play the harmonium, and my daughter Yashasvi, a banker who loves sports. As a person, Laxmi-ji was very religious, gentle, God's own man who always enjoyed being with family and people. He was a keen sports lover, and would invite the Indian, Pakistani and West Indies cricket teams to have dinner with him.' Dr Galvankar recalled asking her brother-in-law once why he did not remember some of his new tunes so that he could sing them at parties, and Laxmikant's unforgettable reply was: 'If I remember what I make, how will I make new tunes?'

Jaya's most celebrated sister, actress Bindu, echoed her sister. 'He would want his house full of people. Food had to be tasty and there had to be at least 10 varieties, though he would eat only small quantities of each.' Getting emotional and wiping tears, she went on, 'Laxmi-ji was so pure at heart; he would respect every human being. If I sent any of our servants to his house for something, he would personally greet them and say, "Come, come, please sit down!" He would switch on the fan himself and ask his servants to get them tea and something to eat, without which they would never be allowed to leave. Forget doing anything bad, he could never even think of such things. So if someone played dirty with him, he would be hurt, but would just say, "*Jaane de na* (Forget it)!"'

But Jaya cannot forget the harsh industry that 'dumped our family after my husband's death.' Boney Kapoor, Nitin Mukesh, Suresh Wadkar, Manhar and Pankaj Udhas, Alka Yagnik and the late Mohammed Aziz (who sang over 200 songs for them in a short span of 12 years) are among the few people who kept in touch. The late Madan Mohla was another person in constant contact, and Jaya recalled with amusement that when he first signed them for *Aasra* (1966), he had told his wife that he did not know what these new boys would do with his film's music. But the calibre of their songs in that film made the producer stick to them for all his films in the next 27 years, in movies as varied and successful as *Sharafat, Raja Jani* and *Dus Numbri*! In terms of years, this was L-P's longest relationship with any filmmaker.

During Laxmikant's lifetime, stars like Manoj Kumar, Dharmendra, Sanjeev Kumar, Jeetendra, Shashi Kapoor, Raj and Randhir Kapoor, Jackie Shroff and Nana Patekar were especially close to him. 'Nana would also insist on my sukhat chutney (a preparation made from preserved fish)!' Jaya remembered.

A popular occasion in the industry was Laxmikant's Diwali-cum-birthday party that started at 9 p.m. and went on till 9 a.m. the following day. There would be no place to stand as top actors, filmmakers and celebrities from multiple fields would be there. Exorbitant amounts for those times would be won or lost in the card sessions. At such times, Jaya's strict instruction to her husband was that he should never gamble with more than ₹20,000!

The actors all held the duo in high regard. For a 1986 concert in Canada, Javed Akhtar had written about 10 lines on L-P's career at Laxmikant's request, which were to be their introduction, spoken by Amitabh Bachchan. The actor reached Sumeet Recording punctually at 6.30 a.m. to record it. She also recalled Bachchan arriving on the dot at 7 a.m. for a rehearsal of 'Chal Mere Bhai' (*Naseeb*) as he had an 8 a.m. dubbing appointment. On another day, he came and whisked the composer away for a long drive, driving his Mercedes himself, as he wanted him to listen to the original Mory Kante number 'Yekeyeke', from which he persuaded them to make 'Jumma Chumma De De' for *Hum*.

1965—A Love Story

But the most interesting story is about how Jaya and Laxmikant met. Four of the six sisters would frequently stroll outside Mumbai's iconic Gaylord's Restaurant, hoping to catch a glimpse of the handsome Jaikishan, who was also their favourite composer. One day, Chandrashekhar, the veteran actor, saw them and asked one of Jaya's sisters, Hema, who wanted to be an actress, if she wanted to do films, and she replied in the affirmative.

Here is the rest of the story, in Jaya Laxmikant's words.

'Chandrashekhar then called all of us to his birthday party, where he was going to announce his new film (which finally was never made), and would introduce my sister opposite him. We sisters were all big fans of Shankar-Jaikishan and I did not care much for the new duo called Laxmikant-Pyarelal, who had just won a Best Music award for *Dosti*, beating S-J's *Sangam*.

'And we were not aware that L-P were to be announced that evening as the music directors of Chandrashekhar's new film. My mother and three sisters were to go, and I was to be left behind. But I insisted on going too.

'When we saw Laxmikant and Pyarelal enter, and everyone congratulated them, I vowed that I was not going to speak to them—I was jealous that they had won the award! But my innocent sister Bindu went and told Laxmikant that we were their fans.

'As the rapport built up, they were invited for dinner at our home to hear my youngest sister, Ila, who was also a singer. I even remember the residential number Laxmi-ji gave Bindu—573357, as they were off for the next few days to Chennai. On the day they were to finally come home, Bindu actually went and bought two expensive and branded shirt pieces and perfumes and a bottle of whisky for them. I was given the task of picking up Ila from school and taking her to their recording studio that was very close to our house on Slater Road, and bringing both of them home.

After the song 'Mere Dushmun Tu Meri Dosti Ko Tarse' (*Aaye Din Bahaar Ke*) was recorded, we came back together. Laxmi-ji was 11 years older than me, but at that time, I had no idea that, for him, it was love at first sight when he saw me. Soon, their coming for dinner became a regular feature, and we also came to know that Laxmi-ji would make excuses to come home, like roads being flooded when there was nothing like that! One day, he told my mother, "I like your daughter very much. My mother is recuperating from a surgery. As soon as she is okay, I would like to bring her and officially ask for her hand."

There was nothing cheap about his approach and my mother was happy. As for Laxmi-ji's mother, she loved her son so much that once he told her that he would marry only me (a Gujarati) or remain single, she agreed to what was then known as an inter-caste marriage. For Laxmi-ji, his mother was the world. So even if Raj Kapoor wanted to sign them, he had to first approach his mother!'

Laxmikant and Jaya had first met on 8 July, and some years later, their son Hrishikesh was born on the same day. Pyarelal had wanted both his and Laxmikant's weddings to be on the same day, but that was not accepted by Laxmikant's or Jaya's families. He got married on 22 May, and Laxmikant on 28 May 1967. Pyarelal married Sunila, a girl he had liked in the neighborhood and was from the Saraswat community. Jaya remembered that Jaikishan presented Laxmikant with a silver violin as a wedding gift—the same was gifted by him to Pyarelal a week earlier. He would tell others that Laxmikant-Pyarelal were doing great work. Laxmikant worshipped him and would imitate his upturned collar, T-shirts and even the loose strap of his watch! Like him, Laxmikant would also appreciate good work done by others. There was no insecurity or jealousy.

Many years later, when he was to have an unusually busy week, Laxmikant suggested that Jaya take their children to her favourite holiday spot, Singapore, as he would hardly be at home. And Jaya had to arrange all his clothes and accessories that he would possibly need for the whole week that she would be away! Laughed Jaya, 'What he wore, at parties, sittings, recordings and anywhere else, was decided by me. He could never do it himself. So I even marked the clothes for each occasion and arranged them for him!'

13

KNOWING THE MAN BEHIND THE MUSIC: PYARELAL

Here is a man, a genius as every associate (including Laxmikant) puts it, for whom life begins and ends with music. Pyarelal and wife Sunila (who is closely related to Girish Karnad, Leena Chandavarkar and Deepika Padukone)[30] continue to live simple lives in Bandra at Deep Bala Apartment. Their elder daughter is Kanal, and their son Gautam lives with them. The couple do not like to speak of their personal lives and all Pyarelal will let on is that Sunila was his sister's friend, and that they chose the apartment they live in because of the vibe it gave when they first entered it as prospective buyers. 'We too had checked on some bungalows in Juhu around Laxmi's place, but Sunila loved this flat for its sea-view and the breeze and we went in for it,' smiled Pyarelal. 'Peace is the most vital need in life.'

Pyarelal, going down memory lane, is full of interesting memories and musical points. Meeting him is not just about chatting with a legend—it is explosive, like stepping onto a mine of music—all aspects of it. I do not remember a single meeting with the maestro in which I did not leave his home without learning something I never knew before—not just about L-P but about music itself! He has even instructed me on the basic taals of Indian music and on a few chords on his piano!

---

[30]Girish Karnad is Sunila's mother's maternal cousin. Leena Chandarvarkar's and Sunila's grandmothers were cousins, while Deepika Padukone's father Prakash Padukone's sister Padmini is married to Sunila's younger brother Nandan Sirur.

Asked how Laxmikant-Pyarelal managed to do so much work in songs and background scores, including multiple assignments in diverse zones, and Pyare-bhai (as people address Pyarelal) gave me an enigmatic simile: 'Let's take a businessman who has interest in multiple and diverse companies. He looks into everything himself, though he has others under him to execute what he wants. A doctor personally has to see to diverse patients in different consulting rooms, but remembers every case.'

Pyarelal stressed that Laxmikant and he had learnt everything hands-on. 'We had this kink—if you can call it that—of going into the depths of everything. This tea we are drinking, a parantha or anything else—I like to know everything about it, about how different it is from the same thing in other places, and why that is so.

God has given taal (rhythm) to every living thing. Our heartbeat is set to a taal. There is music in the way we talk or smile—without tempo, there cannot be expression and sound. Look at our primordial sound Om—it is actually Aum, made up of A, Oo and Ma. So when we chant Aum Namah Shivay or a Muslim speaks Allah-Ho-Akbar, the rhythm pattern is very similar. Today, we wonder about how music can be recorded on 100 or 150 tracks. But we humans also operate on multiple tracks at the same time. You are now listening to me, smiling at me, recording what I am saying, replying and thinking. The way we clap when we are happy, when we want to appreciate or hoot—the sound is different every time.

Human beings acquire knowledge in different ways—from attending a class or by observation. A musician must acquire knowledge. If I am a classical musician, a jazz singer or a folk singer, my perspective of music will be different, and I will need knowledge of diverse things. In music, there is no end. We can only expand our thinking and vision by meeting more and more musicians, as well as other people.'

I kept looking at Pyare-bhai, stunned and in complete awe as he had made me understand the rhythm of life.

The Fount—Pt Ramprasad Sharma

Pyarelal then began to expound upon his unparalleled music base. His father, Pt Ramprasad Sharma,[31] was a very good musician and composer and was not interested as much in playing as a musician as he was obsessed with teaching and talking about music. Ramprasad (as he was then known) was originally from Gorakhpur in Uttar Pradesh, and after his father's death, he came to Vadodara and worked with Babulal, a bandmaster in the Army band there, who advised him to learn music.

After Babulal's death, Pt Ramprasad became bandmaster in his place for a few years. Then he went to Karachi where he made good money within three to four years, running a band and training band musicians. They would play at weddings and other functions. After this, he went to Kolkata, where he played with Mickey Correa[32] (whose roots were in Mombasa, Kenya) in The Grand Hotel despite a sign that said, 'Indians and dogs are not allowed'. Years later, when Correa had aged and was living in Mumbai, Pyarelal came to know about how he had helped his father. He went and met Correa and told him he was like his guru too and asked him to come to their recordings, sit and play a bit and accept his money.

It was in Kolkata that Ramprasad met a simple girl, Indirabai, who also hailed from U.P., and fell in love with her. Pyarelal was their eldest son, born after they had come to Mumbai. After him was born the hugely talented brother, Ganesh, who composed music for about 20 films, but died young. 'He actually worked

---

[31] Pt Hridaynath Mangeshksar, Uttam Singh, Surender Sodhi and Anu Malik and musicians Zarine Daruvala and Mahavir Prasad and of course Pyarelal were among his students. Even Naushad, C. Ramachandra and classical maestros Abdul Halim Zafar Khan and Faiyaz Khan have, to different extents learnt certain notations/techniques from Pandit ji.

[32] Mickey Correa, an Indian born in Mombasa, spent his childhood in Karachi, and belonged to the first generation of our country's musicians to play jazz.

with Manmohan Desai before us, in a film called *Shararat*,' noted Pyarelal.

Pyarelal's real name is Parshuram, but since his mother found him very lovable, she addressed him as 'pyara lal' meaning beloved son, and so he came to be known as Pyarelal. His mother died early, and after two years, Ramprasad married a Maharashtrian girl, Sundarabai, with whom he had six children—two daughters and four sons—Anand, Gorakh, Mahesh and Naresh.

Of these, Anand was the only one who was not musically inclined, though his son, Monty Sharma, is a musician and composer. Gorakh assisted L-P from the beginning. Mahesh formed one half of the Mahesh-Kishore music duo (besides playing for L-P) and Naresh Sharma was composer and also arranger with Nadeem-Shravan and Anu Malik. He is the father of today's composer Mithoon.'

14

THE SECRET SAUCE AND THE CAMARADERIE

*L*axmikant, unlike all other film composers, would never play the harmonium, but only keep his fingers pressed continuously on Sa (the first note) and Pa (the fifth note) while he ruminated on a tune, and even when the song emerged and he was singing it. Musicologist, performer, music author and lecturer Deepak Raja shed light on this mystery and unveiled one of the biggest secrets of the success of Laxmikant-Pyarelal.

'It is common practice in the popular music industry for composers to use the standard harmonium or keyboard for the purpose of composing, and also for imparting their compositions to singers and musicians. The harmonium has a 12-note scale. So, by implication, the composer has limited melodic imagination to those 12 standard notes. But this can be a pragmatic approach because it makes the sharing of melodic patterns between the composer, the singers and the musicians almost effortless,' said Raja.

But Laxmikant was different. He used only the Sa-Pa notes on the harmonium when he composed, and also when he was sharing the composition with singers. And for this, the musicologist has a fascinating explanation: 'Sa-Pa is the standard tuning of the tanpura, because the first and fifth notes are the pivotal notes of the scale, which are achal or fixed. Evidently, then, the harmonium was used by Laxmikant as a substitute for a tanpura. By the principle of harmonics (sound frequencies resonating to the fundamental), the tanpura creates a spectrum of sound, within which the musician can freely access any of the 22 notes (shrutis) constituting the Indian music scale.'

He went on, 'Sa-Pa on the harmonium may not give the acoustic richness of a tanpura. But it will certainly free the melodic imagination from the limitations of the 12-note scale of the harmonium. The composer can then hear all the 22 notes or shrutis in his ear while doing this, and can be said to be in some kind of a subliminal trance, from which he can come out with melodies that can be more complex, even for the singer! Sa and Pa allow you to focus on the entire spectrum of the sound and scale rather than on any particular note. Creative abilities are triggered off in multiple layers and you can focus on them and not be stuck on any particular pitch.'

Little wonder then that Laxmikant-Pyarelal's music makes music lovers go on a different kind of trip!

As we have seen so far, the understanding between Laxmikant and Pyarelal was nothing short of miraculous. In the final analysis, these two disparate individuals from completely contrasting backgrounds came to a common goal when work was concerned. Said Pyarelal, 'My thirst for knowledge was so intense that I would just observe great musicians when I got a chance, and when we struck up a friendship with Hridaynath (Mangeshkar), I would sit in a corner of their house and quietly observe and listen to the great luminaries who visited the Mangeshkars—Bade Ghulam Ali Khan, Abdul Karim Khan, Dagar Brothers and the greats from Marathi natyasangeet (music for Marathi musical plays, a genre in itself). Laxmi would be with me and we would just try to know why music was what it was, like how natyasangeet would also have a strong classical base and yet sound so simple and melodious. As a composer in cinema, you have to compose classical, jazz, pop, cabaret, a ghazal, a thumri, a qawwali, a bhajan, folk, a children's song and so much more.'

He added, 'In films, you have to think both ways. On the one hand, Anand Bakshi's superb poetry in "Khat Likh De Saawariya Ke Naam Babu" (*Aaye Din Bahaar Ke*) or Sahir's "Yeh Dil Tum Bin" (*Izzat*) were both written first. But on the other, even when a song is written to a tune, the thought is already there. While working, your mind has to be open and active. We have seen how the *Shagird* song "Dil Vil Pyar Vyar" was an example of this. Let me give you another example. Shashi Kapoor and we had a lot of mutual affection right from the *Jab Jab Phool Khile* days when we worked with Kalyanji-Anandji. He suggested that we should try and make a song on the Indian musical sargam. The result was "Sa Re Ga Ma Pa", the hit song from *Abhinetri* that was filmed on Hema Malini and him.

Let us take the song "Ek Do Teen Char" from *Tezaab*. It is a tune sung by Mumbai's *rama-log* (groups of young domestic servants) when they are celebrating some occasion. Laxmi loved it and made Javed Akhtar listen to it. And Javed said, "I feel that two people in love will think of how much one waits for the other, so we should use numbers from ek (one) onwards." The prelude ended with the numbers going up to terah (13). This was linked to the mukhda that actually began with "*Tera karoon din gin gin ke intezaar* (I am counting the days as I wait for you)" with a pun on the successive 'terah' and 'tera'. This was the thought, the mood. People accused us of copying the basic tune, but it is all team work—choreographer Saroj Khan and director N. Chandra also did their bit and the final song can be called our song and was a chartbuster.'

Pyarelal continued with their story of camaraderie, 'Laxmi and I firmly believed that while working, the egoistic word 'Main' (I) never interferes. Every song is teamwork, and for us, it was a great shouq (passion) too. A song like 'Dafliwale' (*Sargam*) is not only about our work and how we used 18 daffs (a handheld percussion instrument) when Rishi Kapoor is playing one on screen. It is also about the director's choice of our composition and musical treatment, his vision for the song within the film, the dance director's work, and the expertise of the director of photography, the actor, actress and dancers in a dance number, and also the film's editor. Last but not least, it's about the public that makes it work! Why? Because *yeh public hai yeh sab jaanti hai* (The public knows best)!' And Pyarelal chuckled as he quoted their hit song in *Roti*.

Another frequent Laxmikant-Pyarelal touch was of many songs having differently composed antaras. 'We loved to do that!' affirmed Pyarelal. 'Naushad saab and a few others had this habit, and we picked it up from them.'

How do they decide the orchestration and the ratio of Indian to Western instruments? 'That's very simple. When you go out, you wear clothes as per the occasion: a casual stroll, a formal occasion, meeting a dear friend and so on. In music too, it is the same. What is the song, what kind and for whom? It is the same with raags or with Western music. Taal, bandish, sur—we as composers must know all about them.' Citing their climax song of *Karz*, Pyarelal said, 'The high-pitched and soaring notes at the end of the mukhda of "Ek Hasina Thi" (*Karz*) are to evoke the feeling of the past vis-à-vis the present, and this kind of musical high thinking has to be cultivated. Then we have to think of the interludes and their mood—here the music piece that my brother Gorakh played for us has become iconic. Music is there in everything, and the way we talk and think is all swar (voice). Our thinking has to be multi-dimensional.'

Pyarelal recalled *Mera Gaon Mera Desh*, in which the climax song was filmed on Asha Parekh and Dharmendra tied up by the dacoit Vinod Khanna, with Laxmi Chhaya taunting the hero. 'Raj (Khosla) ji, Laxmi, Anand Bakshi and I were sitting on this song, and Bakshi ji said, "Raj ji, I can only think of the meeting between Alexander and Porus where the former asks Porus, 'Should I kill you or let you go?'" Now see Laxmi's thought-process as he brought in the perfect harkat and sang "Maar Diya Jaaye Ke Chhod Diya Jaaye", with the exact nuance and weight on the word 'maar', which means to kill! The notes have to perfectly meet the requirements.'

He added, 'Whether it is a businessman, professional or even a thief, he must think in multi-faceted ways to approach his work in different places. We composers too have to do that! "Om Shanti Om", "Dard-E-Dil", "Ek Hasina Thi" and "Main Solah Baras Ki" are all part of the same film *Karz*. We used a solo violin piece for the words "*Parda giraya aapne*" in "Dard-E-Dil" to go with the fall of a curtain. Look at Shankar-Jaikishan's short interlude piece between the repetitions of "*Awara hoon*" from the title song of *Awara*—they could have been replaced by more words or by some other music piece. But this interlude became the highlight, so it is all about how a composer thinks.

Film music is a different kettle of fish, but music is an endless ocean. I sit for hours with musicians from abroad when I barely know English. I have studied the smallest details about the intricacies of every Indian and Western instrument and their peculiarities and strengths. Soprano, alto, tenor, bass and baritone—these are all ranges. Today, there is also something known as sopranino. There are various families of instruments (see Epilogue)—the strings family, the woodwinds family and the percussion family.

You also have to know what should be the components of a small, a medium or a large orchestra. We have to learn all these things. While conducting, the count of 1-2-3-4 is akin to making the sign of a cross. This is the first lesson in conducting! In Western music, the sitting posture is specific. The left side of the body is always a little ahead of the right. Learning the basics of music is very simple. But we have to work at it later.

A child learns to walk on his own, with God's blessings. A mother only helps. Then the child tells the mother to leave the hand. That is how we must try and learn as well.'

The maestro continues his musical musings with a note on *Bobby*. He recalled how a senior music critic, judging superficially from the accordion's presence in the songs and general feel, wrote in his music review that the songs of the film were no more than a poor echo of Shankar-Jaikishan's work for Raj Kapoor.

'I called him home, played the music and explained everything from the thought and structure behind each and every song, and rid him of his delusion!' he smiled. 'And do you know that because *Bobby* was our entry into RK Films, Laxmi insisted on formally receiving the HMV Gold Disc from Shankar ji? But in every RK film, Jaikishan would compose a theme piece that he would put somewhere specific within the film, and we kept a piece in similar style in the background where Shashi Kapoor and Zeenat Aman were talking in *Satyam Shivam Sundaram*. And Raj Kapoor appreciated it.

Many years after *Bobby*, Manmohan Desai came to L-P for the song that became 'John Jani Janardhan' in *Naseeb*. He simply told Laxmikant, 'See, I want your tune from *Bobby* as my song.' That 'tune' was the prelude music of 'Aksar Koi Ladki Iss Haal Mein', which became the Rafi hit of Desai's film!

And the same Manmohan Desai had willingly changed the surname of Amitabh Bachchan's character from Anthony Fernandez to Anthony Gonsalves when L-P made the song 'My Name Is Anthony Gonsalves' as a tribute to Pyarelal's guru, the violin player Anthony Gonsalves. Gonsalves also played during that song's recording and Amitabh Bacchan had touched his feet.

I asked Pyarelal about a personal but very true observation that under them, Mohammed Rafi's songs for a Dharmendra, a Sanjeev Kumar, a Jeetendra or a Rishi Kapoor could never be interchangeable in tenor, compositional style and his vocals. What was the special secret that even if one had not watched *Loafer* or *Khilona*, one could still be sure that 'Aaj Mausam Beimaan Hai Bada' from the former film could not be a Rajesh Khanna or Sanjeev Kumar track, and 'Khilona Jaan Kar' from the latter film could not possibly be a Dharmendra or Shashi Kapoor song? With several other composers, it is difficult to pin down a star just from listening to the Rafi song. For example, you could mistake the songs of Naushad's *Mere Mehboob* as filmed on Dilip Kumar, while Rafi's breezy 1960s numbers for Shankar-Jaikishan sounded the same whether they were filmed on Dev Anand, Shammi Kapoor, Biswajeet, Joy Mukerji or Dharmendra. 'That was all Laxmi's doing!' Pyarelal smiled in agreement. 'He was very particular about such things and had a deep understanding of a star's persona and tonality. He would compose the song accordingly and let Rafi saab know what he had in mind.'

Working with musical filmmakers was always special, recalled Pyarelal. 'We had recorded "Haye Haye Yeh Majboori" for *Roti Kapada Aur Makaan* but Manoj (Kumar) ji was not happy. Though he had spent ₹4 lakh, we recorded the song again, and he expressed the wish that Laxmi does the total song—the music, the arrangements, everything. In those days, a James Bond movie had released, and Laxmi reworked its theme as the introductory music.

The world knows how "Accha To Hum Chalte Hain" was made for *Aan Milo Sajana*, where Bakshi ji got up and said those words at the end of an unfruitful sitting, and as soon as Laxmikant asked him, '*Kab mile hum log?* (When do we meet again?)' he stopped in his tracks and said that he had got the song. Pyarelal said, 'But it took a lot of thought to fit the tune after the rest of the words were written, as the conversational mood had to be spot-on, such as in the line, "*Kisi ne dekha to nahin tumhe aate?* (Are you sure no one saw you come?)". Laxmi took care of that!'

Pyarelal continued, 'A director who understands musical detailing was a boon to work with for us. The mocking tones of the line "*Ke tera yahaan koi nahin* (Now you have no one to call your own)" in the song "Yeh Galiyan Yeh Chaubara" (*Prem Rog*) is another example. That last line put life into the song and Lata bai asked us, "How did you think of it?" Why this and why not that—these are all-important points for any song. But a good tune can be made in 10 minutes or can take a day—it is a bit like fishing!'

When the duo composed 'Kajraa Lagaake' in V. Shantaram's *Jal Bin Machhli Nritya Bin Bijli* after Sandhya, the heroine, had composed her dance first, they set the song in Roopak Taal or the 3-2-2 Taal. 'The idea for such a song was Shantaram ji's!' revealed Pyarelal. 'Also, in the title song, Laxmikant introduced a vibration in the words *jal bin* that came in the lines "*Aise tadpoon ke jaise jal bin machhli*", to show how a fish trembles when deprived of water. We cannot study music mechanically. One has to think on what we can do beyond the textbooks on the subject. Indian music is unique. There is no music like Indian classical music, though there is no music like Western Classical in technical perfection.

Speaking of Indian music, don't you find it amazing that our *bhajans* for different deities have distinct tunes and tempos? I realized this just over a decade ago—Lord Ganesh, Lord Krishna, Lord Ram and even Sai Baba bhajans—they are all so different from each other in composition, yet similar to each other in a broad tenor!' Pointing to a key requisite, Laxmikant had added, 'Someone with a deep understanding of classical music need not be a good film composer, but without that knowledge, one cannot sustain. Only when you know the raags and their notes, can you compose. Sometimes, tunes come to fit lyrics, or to fit raags. Anand Bakshi, Majrooh, Rajendra Krishan—they were all masters at writing to a metre.' Creativity, he noted, was 'sublime, interesting and satisfying.' The song 'Humse Tum Dosti Kar Lo' from *Narsimha* was facing some creative blocks and they couldn't quite crack it. Actor Ravi Bahl even brought in western cassettes for the duo to check out! But then, filmmaker N. Chandra had a brainwave. Pyarelal had composed a guitar piece in the interlude of another song, 'Jaao Tum Chahe Jahaan', and he asked Laxmikant to use that as a take-off tune.

The grandeur of a song was everything for the duo. For 'One Two Ka Four' (*Ram Lakhan*), they used a chorus, hardly any melody-based instruments, and more than 82 percussionists. For a dance sequence in *Prem*, they used almost 80 assorted drums, and

Pyarelal split a 9-maatra taal (beat of the rhythm) into halves of four and a half. Seventy to 75 violins alone were used in 'Chanchal Sheetal Nirmal Komal' as well as in the title song of the same film, *Satyam Shivam Sundaram*. 18 sitars played in 'Bada Dukh Deena' (*Ram Lakhan*) and 16 shehnais for a dream sequence in *Karma*. For Pyarelal and his partner, all this was part of a straight passion for a big-screen sound.

In *Khuda Gawah*'s 'Tu Mujhe Qubool', the prelude used thalis (steel plates used for eating food)! Pyarelal invited some Afghan musicians he had seen, to his home to play on their thalis and noted the rhythms they used. For the song, he chose those plates from the market that matched the tones needed. Experimentation was always the name of the game for L-P. For the hit song 'Jaagi Badan Mein Jwala' (*Izzat*), a song filmed on Tamil top star and later politician Jayalalitha, they used a Lebanese folk rhythm that they designed when in Beirut. The song, which featured instruments as varied as the Glockenspiel (a German percussion instrument) and a *Nadaswaram* (a double-reed wind instrument from South India) was written by Sahir Ludhianvi first, with a 26-word mukhda. It was then set to tune by Laxmikant as a heady dance number!

Pyarelal recalled the extraordinary support of Lata Mangeshkar, going far beyond her role as just a singer for them. 'Just for us, she was a part of the theme BGM of *Anita*, reciting alaaps in her voice at my request, and waiting for four hours, from 4 to 8 p.m., to do it'. In 'Kanhaiya O Kanhaiya', a song in *Raja Aur Runk*, she even recited dialogues, as the song was featured in the film as a play on stage. For Sadhana's incomplete film *Yeh Jo Mohabbat Hai*, in a song to be filmed on Madhuri Dixit, she sang in four languages. In *Satyam Shivam Sundaram*, she took on the role of a conductor, waving to our musicians from within the singer's room at Famous Studios even as she was singing. This was because the double-level studio was packed with musicians and chorus and one part of them could only see into the singer's room and were not able to see the conductors! In the song 'Yeh Kaun Hansa' from *Mere Sajana*, she was laughing throughout the song. And in 'Kaise Rahoon Chup' for *Intaqam*, Laxmikant wanted to get a girl to do the hiccups between the lines, but Lata Mangeshkar was firm. She refused to have someone else doing them and promised them that she would really sound drunk—and she did. A nugget shared by Pyarelal here is about the other *Intaqam* chartbuster, 'Aa Jaan-E-Jaan'. Lata's sizzling and soft tenor for Helen offset the visuals of a beast-like man in a cage. The maestro revealed that the beast's voice, the choreography and the overall supervision and concept were by the legendary veteran P.L. Raj.

Another singer who was the epitome of cooperation was Mohammed Rafi. When he had to go abroad for a long concert tour, he recorded five back-to-back songs for them in a continuous session, that lasted almost 24 hours, at Famous Studios. Pyarelal does not now recollect which songs they were, but all five, he remembers, became hits. Another record was for the song 'Woh Maseeha Aaya Hai', the theme song of *Krodhi*. Pyarelal revealed that the complex song was recorded from 8 a.m. on 17 January to 4 p.m. on the following day, almost without a break. He mused, 'There were so many things to be done, but Laxmi and I enjoyed it though we never even slept for those 32 hours!'

Laxmikant would also think of a director's personality and mindset. 'A song like "Ding Dong O Baby Sing a Song" (*Hero*) would fit Subhash (Ghai) ji's flamboyant personality, right? Laxmi was a master at judging that,' Pyarelal smiled.

BR Films' *Dastaan* has some bad attached to it. The 1972 film was their first one with Dilip Kumar. Recalled Pyarelal, 'Whatever could go wrong went wrong. From the start, we never had good relations with the filmmaker, and there was gross interference in our work with people unrelated to the recording (or even to music) insisting on sitting in and throwing in their suggestions. We have always enjoyed complete freedom, but *Dastaan* finally came to a point when we just wanted to finish the assignment and get out, which has never happened either before or afterwards. Despite that, Rafi's 'Na Tu Zameen Ke Liye' remains an evergreen composition.'

An amusing incident is of Anand Bakshi singing two songs for a new hero—Ratan Chopra—in *Mom Ki Gudia*, both of which became popular—'Baghon Mein Bahaar Aayi' with Lata and 'Main Dhoond Raha Tha Sapnon Mein'. With a chuckle, Pyarelal revealed, 'But after the film flopped, the new hero's career nosedived, and his engagement broke off. And poor Bakshi saab felt that he was the jinx. So about five years later, when we gave him the introductory passage of Lata-Rafi's hit duet 'Aaja Teri Yaad Aayi' in *Charas*, he persuaded the director to have many religious icons like the cross, a church, Jesus and Mother Mary seen during his portion of the song!'

Getting more intimate about his bond with Laxmikant, Pyarelal said, 'When we are two different people, it is natural that I may not get along with some people with whom Laxmi was fine, and vice-versa. So we decided that in such cases, what was good or bad for one was good or bad for both. But we both drew a clear line between personal and professional relationships.' When Laxmikant had some issues with Asha Bhosle, for example, they stopped recording with her for a while, but Pyarelal's personal rapport with her remained the same.

In the early days, the two would be together from morning to night, but after their marriages and simultaneous increase in workload, they devised a system for maximum efficiency. Laxmikant would meet six or more producers daily and finalize tunes, while Pyarelal looked after the orchestration, supervise the recordings and the BGM, which had started becoming more complex technically.

Every five or six days, Pyarelal would then go to the music room and in one day, chart out the final graphs of all the tunes approved in that period. Associates would be amazed that two people who seemed to meet so rarely could work so well together.

However, not only did their thoughts run on similar lines, but Laxmikant and Pyarelal would be in constant touch on phone for discussions and ironing out minor adjustments. Laxmikant would thus have a say in Pyarelal's music and Pyarelal would also discuss on his tunes. And Laxmikant had added, 'In over four decades, that I have been in this line, I have never seen a more guni (talented) and perfect composer than my partner, and for me that is an honour and privilege. He not only can convert my tune into gold just with his minor tweaks but is the only musician in Hindi cinema who can read and write both Indian and Western notations, compose, arrange, conduct and record a song—he is the only total composer.'

Laxmikant negated the impression that Pyarelal cannot compose a tune by declaring that some of their finest tunes were composed by his partner. But the aspects Pyarelal now looked after were more time-consuming, so he had no time to sit with filmmakers. On the day there was a song recording, Pyarelal was at work from 10 a.m., whereas Laxmikant went to the studio only in the afternoon.

Said Laxmikant, 'We are different temperamentally. He never lies, I do—in this profession, you have to! For both of us, our partner is the most important person, and everyone else, however big or important, ranks second. One of our biggest filmmakers had some differences with Pyare, so we parted ways professionally.'

And Laxmikant went on, '*Hum logon ki zindagi bas music ke liye hai.* (Our life is for music alone.) We have never thought that we are the best or that we have achieved everything. Each time, we have tried to give our best and something new as well. Many times, our hard work has gone unrewarded or unnoticed. People have rejected some of our favourite songs or scores, but we respect their verdict.'

A crucial reason for L-P's success is that they tried to deliberately create a different style for every filmmaker. This is something neither their seniors nor juniors can boast of doing, and it was, according to Laxmikant, largely due to 'a genius called Pyarelal.' L-P did this even when they had 10, 20 or 30 films on hand, and so their music for Manoj Kumar, Raj Kapoor, Raj Khosla, Manmohan Desai, Subhash Ghai, J. Om Prakash, L.V. Prasad or K. Vishwanath cannot be interchanged.

L-P always kept the filmmakers' individual preferences in focus and worked in the ways the latter wanted. Like Manoj Kumar would always have a stock of poetry and rarely was a tune composed first. Raj Kapoor was a composer himself and had certain preferences that they both had to keep in mind, that too while avoiding S-J-like notes. Also, Kapoor would record a song and spend weeks planning how to film it in the situation he has envisioned. Yet L-P kept the story and setting of the film in mind as well, so though Raj Kapoor's *Bobby, Satyam Shivam Sundaram* and *Prem Rog* were all identifiable as L-P's songs, they were also completely distinct from each other. The music and sound were perfect for each film.

Subhash Ghai mentally visualized songs and then sat with the duo to fashion them. Manmohan Desai liked his songs as 'items' and wanted a lot of Raag Bhairavi in his music, while J.P. Dutta wanted Rajasthani music. Added Pyarelal, 'If you see all our best work, the sound was never repeated again. *Milan, Dosti, Bobby, Ek Duuje Ke Liye, Shor, Roti Kapada Aur Makaan, Mera Gaon Mera Desh, Sargam, Prem Rog, Karz, Hero, Utsav, Saudagar*— have you ever heard that kind of song or sound again in any of our films? That was our key aim.' He added, 'No composer can claim to be 100 per cent original, though some composers are branded as plagiarists. But in over 3,000 songs, we must have copied or adapted less than 60—that is about two per cent! And we would never flatter each other but would be frank if we saw some shortcomings in each other's work, or saw ways in which our work could be improved. And our music, hit or not, good or bad, has always been from Laxmikant-Pyarelal: there was no third person involved.'

Most importantly, the duo remained down-to-earth and cordial with even producers who had left them. One of their filmmakers had signed Raamlaxman and when he had an issue with the management of Mehboob Studios, Pyarelal sorted it out.

Though Laxmikant smiled and said, 'After a point, filmmakers who went to other composers would start missing us and come back, because we became a habit with them!' Pyarelal also felt that their total professionalism also had a big hand in this phenomenon. 'God has given us so much that we can take success without ego and failure without frustration!' he pointed out. 'We are neither taken in by flattery nor affected by malicious criticism. *Bas apna kaam imaandaari aur lagan se karte rahe.* (We kept working with honesty and dedication.) We never thought of any composer as a rival. Shankar ji would be angry with us, make disparaging statements about us, but was still so affectionate, like when he came for our weddings. We had excellent relations with everyone.'

And Laxmikant had continued, 'Great music always happens in a congenial, stress-free, unhurried atmosphere. Look at *Utsav, Sur-Sangam, Anurodh*… Once the basic tune is set, we try to give it shades, add that something extra to improve it further. Suggestions can come in from singers, musicians, lyricists or anyone else, but the final shape of the song on the master-tape is crafted by Laxmikant-Pyarelal.' Pyarelal added, 'A song has to be done like a carefully-prepared delicacy.'

Pyarelal remains dismissive of composers who spend months on a tune in pursuit of so-called perfection. Constant application, he stressed, was a must. 'Look at Shankar-Jaikishan's variety, and how they took up any challenge. They were always working at exercising their tremendous skills,' he pointed out.

However, Pyarelal did not appreciate the short shrift given to BGM in Hindi cinema. 'That is the most important and challenging part of a film!' he said. 'It is the part that brings life to every shot. But sadly, it is the most neglected part of our cinema! Here, there are certain silly rules and requisites. Especially in the South, there is also too much of background score, like they want loud music for even a scene in which the hero is having his morning tea or walking down the stairs!'

So when *Gandhi* was announced in the early '80s, Pyarelal prayed they would be approached for the background score! Pt Ravi Shankar, who was signed for the score along with George Fenton, had earlier replaced them in *Meera*, which they had quit as Lata Mangeshkar had refused to sing for the film and L-P could not imagine doing this musical without her.[33]

Laxmikant summed up their bond: 'We always happen to do things together. We started earning together, we fell in love with women outside our communities together. We got married within six days of each other, had kids more or less around the same time, and have a son and daughter each. We even bought our first cars together.'

And Pyarelal added, 'We would file our income-tax returns together, and the details would be the same. So Laxmi would tell our accountant, 'File one return and then just change the name from mine to his!' And Laxmi was also insistent that our homes should never have name-plates, because the name Laxmikant-Pyarelal should never be separated!'

The Infamous Tiff that Shook the Industry

Yet, incredibly, Laxmikant-Pyarelal's unbreakable bond almost snapped in 1991! In an impulsive decision made during a concert tour abroad, Pyarelal decided not to work with Laxmikant and the latter even recorded a few songs with other arrangers as dates had already been given, because at that time L-P had over 15

---

[33]Lata refused to sing as she had recorded an album of Meerabai bhajans in the same period for her brother Pt Hridaynath Mangeshkar.

assignments on hand. Happily, they came back together in less than a fortnight. But their split and reunion became a 'record' event. Not only were there impassioned pleas by trade magazines and a lot of coverage in the media then, but top filmmakers like Manoj Kumar, J. Om Prakash (who had then signed Nadeem-Shravan out of commercial compulsions), Boney Kapoor, Pankuj Parashar and more came together and helped in the reunion.

Naushad and Lata Mangeshkar also were a part of the peace-making process, it is said.

Incidentally, Laxmikant had also revealed to me that a film industry big shot, whose name he never mentioned, had, much earlier, tried to drive a wedge between Lata Mangeshkar and them, hoping it will affect their careers.

L-P's superstardom at that point was also demonstrated by the fact that Dinesh Gandhi (backdoor producer of films like *Tezaab* and *Hum*) vowed to go on a pilgrimage if they reunited, while Laxmikant's sister-in-law Bindu had vowed to feed 500 poor people if they came back together. On this, Subhash Ghai, Jaya Laxmikant and Laxmikant-Pyarelal shed light. Ghai had told me then, 'Two common "friends" were creating all the misunderstandings between them. But I exposed them.' These two people were retailers in Mumbai's midtown Dadar, and owned the showroom of a reputed cloth brand. They would even address each other as Laxmikant and Pyarelal, revealed Jaya. Intending to soothe ruffled feathers, Ghai had gone to Laxmikant's house while the two retailers were there and later went to Pyarelal's house, and found them there too. They had apparently even told Pyarelal concocted lies about what Laxmikant and his wife had 'stated' about him.

And Ghai told Pyarelal, 'I was there at Laxmi-ji's house. No one said a word against you. These scoundrels are lying through their teeth!' Later, Laxmikant dismissed the matter with a smile, saying, 'Pyare was upset about something,' and Pyarelal remarked, 'It was a stupid tantrum on my part during a show abroad, when

I desperately wanted a glass of water and no one got it, and it seemed that everyone was paying attention to Laxmi. Otherwise, we had always decided that if anyone told us anything derogatory about the other partner, we would check with each other first.'

And that's how partnerships should be, and barring this moment of pique, L-P's relationship was.

15

ANOTHER LONG-LASTING RELATIONSHIP: ANAND BAKSHI

We can almost say that Laxmikant-Pyarelal and Anand Bakshi were incomplete without each other. Three hundred and two films (from *Mr X in Bombay* in 1964 to *Mere Biwi Ka Jawaab Nahin* in 2004)), most of them solo films for Bakshi, was their score. This is unequalled in Hindi cinema, and the best part is that the humongous quantum in no way compromised their quality and range together. Both L-P and Bakshi had similar work-ethics—work was passion, work was religion. Both would say that their creations could not be at the expense of the needs of the situation and the film, done solely with the intention of showing what they could do in creativity.

Bakshi would always say that the real struggle began after one became successful, for that's when the whole situation could easily change for the worse and you could become a passing sensation. L-P, though they did not put it in so many words, clearly believed in the same. If they outclassed Shankar-Jaikishan in six years, they were to keep R.D. Burman, their own mentors Kalyanji-Anandji, Rajesh Roshan and Bappi Lahiri at bay for 24 more years. And Anand Bakshi, once he became the Numero Uno around the same time as L-P, held sway until he left us. Laxmikant-Pyarelal had gone, but Bakshi formed very successful teams with a variety of other composers. Nevertheless, for him, Laxmi-Pyare were always very special. He made his singing debut for them in *Mom Ki Gudia*, and then sang in *Charas*—with a total of three songs, all hits, all mentioned earlier in this book. None of the four songs he sang for other composers were hits.

It is said that Bakshi would often write his lyrics in metre, and thus provide the semblance of a tune to all his composers. It was the composer's prerogative to accept and work on it, or to provide their own melody. And so, Bakshi would often describe film music as 'teamwork', which is actually the case with any film song. This is because the director, producer, lyricist, singer or actor can always give their opinions and inputs. But to say that Bakshi contributed heavily to L-P's music was far from the truth. If the plethora of songs that L-P did without him were not sufficient indication of the duo's talent, the huge L-P-Bakshi repertoire saw songs of every conceivable genre and origin that could not be Bakshi's handiwork. For example, Laxmikant's own inclination towards Punjabi folk (which was Bakshi's forte) was also seen in L-P's work with other songwriters, as with Sahir (*Daag*) or Verma Malik (*Nagin, Jaani Dushmun*). And let us also not forget that Laxmikant also provided some basic tunes to Bakshi too, as we have seen.

So how did their friendship bloom? We have read that Anand Bakshi was one of the struggling lyricists encouraged by Kalyanji-Anandji and that Laxmikant and Pyarelal saw his worth in that phase. *Mehndi Lagi Mere Haath* was the first film in which K-A worked with Bakshi, and he wrote all the songs for the film. Then came *Phool Bane Angarey*, again a full film for him. During this phase and the other songs that Bakshi did for K-A with Laxmikant-Pyarelal as their assistants, the younger duo not only realized that they had found their dream partner ('Our counter to Hasrat and Shailendra' as Laxmikant described him) but also formed a thick and lasting friendship with him. A major catalyst in this process was Raj Kapoor's secretary, Hiren Khera, a big man and a bachelor then, who produced *Mehndi Lagi Mere Haath* and the blockbuster *Jab Jab Phool Khile*. Bakshi and L-P were still struggling, but formed a clique with him. Khera would call the three to his Chembur house, stating that he would make the dal (lentils curry), but that the three youngsters should get the pav (bread) for themselves and for him. Pyarelal thus reiterates that, as between him and Laxmikant, there was no single moment that brought Bakshi and them together. The duo loved all the varied lyrics he wrote so effortlessly and perfectly for the situations, and that too in simple language, in *Mehndi Lagi Mere Haath* and *Phool Bane Angarey*.

L-P had many loyalists among filmmakers, but J. Om Prakash, L.V. Prasad, Raj Khosla, Mohan Kumar, Subhash Ghai, Manmohan Desai (with one exception for Majrooh loyalist A.A. Nadiadwala), Mahesh Bhatt, producers Madan Mohla (with one exception due to leading man Manoj Kumar), Premji and A. Purnachandra Rao were among the many who chose Anand Bakshi exclusively for their films with the duo. Unconfirmed buzz also has it that Bakshi turned down Raj Kapoor's *Prem Rog* for his own reasons after *Bobby* and *Satyam Shivam Sundaram*.

In one of my last meetings with Anand Bakshi, I asked him if he missed working with Laxmikant-Pyarelal. Pragmatically, he answered, 'I do miss those days sometimes. But we worked so much and so well for so many years. Why should I complain? We all came in to replace others. Someone was bound to come in our place. The wheels of Time are always turning...'

Among the innumerable highlights of their work, Bakshi spoke about how he had worked on the timeless songs of *Milan*. 'When writing a song, I never think as Anand Bakshi,' he had told me, echoing another of L-P's qualities. 'So I put myself in the boatman's place and contemplated on the thoughts that would come into his head, and what kind of language he would use. And while Laxmikant contributed the "*Shor nahin, sor, sor, sor*" part in "Sawan Ka Mahina", keeping in mind how some North Indian people pronounced the phonetic syllable Sh as sa, I even read up literature on Lord Shiva—10 books!—when given the situation for "Bol Gori Bol".

Laxmikant himself confirmed Raj Khosla's story on *Main Tulsi Tere Aangan Ki*. Khosla had told Laxmikant about his new film and the title, and Laxmikant had made the basic tune that we all know now for the mukhda. They went to Anand Bakshi's home, where he was lying in bed with a foot raised and in plaster, because he had suffered a fracture. After giving him a narration, Raj Khosla told him, 'We need a second line to complete the mukhda.' And instantly, Bakshi said, 'That is simple. It should be "*Koi nahin main tere saajan ki*"!' The filmmaker broke down as he told me, 'In six everyday words, Anand Bakshi had encapsulated the entire story of my film!'

Among Anand Bakshi's personal favourites of all time (which came out after a long persuasion by me), seven of the 12 songs are L-P's creations: 'Sawan Ka Mahina' (*Milan*), 'Yeh Shama To Jail' *(Aaya Sawan Jhoom Ke)*, 'Bindiya Chamkegi' (*Do Raaste*), 'Gaadi Bula Rahi Hai' (*Dost*), 'Solah Baras Ki Bali Umar' (*Ek Duuje Ke Liye*), 'Chitthi Aayi Hai' (*Naam*) and 'Deewane Tere Naam Ke' (*Saudagar*).

The dream team had no limits, as they broke all barriers in creativity. A song sung while a sport was being played on screen ('Pakdo Pakdo Pakdo' in *Naseeb*), a truck-driver's poetry ('*Tumhari zulf hai ya sadak ka mod hai yeh*' describing a beauty's long tresses, while being drunk in *Dushmun*'s 'Sacchai Chhup Nahin Sakti'), a song by a criminal gang who have found a traitor among them ('Tu Gaddaar Sahi Tu Maqqaar Sahi'), and a song in which three generations of a family are singing out their feelings ('Yeh Kaisa Aaya Zamana' from *Humjoli*)—the L-P-AB team spelt variety with excellence. And whether their friendship was the cause or the effect of their musical brilliance is, perhaps, a headier conundrum than the chicken and egg question.

16

THE LAST CALL…

In 1998, a three-week, 12-concert tour of Europe, USA and Dubai had been fixed, but Laxmikant was not keeping well, and Pyarelal suggested that they postpone the tour by six months. But Laxmikant told him that he would join them soon, and advised his partner to do the first two or three shows alone.

The night Pyarelal and his team were to leave, Laxmikant and Jaya arrived at his house around 11 p.m. with a bouquet. 'He had never gifted me anything ever, and neither had I ever given him a present.' said a moved Pyarelal. 'I only had Indian whisky to serve him, I told Laxmi, and he said he would drink whatever I offered him. Around 12:30, he took my leave.' At that time, Pyarelal was also recovering from a fall in which he had hurt his leg. Laxmikant's health deteriorated further in the next few days. After finishing the New York concert a few days later, Pyarelal asked Shabbir Kumar to dial Laxmikant. It was 3 a.m. there and about 10 in the morning in Mumbai.

Rajeshwari picked up the call, asked how the tour was going, and told Pyarelal that her father was not well and was sleeping. Pyarelal told her that he would just like to speak with him for a couple of minutes. She woke up Laxmikant, and when Pyarelal asked him about his health, he replied, '*Meri chhod* (Forget about me), how is your leg?' Said Pyarelal, 'He also asked me how the tour was going. And since he was in no condition to travel, I told him about the rest of the plans and when I would be back. But he suddenly went off the line, and I was told that he slipped into a coma at that very moment!' This was the last time

Pyarelal would hear his partner's voice. He never came out of the coma, though he passed away many days after Pyarelal returned. Concludes Pyarelal, 'But even today, in whatever I do in music, he is always there, beside me.'

Yes, the L-P bond is forever.

III
MEMORIES AND IMPRESSIONS

Such a book would be absolutely inconceivable and, of course, incomplete, without contributions from Laxmikant-Pyarelal's associates. Here are singers, lyricists, stars, filmmakers and musicians going down memory and melody lanes, and during their look back at the duo, offering stunning and even quirky insights into the creation of some of their finest songs and music. All this helps us comprehensively understand what made L-P the complete, nonpareil composers they were.

A young Laxmikant with his mandolin.
Courtesy: Jaya Laxmikant

Pyarelal with his prime instrument—the violin.
Courtesy: Pyarelal Sharma

At Laxmikant's wedding. Pyarelal had wanted both his and Laxmikant's weddings to be held on the same day, but that was not accepted by both Laxmikant's and Jaya's families.
Courtesy: Jaya Laxmikant

Fine-tuning a composition.
Courtesy: Anil Bohra/ Jaya Laxmikant

With Kishore Kumar and junior artistes at a recording session.
Courtesy: Jaya Laxmikant

In his own rhythm, Laxmikant.
Courtesy: Jaya Laxmikant

Alka Yagnik shows the corner of the still-maintained singers' cabin at Mehboob Recording Studios, where she stood with chorus singers during the recording of 'Ek Do Teen Char' (*Tezaab*).
Courtesy: Rajiv Vijayakar

Laxmikant-Pyarelal's seven Filmfare trophies at Laxmikant's home: for *Dosti* (1964), *Milan* (1967), *Jeene Ki Raah* (1969), *Amar Akbar Anthony* (1977), *Satyam Shivam Sundaram* (1978), *Sargam* (1979) and *Karz* (1980).
Courtesy: Rajiv Vijayakar

With Anand Bakshi, with whom they worked on 302 films (from *Mr X in Bombay* in 1964 to *Mere Biwi Ka Jawaab Nahin* in 2004), most of them solo films for Bakshi. This is an unequalled score in Hindi cinema.
Courtesy: Jaya Laxmikant

Laxmikant with Anand Bakshi and Rajesh Khanna. L-P, Bakshi and Rajesh Khanna collaborated on 21 films, including the L-P presentation *Tinku* (1977). *Roti* (1974), *Aashiq Hoon Baharon Ka* (1977) and *Chakravyuha* (1979) were the actor's home productions, and *Mehboob Ki Mehndi* was unofficially co-financed by him.
Courtesy: Anil Bohra

At the recording of *Ajooba*. Producer-director Shashi Kapoor, Laxmikant, Alka Yagnik, Amitabh Bachchan, Anuradha Paudwal and Sudesh Bhosle.
Courtesy: Sudesh Bhosle

With Shakeel Badauni who penned only one song for them, 'Mere Dil Aaj Tu Maayoos' from *Jurm Aur Saza,* a mesmerizing lullaby.
Courtesy: Javed Badayuni

With R.D. Burman, for whom they arranged the music of his first two films that were produced by Mehmood—*Chhote Nawab* and *Bhoot Bangla.*
Courtesy: Pyarelal Sharma

With Raj Kapoor. L-P had initially refused to compose the music for *Bobby*, but were later convinced by singer Mukesh to do the film.
Courtesy: Jaya Laxmikant

With their mentors Kalyanji-Anandji.
Courtesy: Pyarelal Sharma

At the recording of *Aap Aaye Bahaar Ayee* with producer-director Mohan Kumar, Rajendra Kumar, recording engineer Kaushik, Lata Mangeshkar and Mohammed Rafi.
Courtesy: Late Mohan Kumar

Laxmikant with producer N.N. Sippy, who had told the duo that an incredible one crore rupees in coins thrown by the ecstatic audience was ultimately collected from movie halls where 'Dafliwale' from *Sargam* was playing!
Courtesy: Pravesh Sippy

Raj Kapoor loved to have what he called 'popatiya' words in lyrics, which meant words easily understood and sung by the common man. He would want the tune to be melodious and catchy.
Courtesy: Jaya Laxmikant

At the *Hum Paanch* recording of 'Aaiye Meherbaan' with Usha Uthup.
Courtesy: Boney Kapoor

With Manhar and Mahendra Kapoor at the recording of 'O Door Se Aanewale Bataa' from *Barkha Bahar* (1974).
Courtesy: Jaya Laxmikant

Laxmikant with Anand Bakshi and J. Om Prakash, fondly called Om-ji.
Courtesy: Filmyug

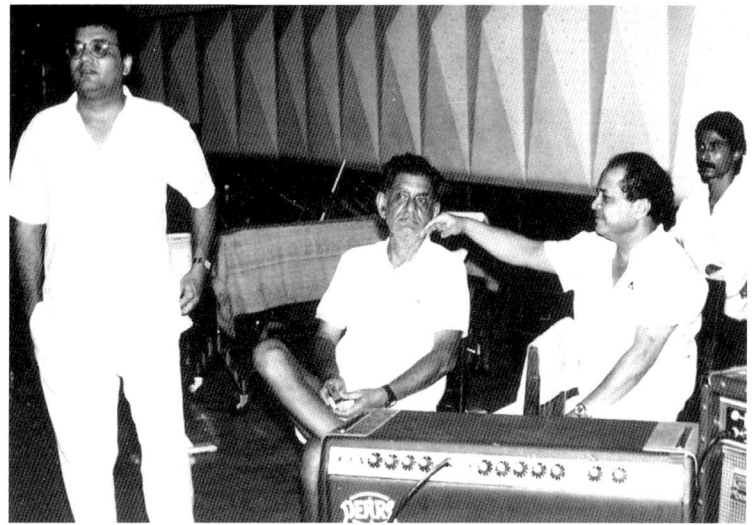

At a sitting for *Karz* with Subhash Ghai and Anand Bakshi. The interlude music piece that Pyarelal's brother Gorakh played in the song 'Ek Haseena Thi' has become iconic.
Courtesy: Subhash Ghai

Laxmikant rehearses Manna Dey for *Satyam Shivam Sundaram*. In the centre is lyricist Pt Narendra Sharma
Courtesy: Paritosh Narendra Sharma

Laxmikant introducing his daughter Rajeshwari.
Courtesy: Jaya Laxmikant

Woh 7 Din recording with (L-R) Boney Kapoor, Surinder Kapoor, Shabbir Kumar, director Bapu and Anil Kapoor.
Courtesy: Boney Kapoor

The poster says it all. Half a song was even recorded by L-P with S.P. Balasubramaniam. Suddenly, the film changed hands and went to Nadeem-Shravan.
Source: Trade magazine poster issued by Divya Films International

Pyarelal, a maverick musician who has a symphony under his name, 'Om Shivam in A-Minor'.
Courtesy: Pyarelal Sharma

17

THEIR SINGERS

Abhijeet

'L-P's music was the toughest—from *sadak chhaap* (streetsmart stuff for the hoi-polloi) to classic, each song had a style, and was popular yet had a status. Look, for example at "Choli Ke Peeche" from *Khal Nayak*. It is such a creative song on which Subhash Ghai and L-P worked. It was 100 per cent L-P's creation, but with anyone else, I dare say it would have been a lousy or vulgar effort.

Among the giants of the past, no one could compete with them, not even R.D. Burman with his blend of melody and western packaging. L-P gave Rafi saab a new life in the late 1970s. They created and changed trends, but never followed anyone else. They competed with everyone in their own style, as if they wanted to say, "We will do what we have always done."

I sang two songs for them, "Prem Doot Aaya" (with Asha ji) in *Mujhe Insaaf Chahiye* (1983), which I sang very badly. Then for your late '90s interview in *Mid-Day*, you asked me what I thought of L-P as they never called me after that. My answer was: "Their music is as good as ever, but they are using a lot of wrong singers who are bringing down their music."

Laxmi-ji read that, called me up and promised he would call me to sing. But at that time, they were going down and barely had a couple of films. Soon I recorded my only other song for them, "Billo Ki Billi Billi Aankhon Ka" from *Barsaat Ki Raat* (1998), which became quite popular. At the studio, Laxmi-ji came and told me that he would have loved to give me more songs, but they had very little work. I was really moved by the statement, coming from a giant who had contributed so much to Hindi film music.'

Alka Yagnik

'Raj Kapoor's Bengal distributor Ashok Desai heard me sing somewhere when we were in Kolkata and asked my mother if I was interested in playback singing. He handed us a letter adressed to Raj Kapoor. I was barely 10, and when we entered RK Studios, Raj saab thought that my mother was the singer! But when he heard me, he wrote a note to Laxmikant-Pyarelal and sent us to them. I was already visiting and learning with Kalyanji-Anandji during vacations.

Laxmi-ji's advice to my mother was simple. "Don't make her a child singer. That stamp is not possible to erase in this industry. When the right time comes, I will call her." Many years later, he called me and asked if I was open to dubbing songs. I said I did not want that. The standout quality of Laxmi-ji was that he could make any singer blossom. I had a soft voice, and they made me open up to throw my voice into the mike so that it could be heard over the orchestra. He liked singers who belted out a song and had a punch and a khanak (sharpness) in their voices.

I remember the recording of "Ek Do Teen Char" (*Tezaab*). Not only was there a huge orchestra, but some 40 chorus singers were there too, and I was sticking close to the wall of the crammed singer's cabin. "*Mike pe maaro awaaz* (Throw your voice into the microphone)", Laxmi-ji told me. I had a sore throat that day and told him that, but he just said, "It does not matter, sing whatever comes out!" Later, when I had recovered, I told him I would like to redo the song, and he replied, "The way you have sung is perfect. I want that same khanak every time you sing!" Imagine!

And L-P were both very particular about a singer's comfort level. They would ask if there was time for us to take a breath between two lines, or should they put in two bars of music as a break for our voices. Today, the music directors just punch in our voice, but L-P would always think of the singer.

Singing a Laxmikant-Pyarelal song was like doing a full riyaaz of the throat. It was like performing vocal acrobatics, with intricate compositions and harkatein and so many ups and downs. The songs were easy on the ears, but pretty tough to sing.

In the classic "Thare Vaste Re Dhola" (*Batwara*), all three of us—Kavita, Anuradha and I—were told what to sing. Laxmi-ji was very intelligent; he knew exactly what suited each singer. They were masters at casting any song.

Pyare-bhai was a strict perfectionist who would praise me a lot, but our interactions were limited. As a person, Laxmi-ji was a larger-than-life personality, always laughing, dressed in bright clothes, and I never saw him in a dull mood.'

Amit Kumar

'The very first time I saw both Laxmi-ji and Pyare-ji was when I had come home from Kolkata during my school vacations. I was in my bedroom when I heard Baba (Kishore Kumar)'s rehearsal for the *Mr X in Bombay* song "Khubsoorat Haseena" and Laxmi-ji's unique voice belting out the refrain "*Tu nahin tu nahin*". I wondered whose unique voice it was.

I came down—I must have been 11 or 12—and Baba introduced me to them. I also went for the recording and that's when I first saw Lata (Mangeshkar) ji. The third or fourth take was approved by L-P.

Some days later, I went to watch the shooting of another song, "Mere Mehboob Qayamat Hogi" and I never imagined that it would soon become a public anthem that remains timeless. At the rehearsal of this song, I remember Baba saying, "*Yeh dono bahut hi guni hai, dekho mere liye kya gaana banaya hai!* (These two are so talented. What a song they have made for me!)" And he had played out the song to all our staff at home.

Both Laxmi-ji and Pyare-ji knew Baba for years, and they had been musicians on many films where he was involved, like S.D. Burman's *Chalti Ka Naam Gaadi*. They had also played on my father's 1959 song "Neela Aasmaan", which is available on YouTube. This song was to be for my father's first production, but it was shelved. It was also to be his debut as a composer. L-P were very close to my father and even played on the songs of his *Jhumroo*.

When they came to know later that I was also interested in singing, Laxmi-ji asked Baba, "*Murqi*[34] *maarta hai?* (Is he able to do murqis?)"

Baba had come for the recording of my first song for them, "Main Bhi To Akela Hoon", which was a duet with Asha (Bhosle) bai from *Zindagi Aur Toofan* (1975). After that, I sang many songs for them in the 1970s, mostly with Baba, like "Bambai Ki Barsaat" (*Aap Beati* in 1976), "Khuli Nazar Kya Khel" (*Parvarish* in 1977) and "Milte Rahiye" (*Prem Vivah* in 1979). Some others were there as well, like the very popular "Aji Suniye Zara Rukiye" in *Parvarish* with Shailendra Singh, Asha (Bhosle) bai and Aarti Mukherjee.

In the 1980s and 1990s—apart from my singing many other notable songs like "Jaaneman Jaan-E-Jigar" (*Ghazab* in 1982), and "Ek Sabz Pari" (*Do Dilon Ki Dastan* in 1985), they made me a regular voice for Anil Kapoor—in the hit songs of *Tezaab* and *Roop Ki Rani Choron Ka Raja* besides some other films.

There were other nice songs in films like *Sachai Ki Taaqat* ("Aisa Ab Tak Hua Nahin Par"), *Narsimha* ("Jaao Tum Chahe Jahaan") and *Hum*—and I personally think that my "Sanam Mere Sanam" was a far better song than "Jumma Chumma De De"!

I was, frankly, a little intimidated by them. Laxmi-Pyare,

---

[34]A short taan, an ornamentation employing two or more notes, which is used in light music forms.

especially Pyare-ji, would never approve a song until he was satisfied—*ghis ghis ke* (by relentlessly polishing) he would take out what he wanted, unlike Pancham, who would be easygoing and make me comfortable and if need be, make me record later.

In retrospect, I think L-P's approach was the right way! I support this strict, no hanky-panky approach: *isse riyaaz hota hai* (It becomes a form of musical training). They would rehearse six to seven times, take a break and then go in for the recording.

I do feel they composed many songs specially for me. However, overall, they gave me lesser songs than I expected and maybe they could have used me much more. But they really gave Baba a lot of variety. I love his "Ek Ritu Aaye" from *Gautam Govinda* (1979), "Jaaneman Jaaneman" from *Jaaneman* and "Neele Ambar Ke Do Naina" from *Asha Jyoti* (1984). Semi-classical, ghazal, qawwali, mujra and all the way to *Karz*, they made my father sing everything.

Finally, there is another of my all-time favourites from Baba's songs, which my father loved a lot: "Tere Baghair Jaan-E-Jaana" from *Anari* (1975). Very few know it was composed way back in 1966 with the words "*Aaja bahaar aa rahi hai / Aaj phir teri yaad aa rahi hai*". My father would rave, "*Kya gaana banaya hai!* (What a composition!)"

No one wanted to change these words, including Majrooh saab, who had written the song, when it was finally to be recorded for a film. But *Anari*'s director Asit Sen insisted on changing the mukhda. And so my father would always sing this song in his shows with the original mukhda and people would go crazy.'

Anuradha Paudwal

'In 1972, I had sung the Marathi non-film song "Pahaa Takile Pusuni Dole" in a popular radio show called *Yuvavani*. Laxmi-ji heard it, found my phone number and called up, saying that he would like to work with me. I told him that I was not interested in films. He coolly said, "Whenever you want to sing, call me." A year later, I had recorded my shlok for *Abhimaan* and Laxmi-ji came to know of it. He called me for the Ramleela song in *Jaaneman* (1976), with Manna Dey and two other singers, Anand Kumar and Vinod Sharma. L-P also soon gave me my first Hindi solo, "Hum To Garib Hai" in *Aap Beati* (1976) for Hema Malini, a fabulous song written by Anand Bakshi.

I learnt a lot from Laxmi-ji and his way of singing, which emphasized the throw of words and the play on them. Laxmikant-Pyarelal's songs were challenging, mostly with differently-composed antaras for every song. They had a huge hit percentage with me, and my voice got moulded just by learning how Laxmi-ji sang, though he never "tutored" me. He was so pleasant and made every singer comfortable. He had absolutely no ego even after achieving so much.

As a trait, Laxmi-ji would never bad-mouth anyone—in fact, he would sometimes tell musicians around that the vaastupurush[2] is always hovering around us and you can never know when he will decide "Tathastu" or "So be it!"

Sweetness and melody were abundant in L-P's music. I was attuned to their melodies temperamentally. Their songs always had that touch of emotion and feelings that is very Marathi in its sojwaltaa (bright purity), and I think that connected with everyone for over three decades.

Look also at their Punjabi-style songs. Thanks to Anand Bakshi, they were never crude or cheap but had decency and dignity, unlike what you hear today. That is why L-P still have diehard fans in North India, which I realize afresh whenever I perform there.

I observed that Marathi audiences were less receptive to their music than those from elsewhere. My personal view of why Marathi people generally prefer some other composers is because we as a race are conservative, and acceptance of something fresh is dicey when we have some set ideas. But in the North and in Bengal, I have seen that people have a much more open mind.

Laxmi-ji had approached me for the title song of *Satyam Shivam Sundaram* as a dubbing artiste, as it was a Raj Kapoor film. I did not want to be a dubbing artiste, so I refused. But later, I agreed to dub for "Tu Mera Jaanoo Hai" in *Hero* (1983) as the muhurat song. That evening, at the launch party, it was being played and everyone thought that since the girl (Meenakshi Seshadri) was new, they should retain my voice. The next day, I dubbed another song, "Ding Dong O Baby Sing A Song", but that too was retained. *Hero* became a major turning-point in my career.

And Pyare-bhai was a treat to watch at work. His khaasiyat (speciality) was that he could create an equally great sound with 50 violins and 100 musicians as he could with just six musicians, like in "Man Kyoon Behka" from *Utsav* (1985).

For "Mere Man Baaja Mirdang", my *Utsav* song, which won me my first Filmfare award, the situation was a mela (fair) in a village in the B.C. era. In any fair, there are always so many things happening at different places, and the main point was that Rekha was running from Shashi Kapoor, who was chasing her. Pyarelal actually arranged different groups of musicians to represent each part of the fair, with different instruments, all ethnic. To maintain the atmosphere of a fair, if the focus was on one musician group at one time, the volume of that group would be at 90 per cent, but the remaining 10 per cent would be "leaked" into it from another group to create an authentic atmosphere. The main mukhda, "*Mera man baaja mirdang*", was sung by me in three different ways for the three groups, who were all playing at different pitches.

So I asked Pyare-bhai, "Which sur (pitch) do I follow?" as I was the one singing throughout. I will never forget his answer: "*Aap dhyan se suniye. Yeh jo alag alag sur hain, unnka milke ek sur banta hai. Aap uss sur ko follow kijiye* (If you hear carefully, all the three different pitches combine to form one common pitch, which is the one you should follow). Then you will be in tune with the song and in sync with all the musicians." It was astounding, and I did exactly that!'

Kavita Krishnamurthi Subramaniam

'I was introduced to Laxmi-ji by Hema Malini's mother Jaya Chakravarthy. That led to my dubbing Hema ji's *Chacha Bhatija* (1977) song "Batli Ko Tod De". It was a strenuous job, rehearsing again and again, and with their huge orchestra. Later, Laxmi-ji would introduce me to everyone as Hema ji's cousin, just so that people would consider giving me songs. L-P gave me my first original song in "Kaahi Ko Byahi Bides" for Moushumi Chaterjee in *Maang Bharo Sajana* (1980). But I kept on dubbing for them just to experience their music and the way they taught me their songs, even if they were finally sung by Lata ji. Among such classics were "Yun Besabab Jahaan Mein" (*Mehandi Rang Laayegi*), the magnificent "Zeehal-E-Miskin" (*Ghulami*), "Jeet Jaayenge Hum" (*Meri Jung*), "Bada Dukh Deena" (*Ram Lakhan*) and some songs in *Nache Mayuri*. In *Sur-Sangam*, I had my own numbers, but also dubbed for Lata ji's songs!

I did not see any difference in the briefing Laxmi-ji would give me and what he told Lata ji, as I was there when Lata ji dubbed some songs I had sung. But it was astonishing how she would bring in changes within the same framework and bring the words alive.

Laxmi-ji would sing a song, if need be, 10 to 15 times and ask me to sing the way he was singing. He had huge affection for all of us singers and would say, "You people are like my army!" On his birthday, he was a great host, but none of the young singers would drink in his presence, as they respected him too much.

And the wavelength of Pyare-bhai and Laxmi-ji was incredibly similar. I have seen many examples of this, but let me narrate one: I was recording a song for *Khuda Gawah* and Laxmi-ji suddenly told me, "After this antara, I think you should sing an alaap. I will tell Pyare." And at that very moment, Pyare-bhai opened the door and walked in saying, "Laxmi, I have thought of an alaap that Kavita can take in the second music." It was uncanny!

Both of them understood music in diverse forms. They had seen the plus and minus points of all the composers, and Laxmi-ji had a strong business sense. All this gave them a humongous edge.

When we were recording for *Sur-Sangam*, they arranged a Benares ang (style) taanpura and gave full freedom to the Misra brothers. For seven days, the atmosphere was just like a temple, and I remember that on the last day, Laxmi-ji's eyes went moist—it was clear he would miss that atmosphere.

Can you imagine the range of what I have sung for them—from Indian classical in its purest form to a "Jumma Chumma De De" in *Hum*?

When my husband (world-renowned violinist Dr L. Subramaniam) and I had visited Pyare-bhai after our marriage, they discussed the intricacies of Western classical music for hours. Pyare-bhai had showed him the notations of the symphony he was writing at the time. When we left, my husband just said, "What's this genius doing here just rusting away? He should be in the west. No one here can compose such symphonies."

I feel blessed that I was so close to such a phenomenal duo.'

Lata Mangeshkar

'I would have objections to the lyrics of some songs, like most of the cabaret numbers. But (Shankar-Jaikishan and) Laxmikant-Pyarelal took care of those aspects. They also made songs that were suited to my vocal cords and left me free to sing them in my style.

They would tell me that I could do whatever I liked with the harkats and taans. They knew that a singer could contribute a lot to the overall quality of a song and that it was not enough for a composer to break his head over a composition. I think that, for me, it was about understanding the way different music directors thought and worked. I had to deliver what each of them wanted, but with my individual touch. Expressions were of paramount importance and I would also be very particular about the taal (rhythm) and also the words, especially the diction or ucchaar.'[35]

Mahendra Kapoor

'There was class in Laxmikant-Pyarelal's most mass-oriented numbers. Or you could put it this way that many of their classy numbers, unlike those of most other composers, had that something that made them mass chartbusters! Like my "Aur Nahin Bas Aur Nahin" from *Roti Kapada Aur Makaan* (1974). People I trust tell me that it is the finest song of my career, and I agree. I think that film music in the real sense ended after L-P!'[36]

Manhar Udhas

'My first song for them was "O Door Se Aanewale Bataa", a duet with Mahendra Kapoor, in *Barkha Bahar*. That was recorded in 1973. And though I had an ensemble song in *Aahutee* (1978) and two in *Rajput* (1982), it was in 1983 that they gave me all the songs for a leading man, because he was new—Jackie Shroff—in *Hero*, followed by *Mera Jawaab* and *Jaanoo*. In the latter was my first solo for them, "Chhodo Mujhe Chhodo". And how *Hero* happened was a story by itself.

I was in New Delhi to do some shows and I had left the phone number of the hotel I was staying at, with my wife. One day, there was an urgent summon from Laxmikant. He wanted me to fly back the next day and go to his music room directly

---

[35] In an interview with the author for Screen in 2009.
[36] In a 2004 interview with the author.

from the airport! In those days, there were not many flights, so there were no seats available.

Luckily, my concert organizer had a contact at the airport and I managed to reach Mumbai. At the sitting, Laxmi-ji narrated the story of *Hero*. Just think of their vision—after due thought they had felt that my voice matched Jackie Shroff's personality. The same day, we rehearsed "Tu Mera Jaanu Hai". Later, I sang "Pyar Karne Wale" and "Ding Dong O Baby Sing A Song".

Laxmi-ji took a clear liking for me, and when they took me for the first time on a tour of USA, West Indies and Canada, the experience was amazing, as I had never heard them live. The response had to be seen to be believed.'

Manna Dey

'Though all the older composers—Naushad, Roshan, S.D. Burman, Salil (Chowdhury) da, Madan Mohan, Pancham da—are tremendous, I feel no one has done such extensively splendid work as Shankar-Jaikishan and Laxmikant-Pyarelal. You just hear some of their work and you sit back awed and think, "*Kya kamaal kiya hai iss gaane mein* (What a fantastic job they have done in this song)". And they have done it hundreds of times, not just once or twice.

I have tremendous respect for both Laxmi and Pyare for their sheer dedication and passion. They are composers in the fullest and trust sense of the word. Give them a subject that demands creativity and they can do wonders. Pyare is young enough to be my son, but sometimes I feel like touching his feet, because he is such an authority! He knows every single instrument in and out. He knows so much about music. I think he can open a school of music for today's composers!'[37]

---

[37] For a 1991 *Mid-Day* interview.

Narendra Chanchal

'Laxmikant-Pyarelal were experts at judging the vocal range of a singer. They would give me the *ooncha naad* (a fundamental frequency used for music, in this case high-pitched) and leave me free. They were like gardeners who, once the seed was planted, would nurture the plant.

They would lay the foundation, while the construction was the singer's domain. And within the ambit of their composition, they would give any singer lots of freedom, and would encourage the artiste to go beyond their song. That was how my first film song "Beshak Mandir Masjid Todo" from *Bobby* was done.

As it happened, my live recordings for them included songs with great singers like Lata ji and Mukesh ji (in *Roti Kapada Aur Makaan*'s "Mehangai Maar Gayi") and Mahendra Kapoor ji and Asha ji (in *Avtaar*'s "Chalo Bulawa Aaya Hai"). But it was a supremely thrilling experience recording their "Tune Mujhe Bulaya Sherawaliye" with Rafi saab in *Aasha* (1980). Just looking at and listening to Rafi saab made me go back to my childhood! It was inspiring to sing with this giant and for me, it was bigger than getting a Bharat Ratna.

My first *Mata Bhent* (devotional offering to Maa Vaishno Devi) for Laxmi-Pyare was a fabulous song in *The Cheat*, "Maiya Beta Tujhko Pukare Bholi Maa". Sadly, the film, though a Vinod Khanna home production, did not work at all, and the song never got popular then, though I often sing it now on stage. I had already begun to sing Mata Bhents outside films when this song happened, and L-P then got me to sing the other Mata Bhents in *Aasha* and *Avtaar*.'

Nitin Mukesh

'My first song for L-P was "Main Kaise Use Pasand Karoon" with Lata ji in *Satyam Shivam Sundaram*. That was Raj (Kapoor) uncle's magnanimity: he called me at once after Papa (Mukesh) passing away. Both Raj ji and Lata ji thought that it was only proper for me to continue the legacy as Papa's last song had been "Chanchal Sheetal Nirmal Komal" for both the same film and the RK banner.

At this point, I must tell you that before Laxmikant-Pyarelal came in, Shankar-Jaikishan were to do *Bobby*, and Jaikishan uncle had taken me for a voice test to Radio Gems, a popular studio, telling my father not to accompany me. He also told me that I was not to sing my father's song, so I sang Rafi's "Badan Pe Sitare" from *Prince*. After that, he told my father that I was fixed as Rishi Kapoor's voice.

But after that, things changed as Jaikishan uncle died, and the next thing I knew was that L-P were doing *Bobby*, and a song recording was held with someone else. I was hurt, but my father told me, "I can't go with a begging bowl to Raj (Kapoor) for you, can I? All this is a part of life and your struggle." The irony was that Papa had suggested Laxmikant-Pyarelal to Raj uncle, but, as Papa put it, it did not mean that they had to take me.

Coming back to *Satyam Shivam Sundaram*, Laxmi-ji had so many rehearsals with me even at RK Studios for weeks, and at the recording, the first take was approved. But a second take was done, as Laxmi-ji said, "for the purpose of *nazar utaarne ke liye* (warding off any evil eye)." Lata ji told me, "*Baazi maar li tune!* (You won the game!)"

But there was an obstacle I did not see coming. A big name close to Raj uncle, did not like my voice! And he suggested dubbing my voice with someone else because I was nowhere close to Papa. I came to know of this, met Raj uncle and wept and told them that I could not possibly reach Papa's heights so early in my career. If my song was dubbed, and word went around, my career would be over before it began!

It was Laxmi-ji here, who called me and said, "Nitu (that's how he would address me), you don't worry. Whatever happens, we will not let anyone overdub your song." And so, I was blessed that my voice was retained, and the song was a hit.

And as you know, I was no stranger to Laxmi-ji or Pyare-bhai. They had known me since the time I would accompany Papa for the rehearsals for *Milan*. Meanwhile, they had also informed Manoj (Kumar) uncle about what was happening, and he called me to Famous Studios and made Laxmi-ji and the legendary recording engineer, D.O. Bhansali, record a few lines of "Yun Lagne Lagi Aaj Kal Zindagani", which L-P had composed for his film *Santosh*.

Manoj uncle then took the recording home and shot himself enacting it on a video camera with my voice! His wife, Shashi aunty, told him, "He is Mukesh's son. You must record with him." The news that I was to record for Manoj uncle got to RK, and that revived a bit of confidence in me. And at the recording, Manoj uncle whispered in my ear, "I am making a very big film next, and you will be singing in that film too." And that was *Kranti*. The common factors were L-P.

At the recording of "Zindagi Ki Na Toote Ladi" for *Kranti*, I was very nervous. Manoj ji had four guests, of whom I remember Sunil Gavaskar, who was also my friend, and Pakistan's Imran Khan. There was a 100-piece orchestra. Laxmi-ji came up during the rehearsal, saying, "*Main kya bolta hoon Nitu…* (What I wanted to say, Nitu…)" and pressed a small piece of paper into my palm.

On it was simply written, "A-One Plus!" It was his encouraging way of saying, "Perfect! Now sing damn well!" I kept that paper for many years till it got misplaced, but I still have the beautiful letter Manoj ji later wrote to my mother, saying, "Your son has done a great job." He would call my father Kripa Ram, and he told me that from now, I was his Chhote (little) Kripa Ram!

One recording that stays with me is of "Chana Zor Garam", also from *Kranti*, in which I was singing with Lata ji, Rafi saab and Kishore da. Kishore da was in a very naughty mood that day and when he finished his lines, he would come in front of the mike and start dancing! He would mime my line, "*Meri chana kha gaye gore*" with eating motions, and I would burst into laughter. Kishore da warned me not to take his name when Pyare-bhai had to halt the take!

After this happened thrice, Pyare-bhai came in and asked me what I was doing, as there were three big singers who were being delayed. And Lata ji told him in Marathi, "Pyare, don't blame Nitin! We have a mischievous brat here." Kishore da was such fun!

The song was recorded in two parts, and the second, which started with my, "*Mera chana hai apni marzi ka*", was with Rafi saab and me. Lata ji and Kishore da had small portions that were dubbed by them later. And Rafi saab was like God. He was so affectionate. He sweetly told me, "Take your time, beta. Relax and sing."

With Laxmi-ji, the relationship was twofold. I knew Jaya bhabhi's family because her sister was with me in college. There was not a mean bone in Laxmi-ji. As for Pyare-bhai, I would say he is nothing less than a computer, a living Beethoven!

Eeshwar, *Deshwasi* and *Jai Hind* were scores that were essentially my albums, and there were also many more songs, like in *Meri Jung*, *Tezaab* and *Azaad Desh Ke Ghulam*. One day, I lovingly complained to Laxmi-ji that he gave me songs only after a long while of waiting. His reply was: "Nitu, I give you my best songs, and songs like those come once in a while!"

Do you know that Subhash (Ghai) ji and Laxmi-ji were considering three or four tunes for "Jeet Jaayenge Hum" from *Meri Jung*? The one you hear was Subhash ji's choice, though Laxmi-ji had liked another one. It was amazing to see Laxmi-ji just ruminate with his hands on his harmonium for a few moments and come out with a great melody that he would record on a tape recorder of the kind then available for about 500 rupees!

On a personal level, I remember Laxmi-ji calling me one day, stating that it was important. Papa had just passed away and he just put ₹20,000 in my hand. I told him that we were doing fine by the grace of God, and that I would sing and earn, and I needed songs, not money. He said, "This give-and-take between your father and me was always there—he would lend me money, or vice-versa. I swear on my son Tinku that I owed your father the money I am giving you."

I then came to know that Laxmi-ji also had a habit of calling up producers and making sure they paid my father's dues even when he was alive, because my father was unworldly about payments and in many cases would let the remuneration go.

When my father had recorded "Sawan Ka Mahina" (*Milan*), he had brought home the song on the old spool tape recorder and played it for half the night. He would put it on, take a sip of his drink, and cry. He had also got together all the kids in our building and neighborhood and put the volume on loud!

When Laxmi-ji composed "So Gaya Yeh Jahaan" for me in *Tezaab*, he told me that he had one of my father's songs in mind— Khayyam saab's "Aasmaan Pe Hai Khuda" from *Phir Subha Hogi*. He told me, "I am giving you a song unique for me as well as you—its entire antara is based on one note!"

I was a compulsory element of all their shows, and every two years from 1984, we would go abroad. From my songs, "Zindagi Ki Na Toote Ladi" (*Kranti*) would get the maximum "once mores". At the end, we singers would go on stage in a parade, singing "Accha To Hum Chalte Hain", their mega-hit from *Aan Milo Sajana*. I would be the boisterous one, rolling an umbrella and waving a red handkerchief as I walked!

When I visited Laxmi-ji's house for Ganpati, I was the one who told him the way the Lord should be brought in home, and the small rituals and their meaning. I also told him that after the daily pooja, he should show him a mirror, for Ganesh ji enjoys looking at himself!'

Pankaj Udhas

'In my house, the radio was always on, as dad was a film music lover, and so were my three brothers and I. I was 11 or 12, and was witness to the transition when Laxmikant-Pyarelal overtook Shankar-Jaikishan. I was a huge S-J fan, and loved the music of *Sangam*, but *Dosti* brought in a tremendous amount of freshness and I could feel the difference from the S-J, O.P. Nayyar era. The new duo was doing small-budget B-grade movies, but in them, their music would always be the A-grade highlight.

In my college days, their scores like *Aaye Din Bahaar Ke*, *Shagird* and *Mere Hamdam Mere Dost* were my favourites and had an amazing aura and atmosphere in their orchestration.

Till the early 1980s, I had no opportunity to meet them, though they had recorded some songs with my brother Manhar, including *Hero*. I had seen them at functions but never been formally introduced to them.

It was in 1984 that director Ravi Tandon called me up and said that he was making *Jawaab*, an interesting subject around a ghazal singer, and he wanted me to sing for it. I had recorded a film song for Usha Khanna in 1971, but never again, as I was somehow cut off from cinema. In any case, I was so busy that I never needed film songs for my livelihood either, so I was hesitant. But Ravi ji said, 'We will create a hungama (sensation)!'

And so I met Laxmi-ji for the first time: we were to become very close later. I noticed that Laxmi-ji had kept my first song ready: "Mitwa Re Mitwa". There were musicians with a tabla, dholak and guitar, and he had a longish tape recorder with piano keys. He also had a harmonium in front of him, but he did not play it like other composers did, but just kept one finger on Sa (the first note) and one on Pa (the fifth note) and sang the whole song. I was amazed at how well he was singing, with perfect murqis. He sang twice, and I sang with him the third time, and we rehearsed again at the recording.

I was quite upset that Pyare-bhai was not there—he was unwell and had written the score and sent it across. His brother Gorakh bhai was conducting the score. It was a small orchestra as the song, within the film, was sung by Raj Babbar at a mehfil.

After a few days, I was again called for what was a proper ghazal written by (Anand) Bakshi saab, "Sabak Jisko Wafaa Ka Yaad Hoga". Laxmi-ji's instructions were to sing it as if I was singing on a show.

His brief was, *'Khulke apne andaz mein gaaiye, alaap lijiye, yeh sur hai, yeh raag hai* (Sing it freely in your style. Use alaaps. This is the scale and this is the raag.). I dare say that this remains one of my better-sung film songs, and Universal Music, which marketed that film's music, would often put it into compilation albums of mine that they would issue until CDs were being made.

Some months later, I got a call from Rajendra Kumar, who was relaunching his son Kumar Gaurav in a film called *Naam*. Mahesh Bhatt was coming out of hibernation and Salim Khan was writing independently for the first time after his split with his partner. I was riding a wave of popularity, and Rajendra Kumar ji told me, "You have to act in my film!"

I was taken aback, as acting was not my area. I told him I will let him know in a couple of days. I was sure I did not want to act, so I avoided calling him. Some days later, my elder brother Manhar Udhas, who Rajendra ji knew very well (he had sung for him too) called and asked me why I was being so disrespectful to the star. I explained my situation, but he told me that I should at least have the courtesy of calling the actor up to tell him I could not take up his offer.

I realized my mistake and called Rajendra Kumar saab. I told him that acting wasn't my domain at all, as I was a singer. And he burst out laughing!

"I did not explain what I wanted properly, so it's not your fault at all," he told me. "I just want you to sing a song that will be filmed on you. And you will be enacting the song on stage as yourself—Pankaj Udhas! You know, if I had wanted an actor, I had many options."

I told him that in that case, I would be more than happy to do his movie, as I had grown up on his films. At the first sitting, Rajendra Kumar ji, Bakshi saab, Salim saab and Bhatt saab were also there, and they were discussing the situation in the film—where Sanjay Dutt attends my live show abroad, and is moved enough by my song to decide to return home to India and family.

At that point, the sitting was over. And at the next sitting, I was seated adjacent to Bakshi ji, and he suddenly said, "*Haan bhai Laxmikant, likho...* (Okay, Laxmikant, write this...)"

And he recited the now-cult words,

Chitthi aayi hai aayi hai chitthi aayi hai
Chitthi aayi hai watan se chitthi aayi hai

(A letter has come from back home)

Just as I was wondering that the words were too simple for what was planned as a ghazal, came Bakshi ji's masterstroke that left me thunderstruck! He went on,

Bade dinon ke baad hum bewatano ko yaad
Watan ki mitti aayi hai

(After a long while, this letter has brought us a whiff of our nation's soil)

Laxmi-ji placed his hands on the harmonium as always, thinking for a few minutes, and the next thing was that he sang the whole mukhda without a pause. I could not believe it. He had just read the mukhda once or twice, and it was such a lilting tune; the unanimous reaction was that it was an awesome mukhda!

Bakshi ji always wrote in the Urdu script, and I could read the language. The briefing continued, and Rajendra Kumar ji told him that he was to try and bring in all our major festivals like Baisakhi, Holi and Diwali for which families always come together, and anyone not present is remembered.

I saw Bakshi ji write the words Holi, jholi, goli, Diwali, and was again stunned when his final lines came in:

Tere bin jab aayi Diwali
Deep nahin, dil jale hai khaali
Tere bin jab aaye Holi
Pichhkari se chhooti goli

(When Diwali came,
it was my heart that was burning, not the lamps
And at Holi,
my water-gun seemed to fire bullets)

Now these are really precious moments to cherish, when I found that I was working with people who were true-blue geniuses.

Laxmikant was born to be a composer: some moments on his harmonium, and a perennial song was out! There was no effort to compose. Everything came spontaneously, with or without the lyrics written! The song was a long one, and I had a couple more sittings with Laxmi-ji to memorize the song and its nuances, and finally I learnt it by heart.

At the last sitting, there was this young boy, so young that his moustache was just coming out, and Laxmi-ji said that he was a brilliant singer, who had left his family in Punjab to come and struggle in Mumbai. He told me, "Let us see his reaction to the song."

As I began to sing, the boy slowly started sobbing, and by the time I finished, he was crying, clearly engulfed in his own memories of his family and hometown. Laxmi-ji asked him, "*Tu gaayega?* (Will you sing?)" The boy nodded.

At the recording, my brother Manhar had come, and so had, in a rare case, Laxmi-ji's wife Jaya bhabhi. Laxmi-ji had so much patience with any singer. If needed, he would sing a song 20 times and never tire. And it would be sung in exactly the same way, with the harkats coming at exactly the same points!

I had rehearsed a lot, but after three takes, Laxmi-ji's combination of a sixth sense and tremendous experience led him to come and sit next to me. He told me that I was singing superbly, but the something extra that was there in the rehearsals was not coming out. He ordered tea for us and reminded me of "Sabak Jisko Wafaa Ka Yaad Hoga". He said, "I want that kind of a mood, of a live concert."

In the singer's cabin, I had to stand while singing, so he asked me, "In your shows, how do you sing?"

I said that I would normally sit with my harmonium in front of me.

"Just give me five minutes," he replied and dashed off.

Would you believe it? In the big musicians' hall, he arranged for some tables on which a carpet was placed to make a makeshift stage, and he made me sit on it with a harmonium! They placed a microphone there and the new sound balance took about 30 minutes. And when he said, "*Take karte hain* (Let's record)", I sang the long song without a single mistake!

After it was over, he came over and smilingly said, "*Aapne kamaal gaaya.* (You sang wonderfully.) It was 100 per cent better than at the rehearsals!"

(I was later told that he did the same thing with Pt Rajan and Sajan Misra during the recordings of their songs in *Sur-Sangam* so that they felt comfortable.)

I had not heard the full rehearsal by the chorus, but at the end of the take, from the chorus, a high-pitched voice sang the lines, "*Bade dinon ke baad hum bewatano ko yaad, watan ki mitti aayi hai*", which went on Akash Khurana in the film as he comes to embrace me on stage. And when I asked Laxmi-ji who the singer was, he said, "Remember the boy who started crying? It was him. His name is Sukhwinder Singh."

Yes, "Chitthi Aayi Hai" was Sukhwinder Singh's first recording! And the song, which is now always played at all my concerts, was special to me also because I met Pyare-ji for the first time! And just look at how the two stalwarts created the interplay of harmonies and interludes for my next song with them, "Aaj Phir Tumpe Pyaara Aya Hai" with Anuradha ji in *Dayavan*.

My last song for them, after "Meri Zindagi Mohabbat" for *Mohabbat Ki Aag* (which did not release, I think) was the hit "Woh Ladki Jab Ghar Se Nikalti Hai" (*Tejaswini*), for which he worked with my favourite lyricist Mumtaz Rashid, because, even as late as in 1996, Laxmi-ji wanted a fresh kind of verse. For him, life was always a king-size celebration!'

Reshma[38]

'There was needless controversy over my song in *Hero*, "Lambi Judaai", only because Raj (Kapoor) saab and Laxmi-Pyare had taken my song "Akhian Nu Rehn De" and adapted it as "Ankhiyon Ko Rehne De" in *Bobby*. But "Lambi Judaai" was 100 per cent Laxmikant-Pyarelal and Anand Bakshi! I also recorded for some more films for them, of which *Pati Patni Aur Tawaif* and *Heer Ranjha* were released.'

Roopkumar Rathod

'Before I sang for them, I was a tabla player and played with several composers. My first film with them was *Sur-Sangam* on the song "Jaoon Tore Charan Kamal Par Vaari". But the joy of the Indian theka (beats) while playing for them was in a class of its own, and would be missing even in the same studio, with the same musicians and recordist, when the composer was someone else. This was absolutely like some chamatkar (miracle) as everyone

---

[38]The renowned singer from Pakistan spoke to the author when she had come to India in 2004.

futilely tried for that sparkle that just would not come! Their work just had an aura, a kick.

Pyare-bhai told me once that my father, Pt Chhaturbhuj Rathod, would teach Laxmi-ji and him small things about raags and nuances whenever he would go to teach Kalyanji-Anandji, when L-P were their assistants. He knew of them and their talent.

Though I had interacted only with Pyare-bhai, somehow, I had always been under an impression that Laxmi-ji was very strict. This seemed to be vindicated after director K. Shashilal Nair had told me to go to Laxmi-ji's music room and I had to wait for many hours a few times, only to be regretfully told to come some other day!

When he finally called me in, the first question he asked me was, "You are the brother of Shravan, of Nadeem-Shravan, right?" He showed me an issue of the Hindi magazine *Mayapuri*, which had published an article in which Nadeem had said that L-P should now pack up! So I replied, "I have never worked with them, and do not really wish to. But I have come to you because I am your big fan and would love to sing for you!"

"But you are a ghazal singer," he told me. He did not even hear my singing and later I came to know that he was planning to record "Kitni Jaldi Yeh Mulaqaat" with Amit Kumar and didi (Lata Mangeshkar) for K. Shashilal Nair's *Angaar*, the song Shashilal had hoped I would get to sing! Shashilal had earlier given me a cassette of the song and told Laxmi-ji about it.

As it happened, on the day of the recording, Amit got stuck at the passport office and there were no mobiles then for them to know what had happened. Lata didi dubbed her portion and left, and Shashilal spoke to Laxmi-ji again about me. "How soon can he come here?" Laxmi-ji asked, and Shashilal called me up at home and asked me to reach Mehboob Studios pronto!

When I reached, Laxmi-ji asked me, "Do you remember the song?" I nodded, and when I sang the mukhda, he came immediately into the singer's cabin and told me, "You never told me that you could sing well!" And, believe me, and probably because I had just copied his style, he told me, "Okay, I am going home! When you finish, just get the song transferred on a cassette and bring it home."

When I went that evening, he was so happy he called Jaya bhabhi and his children and made them all hear the song. Later, our relationship had come to the stage when I remember that one day, I was just sitting pensively and he put a hand on my head and said, "Why are you worried? I am there."

My next song was for a film starring his son Hrishikesh. Aadesh Shrivastava was producing the film and Ashok Gaekwad was the director. We recorded the muhurat song—Aadesh's wife Vijayta Pandit and me. That was the first time Pyare-bhai did programming with Ranjit Barot.

Shortly afterwards, I went for a concert tour of Africa. Laxmi-ji's son Hrishikesh's in-laws are based there, and they got a call from Laxmi-ji asking them to locate me. When we managed to speak, I told him that I would be there for a month.

He told me that he was giving me a very big break, if I could manage to come back for a day. I put forward my case to the organizers and landed in Mumbai the very next day. But the recording was cancelled for some technical reasons! I went back and a week later he called me again, promising there would not be a hitch this time. It was a beautiful song by Anand Bakshi that went,

> *Mere janam tere liye tera janam mere liye*
> *Yehi geet gaane laga*
> *Zamana bulaane lagaa*
> *Tujhe mere naam se mujhe tere naam se.*

Laxmi-ji's son Hrishikesh was playing a rockstar in the film, but the film never got going. After that, I was called for *Gumrah*. I remember that during my recording, Laxmi-ji, child-like in his innocence, asked Mahesh Bhatt, "Bhatt saab, your music director

Nadeem has been badmouthing us. What do you think?"

Bhatt saab replied, "At your time, who were you competing with?"

"Shankar-Jaikishan," replied Laxmi-ji.

"At that time, you must have said something not so good about them?"

He admitted, "Yes, we did sometimes."

And Bhatt saab told him, "So what does that prove? Just as Shankar-Jaikishan were No. 1 then and you wanted to replace them at the top, Nadeem's statement only proves that you are No. 1 today. People only get jealous of the top person who is standing between them and the peak."

Laxmi-ji was so thrilled with this answer that he got up, saying, "C'mon, let's get on with the song!"

Of the two songs I had in the film, I had doubts about being able to sing the fast-paced "Main Tera Aashiq Hoon", but Laxmi-ji was adamant: "Pandit ji (that's how he would address me), I know you can do it," he said. Yes, Laxmi-ji knew what was there within me better than I did!

I have spent such great times with Laxmi-ji. When a man attains success and riches, he never talks about his humble beginnings, but Laxmi-ji is the only exception I have seen! Once, during a sitting in the monsoon, he pointed to water dripping in the sitting room and told me, "*Yeh paani mujhe chhodta hi nahin hai—50 saal ho gaye!* (This water never spares me—it's been 50 years!)" He then went on to talk about the time they lived in a hutment and they would have to keep four or five vessels at night to collect the water that dripped from the roof.

Laxmi-ji also told me about a drunkard neighbor, who would give him a rupee every night to get him an omlette from a nearby Irani restauarant. "I would eat its borders before giving it to him because he would be too drunk to notice. And because it cost 75 paise, he would tell me to keep the change," he told me. Who talks like this unless he is a saint within?

Laxmi-ji would always wear his watch loose, because Jaikishan did that! One day, I was in Switzerland with filmmaker J.P. Dutta and we went to buy a watch for me. It was loose and I refused to adjust the strap. J.P. ji cottoned on and said, "Oh, I get it, you want to wear it loose like Laxmi-ji does!"

The same evening, we got the news that Laxmi-ji had passed away. I wept so much I doubt I have done so even when my father died. Laxmi-ji had always encouraged me, charged me up, made me feel comfortable and had given me so much love. He was a bright, fulfilled individual and he went too early. At that time, we had planned to do some projects.

Even today, when I sit to compose, his colour, so strong in my mind, comes into my compositions. He would never belittle a singer, and if he wanted to correct him, he would speak to him in person. "*Harkatein kam kar, murqiyaan kam kar* (Sing straight without any needless modulations),' he would say, away from the ears of anyone else at the recording studios. He would never make anyone feel he was *the* Laxmikant.

He would always tell me that my voice must convey heroism and not sound like a classical singer. Many years later, Lata Mangeshkar also told me the same thing when I was recording with her for a song in a film composed by her brother Hridaynath Mangeshkar—"Lal Salaam".

Laxmi-ji was clear about minute nuances of pronunciation, of every letter and syllable. His voice had such resonance that it would fill the music room. If a singer just copied him, it would be enough to make him a star. And he would take out something from a singer he never knew he had.

Take any singer he composed for—Shailendra Singh, Suresh Wadkar, Nitin Mukesh, Shabbir Kumar, Mohammed Aziz, Sukhwinder Singh, Talat Aziz—their best songs are with L-P! And L-P were the only entity whose name got smaller as they became bigger! By that, I mean that from Laxmikant-Pyarelal, they began to be known affectionately as Laxmi-Pyare and then, simply, L-P.

Among the classics I sang were "Duniya Qismat Aur Khuda", my other song from *Gumrah*, the very Rafi-like "Raha Jo Dil Mein Mere" (*Mohabbat Ki Arzoo*) and of course the two songs for *Bhairavi*. "Om Namah Shivay" is so popular now, it's even sung at temples and on reality shows. Recently, a young girl had come to visit me from Karnataka and she knew the song! The other song "Moh Maaya Ko Tyaag Re Praani" is another timeless beauty.

Pyare-bhai has this unique quality: normally, classical musicians look down on film music makers, but not so with Pyare-bhai. Four *babbar sher* (ferocious lions) from the classical music world were always present for Pyare-bhai's recordings: Pt Shivkumar Sharma on the santoor, Pt Hariprasad Chaurasia on the flute and Pt Ramnarain and Ustad Sultan Khan, the sarangi maestros.

In "Jaoon Tore Charan Kamal", my first song as a musician for them in *Sur-Sangam*, the South Indian chhand (metre) introduced in the first and third music could only have come from Pyare-bhai's creative brilliance. It was so technically complex, but the way he brought that into North Indian music and made it easy for musicians here was remarkable. With the veena, rudra veena and mridangam, he created such a sound that I was awe-struck. And I remember thinking, "My God! This man is beyond a genius!"

Pyare-bhai had studied world music so much. One day, at his house, he brought out some old music sheets, and what he made me listen to made my eyes pop out: this was a project he was planning to do with Pt Hariprasad Chaurasia and internationally-renowned American jazz saxophone player Kenny G! He has several such magnificent scores ready with him. That restlessness is there even today, it's not as if he thinks he knows everything and has done it all.

Pyare-bhai is just like some ringmaster. Just imagine what he must be made up of if he could handle titans like Shiv ji and Hari ji. He would first see which musician was there at his recording and then compose!

There was this shelved film of J.P. Dutta called *Sarhad*. The unit had left for a shoot and the song had not been recorded. J.P. ji had just given L-P the brief, and the song sent by them was so perfect it seemed that L-P had made it after the shooting was done! Look at their songs and BGM for all of J.P. ji's released films—*Ghulami, Yateem, Hathyar, Batwara*... A lot of their BGM has been used as stock music in so many other films!

Yeh log aisa kaam karke gaye hain ke innka koi muqabla hi nahin. (These people have done such work that they have no equal.)

I would like to tell you something supremely interesting about Pyare-bhai, told to me by the junior recording engineer of didi's [Lata Mangeshkar] LM Studio. Pyare-bhai had gone there and recorded a dholak. After that, he told the engineer, "There is a 1.4 kb (kikabytes, a measure of frequency) drop in the left speaker, and there is a 1.8 kb drop in the right. Just have them checked."

So they called a foreign technician to check and he used a meter that measures these technical aspects. The engineers were left clutching their heads when the result was exactly what Pyare-bhai had assessed with his ear!'

S.P. Balasubramaniam[39]

'They took the industry by storm with their first film *Parasmani*. My introduction to their songs was on radio at a milk vendor's shop in my town at the age of 17 or 18 when the song "Woh Jab Yaad Aaye" from *Parasmani* was being played. I was amazed by the song. It was not Roshan, whom it sounded like, nor Shankar-Jaikishan, it was someone else!

---

[39]From interviews with the author in 1991 and 2011.

I soon came to know from magazines and from the radio that the composers were a new duo called Laxmikant-Pyarelal! I came to know that one played the mandolin and the other the violin and that they remained busy musicians for other composers until they became very popular! I become their great fan, but never dreamt that one day I would be singing for them!

I had sung in *Maro Charitra*, the original of *Ek Duuje Ke Liye*, and my director K. Balachander saab was keen that I sing in the Hindi version too. So was (producer) L.V. Prasad ji. I wouldn't say that Laxmikant-Pyarelal were reluctant, but they had heard my South Indian songs and they were definitely apprehensive as they were very particular about diction.

But Balachander saab explained the logic that the hero too was a South Indian boy who starts learning Hindi for his love, and so a faulty accent would sound very natural. After the composers were convinced, the Prasad team called me to Mumbai.

I remember that I was in America on a concert tour and it must have been cumbersome for them to make international calls then. All overseas flights were then from Mumbai and they told me to stop over for a day in Mumbai on my return journey.

I went to Laxmikant ji's music room and he asked me to sing a semi-classical song. I sang Naushad saab's title-track by Mohammed Rafi saab from *Mere Mehboob*. He then told me to sing a simple song and my choice was obviously their own "Jaanewalon Zaraa" from *Dosti*. This was a favourite song of mine for any audition.

My first recording was the duet version of "Tere Mere Beech Mein" at Mehboob Studios. As you know, it is sung entirely by Lata (Mangeshkar) ji and I only recite some interpolations. I was very nervous, even though Lata ji had praised and congratulated me during rehearsals and said that she had heard a lot about me. I was so nervous that I spilled tea accidentally on her saree, and thought, "My career in Mumbai is over!" But she was so gracious about it and praised my final take. Of course, after that I sang so many wonderful songs with Lata ji.

But the most interesting part was that at one point, Vasu tells Sapna through my voice, "*Nee rhomba nalla paadrae*," which means "You sing very well." Imagine the irony that through my voice I was certifying Lata ji's expertise as a singer!

After this, I had to record my solo version of the same song. I was 13 years into singing down South, but I was still quite nervous. After seven or eight takes, the song was over but there were hardly any compliments! So I could never have dreamt that this first song in Hindi would soon get me the National Award for Best Male Playback Singer! I did not even have their landline numbers, but I managed to get Laxmikant ji's and Pyarelal ji's addresses and sent them a telegram saying, "You made it possible!"

Besides the remaining songs of *Ek Duuje Ke Liye*, I soon sang great, great numbers for them in *Ek Hi Bhool* (which included a duet "Hey Raju Hey Daddy" with Rajeshwari, Laxmikant ji's daughter), *Raaste Pyar Ke*, *Zara Si Zindagi*, *Andhaa Kaanoon* and others.

In an interview, Laxmi-ji even said, "There are so many playback singers, but only one S.P. Balasubramaniam!"

One final story I would like to narrate: I had composed the music of *Mayuri*, which was remade with L-P's music as *Nache Mayuri*, for which I had also composed the background score. My tune of a song during the credit-titles of the original film was retained in the Hindi film and (Anand) Bakshi ji wrote the lyrics that went "*Pag padam*".

In those days, there was an institution, Sur-Singar Samsad, which awarded the best classical music-based song of the year in Hindi cinema. In 1986, "Pag Padam" won and L-P took the award as that film's composers. I was not credited by the producer for it, so I guess it was his fault. But what's one award in such a wonderful association—it is really immaterial.

L-P's music never lost touch with classicism, the roots were so solid. Their contribution to film music is extraordinary.'

Shabbir Kumar

'I had no ambition of becoming a playback singer. In 1967, the song "Mere Dushmun Tu Meri Dosti Ko Tarse" (*Aaye Din Bahaar Ke*) was loved by my friends whenever I sang it in my hometown Vadodara. I was gradually persuaded by them to sing at Ganesh festivals and in musical shows like the Opera Music Circle, where Ashok Jagtap, who played the violin, and the drummer Suresh Soni, who worked with L-P in Mumbai, also played. I also came down to Mumbai occasionally and became a part of the famous troupe, "Ek Sham Rafi Ke Naam", and Usha Khanna ji came to watch the show and soon gave me a break. I was a Rafi devotee and because I would get calls for doing shows, I had given a "care-of" number of a transport company in the building in which I stayed.

One day, I got a call, and when I asked who was speaking, the voice said, "*Laxmikant bol raha hoon, Laxmikant-Pyarelal ka Laxmikant! Naam to suna hoga.* (I am Laxmikant of Laxmikant-Pyarelal! You must have heard the name.)" Stunned, I greeted him with "Pranaam, sir!"

He said he wanted me to come to Mumbai the very next day, gave me his address, and when I reached his home, he asked me to sing any song I liked. Confident that he would be supremely disappointed, I sang L-P's "Kahan Tera Insaaf Hai" from *Sargam*, and his rhythmist Sudhir accompanied my singing. When I finished, he said, "Come tomorrow." I now know that in those 24 hours, he spoke about me to Pyare-ji and Manmohan Desai ji.

The next day, he told me, "You have been singing Rafi saab's songs and learning them by heart uptil now. How will you sing a fresh song where you have no guidance from the original singer?" He offered me the song he had made: "Mujhe Peene Ka Shouq Nahin".

Now I had grown up on greats like Rafi saab, Kishore da, Lata ji, Asha ji, Mukesh ji and Manna da, and I knew that they focussed on expression and diction and brought forward the honesty in the words. So I remembered all that and sang the new song and I did not know that he had taped my voice!

Laxmi-ji then told me to come that evening and I saw that Man ji, his son Ketan Desai, Boney Kapoor ji and Anand Bakshi saab were all present. He later told me that he had played the tape on phone to both Pyare-ji and Man ji! The next morning he called me to Mehboob Recording and taught me a fresh song, "Mubarak Ho Tum Sab Ko Haj Ka Mahina".

I must be the only singer whose voice-test was thus taken with a 150-piece orchestra, including 25 to 30 senior chorus singers! They played back the song to see how my voice would come across on the big screen, and then officially declared that all the songs of *Coolie* would be sung by me. A few days later, I recorded another song with Asha ji for *Farz Aur Kaanoon*.

The world of their recording was like a different planet, and I would be hypnotized by it. I remember Man ji telling me, "If you want to be a perfect singer, sing exactly like Laxmikant does. If you even catch just the expressive nuances and his throw, you will not need anything more."

Laxmi-ji was always a source of great encouragement. He would tell me, "*Tu mera sher hai, jamaa le.* (You are my lion, rock the song.)" I look on them as God's prasad.

And Pyare-ji is Pyare-ji! I remember him praising me after "Zihaal-E-Masti" in *Ghulami* and "Kahan Ja Raha Tha" in *Qatl*, and he told me that the latter song might well get me an award. Sadly, they had to dub the song from Kishore da, probably because the director did not like my voice!'

Shailendra Singh

'I was training as an actor at Pune's Film & Television Institute of India (FTII) when my father, who was working with Rajshri Productions and was friends with publicist V.P. Sathe (who also co-scripted *Bobby*), called me to Mumbai for two days.

Sathe uncle had told dad that Raj [Kapoor] saab was looking for a new voice. He took me to RK Studios and my music guru here, Iqbal Gill, and my tabla player came with me. I sang a few ghazals for Raj saab. Then they took me to a shooting floor with big microphones and his legendary recording engineer Alladin taped my voice as I sang, and I caught a glimpse of Rishi Kapoor observing me from a corner.

Raj saab liked my name for obvious reasons—it brought back memories of his late friend (lyricist) Shailendra. He said that he would take me to Laxmikant-Pyarelal. When we went to Laxmi-ji's music room, Premnath, Bakshi saab and Pyare-bhai were also there besides Raj saab. Laxmi-ji offered me his harmonium, but I said I could not play it. I again sang some ghazals, but he asked me to sing a film song. And do you know the song I chose? R.D. Burman's "Dekha Na Haye Re Socha Na" from *Bombay to Goa*, which I only realized later!

Then Raj saab asked Laxmi-ji to sing for me the song they had made. When I heard "Main Shaayar To Nahin", I thought it was fabulous. Raj saab asked them to give me the song on a cassette, but there was nothing formal yet! After that, it took a few months for me to be called. I heard that L-P wanted Rafi saab, but Raj saab was insistent that there should be no known voice, as the hero was about 17 and a fresh and young voice was needed. Ajit Singh, then a known pop singer, and Mehboob Chavan were others who had been auditioned.

I also came to know that the reason why even Amit Kumar and Nitin Mukesh lost out was that Raj saab did not want even a voice that resembled an existing singer!

Two points of interest that music lovers may not know: one. "Hum Tum Ek Kamre Mein Band Ho" was not a part of the score first. Raj saab incorporated it when Bakshi saab got lost on his own in Laxmi-ji's huge then-under construction bungalow and thought of the concept, which Laxmi-ji composed and made Raj saab listen! On the other hand, "Yeh Public Hai Yeh Sab Jaanti

Hai" that was heard in *Roti* was to be a part of this music![40] Working with them was great fun—Laxmi-ji was so cleanhearted, and Pyare-bhai's level was of someone who should have been making proper symphonies in his prime! I soon realized that the greatest singer can only sing 50 per cent of what a composer does when he sings his own creation! And that L-P's singers had to have a great throw and loudness because of the volume of their orchestra.

A cute memory I want to share is of Laxmi-ji requesting me to help in getting R.D. Burman to record a song for them. I asked him why he could not ask Pancham himself, and he said that he had tried and failed to convince him!

To date, I have never understood why Pancham flatly refused even when I cajoled him, and I remember telling him that Laxmi-ji would compose only an extraordinary song for him, that their combination would be unmatched, and that their coming together would be historic and a mega-scoop. Laxmi-ji later himself sang in Pancham's style in "Gore Nahin Hum Kale Sahi" (*Desh Premee*), and made Jolly Mukherjee sing in that way in "Chahe Meri Jaan Tu Le Le" (*Dayavan*)!'

Sudesh Bhosle

'Kishore Kumar spurred my interest in playback singing, so I started approaching all the top composers. Laxmi-ji welcomed me because Jeetendra had watched my show and praised me. He made me sing a few songs and told me, "Come every evening at 7 and see how we work." He used to address me as "Bhosle saab" and promised me a break in the months to come. But before that, they first gave me a chance to perform at a show

---

[40]Interestingly, *Roti* was to be made with *Bobby*'s heroine Dimple Kapadia, but she quit because she married ther film's hero and de facto producer Rajesh Khanna, and Mumtaz replaced her!

and saw what I could do.

While sitting with them every day, I saw the kind of amusing things that went on, like this rowdy young producer who came and threw a cassette on Laxmi-ji's harmonium and told him, "This is a hit song in Pakistan. I want to record it tomorrow!"

On another occasion, there was this producer indulging in small talk long after work was done. Pyare-ji was also there and it was past 10:30 p.m., and Laxmi-ji picked up the harmonium and began playing the tune of our National Anthem "Jana Gana Mana" to signify that the day had ended and the producer must leave!

One day, I was driving in town when Laxmi-ji's cousin, Chandrakant, who dialled up singers and musicians for them, called up and ask where I was. He would talk to everyone in his rural way and told me, "Bhosle saab, turn the car, everyone's waiting for you at Mehboob! It's going to be your first song for us, sing with force!"

When I reached there, I saw about 80 musicians, and Laxmi-ji told me to write down the song—it was "Ya Ali" for *Ajooba*. He said that Shashi Kapoor, who was standing there, was the director, and the song was for Amitabh Bachchan. And along with my delight, I was petrified as well. Laxmi-ji said that if I sang it well, it would be kept in my voice.

He also told Shashi ji that I imitated Amitabh Bachchan very well, and Shashi ji asked me to sing that song in Amit ji's style. When I did so, he told Laxmi-ji, "Make him sing this one as well as the song that we are planning to record the day after tomorrow."

So even before I recorded my first song for them, I was booked for the second one—"Jalnewalon Ko Jalne De" with Mohammed Aziz, which they had planned to record with Amit ji himself! And after I recorded for them, every music director began to call me, and I began recording songs for all those names I would visit to ask for work! For my third song in *Ajooba*, Amit ji himself came and told me, "*Arey bhaiya, hamari aapki awaazein to milti-julti hain.* (Our voices are very similar.)' After that, I recorded regularly for L-P till the end.

One day, Laxmi-ji called me and said, "I have written something. Sing it to me the way Amit ji would." He began singing lyrics he had himself written—"*Arey o Jumma, meri jaaneman, aaja aaja*". The next day he called me, saying he had written the main line, which was 'Jumma Chumma De De'. Part by part, he asked me to sing the complete mukhda the way Amit ji would, and then excitedly told me that he would get the antaras written by Anand Bakshi. We had seven or eight sittings later with Pyare-bhai, Bakshi ji and his musicians and then we called Amit ji to hear the song.

The next day at Mehboob, we began recording at 9 a.m. but completed it at 2 a.m. Out of sheer nervousness, I did not eat anything at all in that period, thinking it will affect my singing, and instead, I consumed 25 cups of tea! Amit ji was shooting there for Manmohan Desai and came in-between, and when I asked him how I was sounding, he said that he liked what he heard but that I should pay attention to the conversational lines in the song.

I was already nervous and told the recording engineer Tagore saab that we will dub those parts of the song later, but he said that would not be possible in a live take and explained some technicalities. I went and told Laxmi-ji I could not sing the song. He said, "Alright, sing in your own voice." I sang a few lines and he said, "Very good!" Then he asked me to sing the same lines in Amit ji's voice. When I did, he exclaimed, "Superb! This is what we want. Go and sing like this." And I did it! Laxmi-ji knew how to handle nervousness in a singer.

I had lesser interaction with Pyare-bhai then, but I still meet him at his home now and we travel down memory lane, like revisiting the recording of "Yeh Jeevan Hai" where Kishore da was singing first in his normal voice until L-P told him to go very soft, and when he gave them that husky option we hear now, they instantly went for the take! Pyare-bhai once told me, "*Laxmi-ji jab tak the, tab tak main bhi tha*. (I was there until Laxmi-ji was there.)" He does feel incomplete without him.

But to sum Laxmikant-Pyarelal up, who would have thought that their one song, "Jumma Chumma De De", could give me a living for 30 years? I remember musicians would tell me, "You can sing 100 songs outside, but one L-P song will be equal to them all and will be like a certificate." Today, I even sing "Jumma Chumma De De" on stage in various actors' voices!'

Sukhwinder Singh

'When I came to Mumbai, there was only one address in Mumbai I wanted to go: Parasmani. I was staying far away, but almost every day I walked to the bungalow and stood outside, waiting for my chance to get in. Then one day, I went in because somebody knew me. When he heard me, Laxmi-ji arranged that I stayed with him, just observing his recordings and sittings every day.

Laxmi-ji would never be dully dressed. He wore bright shades and was a rangeen (colorful), good-looking personality. He had a calm happiness in his nature. He genuinely loved and respected everybody, including the humblest musicians and chorus singers, and he showed it. I never saw him musically stressed. He would also joke around with the musicians, just so that they would not think of the difference between his status and theirs! Everyone used to think of their recording sessions as a family gathering.

Pyare-ji went one notch higher than Shankar-Jaikishan in symphonic orchestration, because the Indian colour in his work was more. When they came together with another colourful and royal man in Anand Bakshi, they could not be matched. You never saw lobbies or plans to attract producers, just a passion for work.

I remember I was in school in Amritsar and there was a big musical event with top folk and classical singers coming to perform. I was barely six and threw a tantrum that I wanted to sing. The school authorities finally relented and the song I sang was L-P's "Sa Re Ga Ma Pa" from *Abhinetri*. I remember everyone

loved it so much that I had to sing it thrice. Later, I would even collect their pictures.
I was crazy about their songs. Listen to "Rang Mahal Ke Dus Darwaze" [Saiyyan Nikas Gaye] from *Satyam Shivam Sundaram*— for the first time I heard such utter calmness in music, such that you feel there is God in that song. The Indian percussion like dholak (the two-headed hand-drum) and taashe (a variety of kettle-drum in Indian folk) that have been played on their songs has never been replicated by anyone else. Laxmi-ji was a master at forging relationships, while Pyare-ji followed the tradition set by O.P. Nayyar that musicians at a recording had to be immediately paid.

Having said that, ordinary musicians never dared to come for their recordings, for if one musician in a 100 made a mistake, Pyare-ji would know who it was and call him by name! Such concentration is unique.

40 years of glory—who else has seen that among composers? I have sung so much for them, and my work in *Yateem*, *Saudagar* and *Khilaaf* is proof of what we could do together.'

Suresh Wadkar

'My first song for L-P was "Chal Chameli Baagh Mein" for *Krodhi* with Lata bai, who was the one who recommended me to them: it was my first also with her. When I went to meet Laxmi-ji, he offered me his harmonium and asked me to sing, and he heard me for 30 to 45 minutes.

The title song of *Hum Paanch* was recorded after a long gap, though that film released before *Krodhi*. Then in the same year later came my songs "Megha Re Megha Re" and "In Haseen Vaadiyon Se", again duets with Lata bai for *Pyaasa Sawan*.

In those days, whenever the L-P stamp fell on singers, their position went to another level and they were discussed. But you take the A to Z of composers and you will see that no one has ever given that kind of variation and variety.

While singing, Lata bai had told me, "Listen to how Laxmi-ji sings, and follow the detailing, but in your voice. I did that. Yes, I got a lesser number of songs from them. Maybe because they could not look beyond Rafi saab and Kishore da after they had passed away, but still, *Prem Rog, Hero*'s "Mohabbat Yeh Mohabbat", *Utsav*'s "Saanjh Dhale", *Sindoor*'s "Patjhad Saawan Basant Bahar", *Sheshnaag*'s "Chhed Milan Ke Geet O Mitwa" and many more—they gave me such fabulous songs, and they would always call me for something different. The creative juices they would extract from any singer—none of us experienced that elsewhere.

And it was after "Qismat Mein Likhi Koi Baat Ho Tum" with Anuradha Paudwal was recorded for *Triveni*, a film delayed for long, that Laxmi-ji began calling me regularly.

Prem Rog happened because my "Megha Re Megha Re" had been recorded and Raj Kapoor was looking for a new voice. Laxmi-ji recommended me and made Raj Kapoor saab listen to my song. And Raj saab loved my voice and told Laxmi-ji, "*Issi ko bulao, yehin gaayega Prem Rog.* (Call this boy, he will sing for *Prem Rog*.)'

Raj Kapoor loved to have what he called "popatiya" words in lyrics, which meant lyrics easily understood and sung by the common man, so he would want the tune to be very catchy but melodious. When I was making the humming sound of a bhanwra (a bumblebee) for "Bhanwre Ne Khilaya Phool" to myself during a rehearsal, Pyare-ji loved it and told me to incorporate it in the song along with the algoza (a double flute).

Give Laxmi-ji any poetry and he would tune it in the perfect colour it deserved. And Pyare-bhai's solid command on Indian music ensured what could enhance the song. For "Patjhad Sawan Basant Bahar", he used about six sitars and two or three sarods! Innovation was their middle name.'

Talat Aziz

'When I first came to Mumbai in 1978, I met Shankar of Shankar-Jaikishan who was doing a film called *Wattan*, and Anand Bakshi also through some friends, and Bakshi ji took me to Laxmi-ji. There was a film being made called *Aurat* then, directed by K. Vishwanath. Laxmi-ji liked my voice and the result was my first song, a superb duet, "Chhota Sa Ghar Banaaye", with Lata ji, which was recorded in May 1980.

The film was produced by a big name, Premji, and in those days, recording for a big-banner film, Mehboob Studios and Laxmikant-Pyarelal-Anand Bakshi was a very big thing. I had just released my first album, *Jagjit Singh Presents Talat Aziz*, three months earlier, and I found Jagjit ji walking in for my first recording, and also my friend from before, Yash Johar. Jagjit Singh told me, "*Arey bhai*, I heard you are singing Laxmikant-Pyarelal's song, so I thought I should come!" Sadly, the film was so delayed that it released only in 1996, with some other director completing the movie, the music marketed by some unknown label, so much so that I had to ask you to give me a copy of that wonderful song, which is luckily available online now! The film was released as *Aurat Aurat Aurat*!

And from that recording, I remember I went straight to the airport as I had my first show in Kolkata as well!

Laxmi-ji would be very warm. You know he had this permanent smile on his face, with the paan inside his cheek. He had this habit of telling producers, "Now listen to this song at Mehboob after Pyare completes the orchestration. Then you will understand the song." Producers would not have the guts to challenge that!

Both of them treated the musicians like family, and it was a family operating with clockwork skill—60 musicians or more coming in at 10.30 a.m., meeting and greeting each other, and Pyare-bhai recording the live harmonies first. There would be eight to 10 people in the rhythm section, and recordist Tagore would come in around noon. Then the recording would start, with a lunch break at 2 p.m., and then after 4 p.m., there would be the strings section and so on, and Laxmi-ji and the singers would come in.

When my wife Bina and I launched our production *Dhun*, a musical with Mahesh Bhatt, in which I was also the hero, my first thought for the music was that we have to get L-P, as they would be the best bet. And Laxmi-ji and Pyare-bhai both took special interest because it was my film! I will never forget two things that very few people know.

'The first is about the song "Laagi Prem Dhun Laagi", which were the words Bakshi ji had given Laxmi-ji, who called me and asked me what I thought of the tune he had made for it. I loved it and said so. Laxmi-ji then told me that he wanted my opinion as I was the singer as well as actor—just imagine, he was waiting for my approval before making the rest of the song! By the time Bakshi ji completed the lyrics and Pyare-bhai added his flourishes, it became a very big song!

The other story is of a father-son song that I wanted, where the traditional father sings a bhajan and I accompany him. He asked me my suggestion for the other voice, and I suggested Mehdi Hasan, who I consider my ustad, who was in India at that time. Laxmi-ji replied, "You speak to him, and look after him at the recording!"

Not many know that in Mehboob Studios at that time, the voltage used to fluctuate a bit after 4 p.m., and though we recorded the song, things went wrong with the surmandal (Indian harp, also known as the swarmandal)'s piece, and Pyare-bhai after four fluctuations, announced 'Pack up!'

We had to dub the song after a couple of months when Mehdi saab had come back. And after he left, a flute piece was left, and Pyare-bhai got a flautist and recorded it, saying, "This is my gift to you!" He did not take money for that extra session and the musicians needed! Even Laxmi-ji never talked money with me but accepted what I gave them as fees.

All they were interested in was in excelling in the music, and Laxmi-ji said that they wanted to ensure that the music should make them proud. In fact, we had recorded a song, "Yeh Zindagi Ka Safar", my duet with Kavita Krishnamurthi, which was not used in the film, and Bhatt saab asked me for it when he was making *Gumrah*. I had no problem, but told him that ethically he should ask Laxmikant-Pyarelal too, and he told me that they were doing that film too. But somehow, they did not use the song in that as well!

Another recording I remember was of the song "Iss Duniya Mein Saat Samandar". As I said, the strings section would record after 4 p.m. and the rhythm players would dub earlier, take their remuneration and go away.

Later, I was perplexed to see about seven of the rhythm players sitting in the hall along with the 50 strings. When I asked them, they said, "We are just listening, and enjoying this. We want to listen to the runs Pyare-bhai is giving to the violins." When a musician appreciates your work to this extent that you want to listen even after your work is over, it speaks volumes for a creative artiste.

And Pyare-bhai deserves 10 times whatever fame and success he has got. He is the only Indian musician who could have written a symphony, and he can write a proper international score. I believe a conductor abroad was flabbergasted when Pyare-bhai sent him a score and he came to know that an Indian has written it! Though we have not met in some time, I still remember a great evening with him at his house when he made me sing on his harmonium.

Coming back to *Dhun*, though the film could not finally release, its audio release event was a major hit in 1991, and so was the music. And the who's who attended the event—from Yash Chopra to Subhash Ghai and the producer of *Gumrah*, my friend Yash Johar. Laxmi-ji called me a few days later and said that all the kids in his son Hrishikesh's college were singing "Laagi Prem Dhun Laagi" and it was a super-hit! Bakshi ji called me and said,

"Miyan, our music is doing well. The film will do great business!" Our association is full of such terrific memories.'

Udit Narayan

'Their music always charged me since childhood. I would always wonder where such people must be staying, in which world, and meeting them, even when I landed in Mumbai, seemed like a dream! I would sing their compositions, like Rafi saab's songs in *Dosti* and *Mere Hamdam Mere Dost*, in the fairs in my village where I grew up. But as they say, '*Jahaan chaah, wahin raah!* (When you want something intensely, the path leading there opens up for you!)'

I would see a line of producer-directors waiting for Laxmi-ji in his sitting room, and would try to go to their recordings, even if I was sometimes stopped at the gate, for two years!

When I finally met Pyare-bhai, he said, "We will listen to you when we get the chance." That happened one evening after midnight at Mehboob Studios, and after that, in front of some 10 people, he just told me, "Don't leave the city. I think your day will come." I was thrilled! He then asked me how I managed to live in Mumbai with a wife and a son, and I said that I recorded songs for small films and jingles. I then asked if I could sing in their chorus. He suggested that I should not become a chorus singer and asked Laxmi-ji to listen to me, and Laxmi-ji advised, "Keep doing your riyaaz."

Meeting L-P was thus like meeting some gods! I would go for the recordings of Lata ji, Asha ji, Rafi saab and Kishore da. But the chance to record for L-P took eight years! Shabbir Kumar, Mohammed Aziz, Amit Kumar, Nitin Mukesh, Suresh Wadkar and Shailendra Singh were all singing for them. Once during that time, I met and requested Laxmi-ji, "I will be happy with even one or two songs a year."

But God writes such unusual screenplays! One day, when despite *Qayamat Se Qayamat Tak*, I was still not successful, Laxmi-ji told Boney Kapoor at a recording, "He is the singer of the song 'Papa Kehte Hain' (*Qayamat Se Qayamat Tak*). One day he will sing for both your brothers!" And that came true as I sang for both Anil Kapoor (including in L-P's *Ram Avtar, Rajkumar* and *Deewana Mastana*) and for Sanjay Kapoor under other composers!

Laxmi-ji soon began to give me several songs in their films, like *Aashiq Aawara* in which I was the only male singer, *Narsimha, Prem Deewane, Dil Hai Betaab, Mohabbat Ki Arzoo, Bhairavi, Trimurti* and others. I even sang for Laxmi-ji's son Hrishikesh in his debut film *Dilbar*.

I am especially happy that I was the only singer of my generation—the 1990s—who sang regularly for them. I firmly believe they were like emperors in the quality of their music, their long rule and their world-class orchestration. You can immediately make out the deep melody in their songs, with a stamp *jiska khumaar kabhi utrega nahin!* (those whose hangover will never go away!)'

18
THEIR LYRICISTS

Amit Khanna

'Though we finally worked together only in *Bhairavi* (1996), L-P and I knew each other since the 1970s as we had a lot of common friends. In fact, I was to make my debut with them in a film launched in 1974 with producer Attam Prakash, who had produced their musical crime drama *Geetaa Mera Naam* the same year. The film was to be directed by Ashok Roy with Feroz Khan, Shashi Kapoor and Hema Malini and we even had a sitting for it. But the producer died in an air-crash.

Before that, we were to do producer Amarjeet's *Prem Shastra* (also 1974) starring Dev Anand and Zeenat Aman, and I was very close to both Dev saab and Amarjeet. But Amarjeet had already spoken to Anand Bakshi, so I volunteered to leave the film. My first two films would actually have been with them!

For me, as everyone knows, songwriting has always been a hobby. And when Mahesh Bhatt and I decided to make *Bhairavi* for Plus Channel, L-P were the obvious choices for the musical. After *Sur-Sangam*, which was all classical, and in which they used the topmost classical musicians, there was really no other option.

We mutually chose Kavita Krishnamurthi (now Subramaniam) as the female voice, and I remember Laxmi-ji was quite surprised how fast I was in writing to his tunes. I made a conscious effort to incorporate a Hindu ethos in all the songs, and "Om Namah Shivay" and "Moh Maaya Ko Tyaag Re Praani" were both bhajans.

Today, "Om Namah Shivay" is no longer just a film song. It is now played in Lord Shiva's temples and on devotional occasions. We used very sparse instruments in the songs, maybe four or five. The tanpura came in all the songs. We used the sitar and Pyare-bhai even avoided his instrument, the violin. Both of them had clear views on their music, and were meticulous in their sense of rhythm, sound and instruments being used. Chronologically, *Bhairavi* was their last creative ace.'

Majrooh Sultanpuri[41]

'My best work among all my films, according to me, was in Asit Sen's *Mamta* and V. Shantaram's *Jal Bin Machhli Nritya Bin Bijli*. Besides the subject and the filmmakers, it was also because of Roshan saab and Laxmikant-Pyarelal. Even in all the other films I have done with them, these are the only two names who have never asked me to change even one word—not for metering or any other reason! They changed the musical phrase instead to fit my verse.'

Sameer Anjaan

'I have always been L-P's fan since I can remember. Papa (lyricist Anjaan) would call them his mehboob (beloved) music directors even before they worked together. "Ganga Mein Dooba", which was the first song they recorded with him, was always considered by my father to be one of his very best. And, since, from the '80s, I would accompany my father to his sittings and recordings—as his son and not as an aspiring songwriter—I enjoyed my sittings with them the most.

The reason was very simple: when Laxmi-ji sang, he sang the feel, and that got to you. Pancham da (R.D. Burman), to a good

---

[41]In an interview to the author in 1995.

extent, was also like that.

Laxmi-ji never just got lyrics written. Pyare-bhai and he actually studied and absorbed the words to understand what the musical requirements of those verses should be.

Laxmi-ji kept a notebook, and if he wrote your mukhda in it, it was like a confirmation that the song would be recorded! And then simultaneously, his mind would start racing for its tune! He would go into the deep waters of the poetry, and his assistant Sudhir would also have an idea of what was going on his mind and would play the right theka or beat. And then he would keep a napkin on his shoulder, put his paan in his mouth and start singing. And that would remain in his mouth until the final tune emerged, by which time his face would be fully red. This was actually like some delivery pains between conceiving a tune and giving it birth.

After that, he would perceptibly relax and start chatting about everything else! And the way he would sing a tune, 99 times of a hundred it had to be passed! In my career, besides Laxmi-Pyare, I have seen three other composers—R.D. Burman, Nadeem and Himesh Reshammiya, who had this knack to a good extent. So it was never about the words or the instruments, but about who was playing them and who was singing the feel of the words.

Laxmi-ji had this habit of taking an evening stroll of his bungalow and then standing at his main gate, his napkin around his shoulder, in his bright shorts and T-shirt, just looking at people passing by. Obviously, many strugglers would wait for him there and try to talk to him. If he liked a person, he would put a hand on his shoulder, which meant, infallibly, that the lyricist or singer would be taken to his sitting room.

One of my father's most memorable songs for L-P was "Meri Saanson Ko Jo Mehka Rahi Hai" from *Badaltey Rishtey* (1978). Laxmi-ji told my father to write to the situation and that he would tune it, and he wanted Lata ji to sing it. And when my father gave him the mukhda, he was thrilled. He told my father that he would make it in Raag Puriya Dhanashree, a raag whose name I heard for the first time, and I don't think that I have seen Laxmi-ji take so much time over any song. His top favourites were Lata and Rafi. And he wanted them both. But at that time, Rafi saab was not available and he took Mahendra Kapoor, who, of course, sang the shorter male version very well.

Now let me tell you something very significant that Laxmi-ji told my dad in my presence, and maybe my father and I both felt bad at that time, but we realize now that he was perfectly correct in saying it. Dad, as I said, had never told him that I too write songs. One day, when I had recorded a few songs here and there, he told Laxmi-ji about it, and said, 'If you see fit, please give my son a break.' And Laxmi-ji said, "You have told me this today, but don't say it to anyone else! *Baap ki dukaan baap ki hoti hai, aur bete ki dukaan bete ki.* (A father's shop and a son's store are different from each other, implying that a father's legacy is his own and not the son's.) I will give him a song if he impresses me with a mukhda, I will not give him a break because you have told me to do so.'

And that happened when I gave him the words, "*Qismat apni khul gayi / Ab kisika dar nahin koi*" for *Love '86*. Many more songs and films followed, but I think that *Kudrat Ka Kanoon* and *Jawab Hum Denge* were our best work together.

I had, comparatively, very little contact with Pyare-bhai. But I have long realized that no one understands music better than he does in our industry. After Laxmi-ji had gone, we did five or six songs for an album that did not come out. And that's when I had this fascinating experience of watching him compose and sing on his piano. It was like a shower of melody. His work in orchestration is like an institution from which generations can learn. I was so inspired I wrote two lines in his honour and he loved them:

Tumne kabhi suna hai alfaaz bolte hain
Khamosh rehke bhi to kuch saaz bolte hain

(Have you ever heard words speak by themselves
Instruments too express something through their silence)

What a combination they made—I do not think there was a duo like them! Laxmi-ji, in the late '90s, once told my father, "Only one man understands me: Pyare. I raise an eyebrow and he understands what I want!"

I was driving past his house during the year 1997 when I saw him standing outside his gate as usual, but looking very forlorn. I stopped the car, and he smiled and said, "*Aaja laale*, I am so happy you are doing great work." We chatted and suddenly his eyes became moist. I asked him why he was unhappy, and with candour, he told me, "The day you understand that, you will understand Laxmikant." Here was a man whose name had reverberated for decades in this industry, who gave so much to so many people, to meet whom I had waited for hours outside studios, and whose songs made me shiver in admiration as they seared my soul, and here he was, in tears before me.

I gently told him that he had a family, money, fame and everything else. So what was making him sad? And he told me that the one thing he wanted most in life was missing—work! "For a real artiste, everything else is secondary. A real artiste lives for work," he told me.

That's when I realized that the world can be ruthless if Destiny is not with you. If someone of his calibre could be ignored, what is there to be said?'

19

THEIR STARS

Anil Kapoor

'My father, Mr Surinder Kapoor, was already great friends with Laxmikant-Pyarelal when I did my first film with them, *Woh 7 Din*. After that, Laxmikant-Pyarelal scored some phenomenal music for my films, including terrific songs in my home productions *Mr India* and *Roop Ki Rani Choron Ka Raja*. And *Karma, Tezaab, Ram Lakhan, Eeshwar, Heer Ranjha, Rajkumar, Deewana Mastana* and others—what fabulous music they made for me. I remember Laxmi-ji wanting me to sing "Na Jaiyyo Pardes" from *Karma*, because he came to know that I had learnt singing from Kalyanji (and Anandji) bhai. I did record the song, but was not happy, and I told them that they should get it dubbed from a proper voice, and so Kishore Kumar sang it.

L-P used multiple voices for me, and as composers, they would decide who would sing. *Eeshwar*, for example, was a milestone score, and Nitin Mukesh was selected as my voice. The way Laxmikant and Pyarelal completed each other, complemented each other, remains something to be experienced. I would attend many of their sittings and recordings and I do not think *any* composer can match their sheer range and talent. If anyone deserves the government's Dadasaheb Phalke award today, it is them, and I hope that the government and the Ministry for Information & Broadcasting wakes up to their work. They are, simply, incomparable.'

Bindu

'My first song was in *Anpadh* with music by Madan Mohan, in which Lata Mangeshkar sang "Jiya Le Gayo Ji Mora Sawariya". So whenever Laxmi-ji, my sister Jaya's husband, had to compose songs for my character, I would request him to use Lata ji's voice for me.

Lata ji would not readily sing the kind of songs filmed on me, but Laxmi-ji did end up striking a balance and made lovely songs for me that she did sing, which were popular as well— like "Dard-E-Dil Badhta Jaaye" (*Buniyaad*), "Yaad Yeh Rakhna" (*Lagan*), in which my portion was the fast-paced one, "Purab Disa Se Pardesi Aaya" (*Suraj Aur Chanda*) and "Iss Qadar Aap Humko" (*Apne Rang Hazaar*).

We four sisters would attend so many recordings of their songs for others, and I recollect being present for songs like "Sawan Ka Mahina" (*Milan*) and "Suno Sajana" (*Aaye Din Bahaar Ke*). Whenever Laxmi-ji made a song for me, he would make me listen to it, like a "Hungama Ho Gaya" (*Anhonee*) or "Dekho Idhar Bhi Jaan-E-Tamanna" (*Imtihan*). He would grin and say, "Bindu ji, see what a good song I have made for you! *Ab jamaa dijiye* (make it look great on screen)!"

There was a song in *Suntan* (1976), "Jawani Ke Din Char", which needed about 10 costume changes. When someone complimented me after watching the song, Laxmi-ji just smiled and asked him, "*Aakhir saali kiski hai?* (After all, whose sister-in-law is she?)"

When both of them would record at Famous Studio, Tardeo, they would come to my nearby Worli home during the lunch-break. Even here, we had a harmonium and a tabla as one of my sisters loved to sing, and they would start singing. In fact, Laxmi-ji had made some of his tunes in my home as well!

When I was rehearsing with P.L. Raj for "Hungama Ho Gaya", Laxmi-ji dropped in to discuss something else with the choreographer and enquired whether everything was going 'first class' with our song! After the song was shot, Raj ji enthusiastically showed the song to Laxmi-ji as well as Shammi Kapoor, as cinematographer Ramchandra had used the zoom technique and disco-type lighting. Laxmi-ji raved about it, and I heard that Shammi Kapoor watched it 19 times back-to-back at Natraj, Shakti Samanta's studio. Shammi ji had then called me and complimented me lavishly.

I also was to have a song in *Hero*, one of my best and very different roles, but then Subhash Ghai decided against it. I have been a part of many of L-P films like *Prem Rog* too in which I had no song. But what superb music L-P gave in all of them! There was no one better than them, and if you accuse me of being partial, it's okay! Their music is unforgettable and every song had a classical touch. What a combination they were!

In fact, my break as an actress happened indirectly because of Laxmi-ji. Both Laxmi-ji and Pyare-ji would frequently come to our parents' home in Slater Road for dinner after their recordings. By that time, Laxmi-ji and my sister Jaya were already engaged. One night, at 11 p.m., we walked down to Famous Studios to check why they were delayed—a BGM session for Raj Khosla's *Anita* was on.

Raj ji saw me with Laxmi-ji and asked who I was. He said, 'She is my *saali* (sister-in-law)' and he straightaway asked me whether I would like to act—after *Anpadh*, I had not done any film! I was tempted, and Laxmi-ji advised, "Try your luck!" Raj ji told me that my character was the central character in the story, but a negative one. I finally accepted the film—which was *Do Raaste!*

By that time, (Anand) Bakshi ji had become like a family member. And he would address me as Bindiya. So after the song "Bindiya Chamkegi" was recorded, he came and told me, "This song is written for Mumtaz in the film, but I have actually written it for you! *Tu chamkegi* (You will dazzle)!" And he was so right—after that I had a long, long career!'

Jackie Shroff

'I have been L-P's fan since I heard their classic songs from *Sati Savitri* like "Jeevan Dor Tumhi Sang Bandhi", "Tum Gagan Ke Chandrama Ho" and "Kabhi To Miloge" and also "Mere Mehboob Qayamat Hogi" from *Mr X in Bombay* at my friend Anees Sabri's house.

Their music for my first lead film, *Hero*, made me a musical star. The title song and "Pyar Karne Wale" were so beautiful and I still remember Subhash (Ghai) ji's recordings, with Pt Hariprasad Chaurasia on the flute. Later, there were so many films we did together. Laxmi-ji even sang for me in *Mera Jawaab* and made me record my voice for a song for *Dil Hi To Hai*.

Soon, our relationship became more personal, and I would go for parties and for Ganpati celebrations to Laxmi-ji's house. And while they gave me such great songs like in *Ram Lakhan* or *Khal Nayak*, I still go back, when in a nostalgic mood, to their lovely songs in their older films, like *Night in London, Patthar Ke Sanam* and so many others that form the music of my growing-up years! Laxmikant-Pyarelal's songs always stand the test of time.'

Jeetendra

'We have had a 30-year association from 1967's *Farz* to 1996's *Paappi Devataa*, including six of my home productions. Whenever Laxmikant sang a tune with his paan stuffed in his mouth, it sounded better than in the recorded version! Can you beat that? A recording can become too technical, too mechanical. But with Laxmikant singing, it was the sheer passion that came through. He would sing from within! I feel the essence of any song reduces with the mechanical aspects of a recording, even if the singer delivers technically better than the composer.

When I would hear "Yeh Kaisa Aaya Zamana", which Mukesh, Kishore and Mehmood himself sang for the three Mehmoods in first home production *Humjoli, kya mazaa aata tha* (it would be so enjoyable) on just the rhythm! The song became very popular as filmed on all his three characters modelled on Prithviraj ji, Raj ji and also Randhir Kapoor, who had still to come in!

But forget my films—what a phenomenal contribution these men have made to film music! You name the filmmaker—Manmohan Desai, Subhash Ghai, Raj Kapoor, L.V. Prasad—even today their songs shake you up, like "Khilona Jaan Kar" from *Khilona*—see how well they got Rafi saab to sing!

Personally, I would like to mention one film of mine: *Roop Tera Mastana* (1972), which flopped very badly. It was such a sad thing, because Laxmi-Pyare made such fantastic songs for me—"Bade Bewafa Hai Yeh Husnwale", "Haseen Dilruba", "Akash Pe Do Taare", "Dil Ki Baatein Dil Hi Jaane", "Pakdo Pakdo Re Jawani"—and how well the songs were shot and choreographed by Kamal Master! This was Laxmikant-Pyarelal's hundredth film. Today, I would say that I owe them at least fifty per cent of my success!'

Madhuri Dixit Nene

'I remember going to the "Ek Do Teen Char" (*Tezaab*) song recording. I was very raw, very young, but I sensed it was to be an important song and understood the concept. It was a folk tune played on a mandolin but set to a modern dancing beat. Saroj ji and I were both excited, because the so-called Bollywood dancing was so different from Kathak. I wanted to rehearse and we got two weeks.

As late as 2020, I launched a Hook-Step class on Tik-Tok and the response floored me—32 years later, the song is as loved! L-P were so versatile and both Saroj ji and I were big fans of their music. The songs, the beautiful instruments—it was all so terrific. Their concepts took you into a different world.

Laxmi-ji was very good at knowing how to place words. When

Lata Mangeshkar ji sang "Ho Ramji Bada Dukh Deena" for *Ram Lakhan*, I could not believe she was singing for me. And Pyare-ji would be so calm. Among eight violinists, he would make out which one was making a mistake.

With L-P's songs, you remembered even the *interludes*. The music of *Jal Bin Machhli Nritya Bin Bijli*, "Dard-E-Dil" from *Karz*, "Sawan Ka Mahina" from *Milan* or even the song filmed on me, "Dhadkan Zaraa Ruk Gayi Hai" from *Prahaar*—what a range they had. And the movements we did for the last song were so challenging, fans still write to me about this one.

I also remember Saroj ji's assistant tell me how they set a rhythm to the vilambit (fast) taal for their early song "Allah Yeh Ada" from *Mere Hamdam Mere Dost*.

In Subhash (Ghai) ji's films they were also brilliant. I would hear their enlightening conversations on music. Of the two of them, Laxmi-ji was more talkative.

I have no idea how many awards they have received, but their biggest award of all is that people love them still. Soul is the correct word to describe their music. Nobody can touch that level here. And what they did with Indian instruments, especially, was mind-boggling.

They played a major role in my success, and I can never forget that.'

Manoj Kumar

'I have never believed in getting a song written after a tune is made! To me, a song is a scene that has to be narrated lyrically, and so it has to be written first and then given to the music director to compose!

It is therefore unfortunate that Laxmikant-Pyarelal missed out on the Best Music awards for my films even though they had worked so hard on the songs of *Shor*, *Roti Kapada Aur Makaan* and *Kranti*. Especially with *Roti Kapada Aur Makaan*, it was no mean task to set to tunes complex lyrics like "Aur Nahin", "Main Na Bhoolunga" (which was an 18-minute-long song recorded in two parts!) and "Mehangai Maar Gayee", besides "Haye Haye Yeh Majboori". And Mahendra Kapoor and Santosh Anand got Filmfare awards for Aur Nahin! Also, one of the finest songs in that film was the fifth song, "Panditji Mere Marne Ke Baad", recorded by Lata bai and adapted by Verma Malik from a Punjabi poem I had loved by a writer called Barqat. We took the rights from him. Later, when another lyricist accused us of plagiarizing his song, Barqat had backed us because the lyricist had lifted that song from Barqat himself!

But I must tell you that I broke my verse-first-tune-later rule once, when Laxmi-ji offered me "Zaraa Sa Ussko Chhua To", the frothy title song of *Shor*. L-P also gave me "Shehnai Baje Na Baje", "Jeevan Chalne Ka Naam" and the two Lata-Mukesh duets, "Ek Pyar Ka Naghma Hai" and "Pani Re Pani Tera Rang Kaisa". I had been impressed by their music even in the three films they had done with me as actor before these—*Anita*, *Patthar Ke Sanam* and *Sajan*—and would recommend them to others.

When I shifted from Kalyanji-Anandji to them, Laxmi, Pyare and I went with Mukesh, Lata bai and Dilip Kumar to Kalyanji bhai's house for lunch after the recording of "Ek Pyar Ka Naghma Hai". That was Kalyanji bhai's greatness!'

Sadhana

'My two home productions *Intaqam* and *Geetaa Mera Naam* had exceptional music, but it was all because of Laxmikant-Pyarelal, who always wanted to excel. R.K. Nayyar, my husband, had a great sense of music, but I rarely went to music sittings. However, sometimes Laxmi-ji would make me listen to a song. They formed a great team with our favourite lyricist, Rajendra Krishan, who was nothing less than a genius. His contemporaries like Sahir saab and Kaifi Azmi saab would have a PR mechanism in place, but this genius believed in just doing great work.

Outside our films, L-P also scored music for my *Anita* and *Aap Aye Bahaar Ayee*, and from the second film, "Mujhe Teri Mohabbat Ka Sahara" by Lata ji and Rafi saab is one of my topmost favourites! L-P continued to work with my husband after I left acting, in films like *Qatl* and *Pati Parmeshwar*. We had also launched a music-based television serial with their songs.

There is a funny story about my Binaca topper song "Kaise Rahoon Chup" from *Intaqam*. My husband, who was no singer, came to me and sang the song he had approved, and I could not figure it out! The next day, rather doubtfully, I attended the recording and told Lata (Mangeshkar) ji about it. She sweetly hummed out the mukhda and I said, 'Wow! It sounds great!'"[42]

Shammi Kapoor[43]

'Laxmikant-Pyarelal were the natural successors to Shankar-Jaikishan. They had turned down my offer to score music for *Sacchai* for their own reasons, but we knew each other for years and I was following their music right from the beginning, and there was so much to admire in their songs.

They were to compose the music for *Aaghaaz Aur Anjaam*, which I was to direct with Dharmendra, my brother Shashi Kapoor and Zeenat Aman. But I soon left the film as I could not vibe well with the makers. It was dropped, and later made without L-P and with a different setup as *Aap To Aise Na The*.

When I heard the music of *Hero*, I was blown and enthralled and went and told all my friends about it, though I had no song in it.

Yes, I know they gave me Shailendra Singh's voice in their hit "Hum Premi Prem Karna Jaane" in *Parvarish* when my favourite

---

[42]During a *Screen* interview with the author.
[43]During a *Screen* interview with the author.

voice Mohammed Rafi was singing in the same song for Vinod Khanna. But that's okay, because Rafi sang for the hero. I was the old man who came in at the end of the song!'

20

THEIR FILMMAKERS

Boney Kapoor

'I was the whip on *Ponga Pandit* (1975). At that time, I was also assisting Shakti Samanta. Films then would be routinely made over 15 to 18 months. In between, I would look after my father Surinder Kapoor's productions, and would be there at most of the music sittings too. For *Ponga Pandit*, our first film with Laxmikant-Pyarelal, I used to drive our lyricist Rajendra Krishan ji to Laxmi-ji's house, and the first song we did was the hit "Ganga Ghat Ka Paani Piya Hai" which he composed instantly. We made seven films with L-P on the trot in 20 years.

For *Phool Khile Hain Gulshan Gulshan*, I walked into a discussion going on between Laxmi-ji and one of their Gujarati musicians, Dilip Dholakia, and they were jamming on a song that I ultimately insisted on—which became "Manubhai Motor Chali Pam Pam Pam", which my son Arjun (Kapoor) was later crazy about as a kid. The song was an instant hit.

I also used to love the sound of an instrument called French horn. I told Pyare-ji to use it in Bhupinder's unusual ghazal, "Pyar Pardon Mein Chhupane Se" in *Phool Khile…* and he incorporated it.

Anand Bakshi and my father were the best of friends because he had written a qawwali for his film *Jabse Tumhe Dekha Hai* and all the songs of *Tarzan Comes to Delhi*, two of his earliest films. So after *Phool Khile…*, which was a setback to our banner, we decided to retain only L-P and our stunt director Veeru Devgan

(Ajay Devgn's father) in our next, *Hum Paanch*, and Bakshi ji came in. With Rajendra Krishan, there was awe and respect, but with Bakshi ji, we could be free and ask for changes if we were not satisfied.

At the time of *Hum Paanch*, our director Bapu was very busy, as he was simultaneously making a Telugu film too, and I have always believed in doing a full background score and not using stock music pieces in between recorded themes, like even top filmmakers would do. Bapu, who was also on a similar wavelength, suggested that he get S.P. Balasubramaniam to compose the BGM in Chennai itself so that he could be present for it, and I too went there. That is how S.P. Balasubramaniam came in for the background score!

Because I was fond of knowing every aspect of filmmaking, after a working day with Shakti da, I would go to Laxmi-ji's music room and just sit there, usually also having dinner with the family later. Sometimes, after all the sittings were over, Laxmi-ji would make me sit and listen to some other tunes he had made. So there was a very friendly rapport with him, and I also got along very well with his wife Jaya ji.

In the '80s, I loved "Man Kyoon Behka" from *Utsav* so much that I had recorded it again and again on one side of a musicassette to hear in my car—Who would go through the effort of rewinding it again and again?

I was quite fascinated by the way the two used to work. How Pyare-ji would come into the music room, write his notes, discuss, the way they used to pick up small nuances and the way Laxmi-ji used to teach the singer with his mouth full of paan—it was all so interesting. But they always had a small part in each other's work, and an important one. More significantly, they were in total sync. In fact, Laxmi-ji bore the brunt of the pressure of work and would be irritated with me for indulging Pyare-ji, who used to enjoy doing my BGM at length!

The busy era had started when Laxmi-ji would have to dub a

song if the singer was not available in time for the shoot of the song. I noticed then that when a composer himself sings, *unnka josh kuch aur hota hai* (they take the song to another level).

So I was there when he dubbed "Om Shanti Om" for *Karz*. I freaked out when I heard the song, though Chintu (hero Rishi Kapoor) did not care much for it! I said, "Chintu, this is going to be massive!" He did not believe that then, as he has mentioned in its autobiography as well.

When L-P shifted from Famous, Tardeo to Mehboob, it became closer and more convenient for me, and I would attend even more recordings. When "Chal Mere Bhai" (Rafi with Amitabh Bachchan in *Naseeb*) was being made, I was there, and when it was being recorded, I was present too.

During *Mr India*, there was a romantic moment in the climax between Sridevi and Anil as Mr India, and during the background score, Pyare-ji requested that we increase the footage a bit so that he could fit in just the melody of the words "I love you" from the song "Kaate Nahin Kat-Te".

Both of them were so innovative even then—today, with so many tracks, such things are child's play for music makers! I think it was Laxmi-ji who had the brilliant idea of using a single sitar in the mukhda of "Kaate Nahin Kat-Te" before the soft "I love you" as a counter to the heavy beats, but it could have been Pyare-ji. In those days, singles would be issued on EP discs, and Pyare-ji would come and edit the music pieces as the length was stipulated and the songs had to be between 4.5 to 5 minutes.

Later, in the 1990s at Mehboob, multi-track recordings became possible, and Pyare-ji would often make changes in the songs later. If you check, the title song of *Roop Ki Rani Choron Ka Raja* (1993) is different within the audio and in the film! We had recorded the song for the launch, which was at the Silver Jubilee function of *Mr India*. Anil and Sridevi danced live to the whole song and everyone loved it. The film was completed in late 1991, but I had to hold the film for 18 months, because of the riots, bomb blasts and other things. Unfortunately, by the time the film released, things had changed. Nadeem-Shravan had finally made a big mark and then A.R. Rahman's *Roja* came in and the music scenario changed for good.

For *Roop Ki Rani Choron Ka Raja*, we did 60 shifts for the BGM. Just watch the train robbery sequence, where for the first time we had used a rapper—Bali Brahmbhatt. The BGM was, in one word, spectacular! Not many know that Pankuj Parashar had directed the titles of *Roop Ki Rani Choron Ka Raja* and Arshad Warsi had choreographed and danced to the title-music. I had wanted the titles like James Bond films.

Musicians used to wait for our films' BGM to start! Pyare-ji would have a full house and they would end up buying bikes or other big things with their incomes! The BGM of *Prem* also took very long, and we had called percussionists from Benares and the South besides names like Ranjit Barot and Aadesh Shrivastava. Its background score was outstanding—it won the first *Screen* award for Best Background Music.

There were two dances of Tabu that were not songs but offbeat rhythms. It would cost me about ₹24,000 per shift as there would be 100 musicians, and every musician had scope. Some did not play every day but would be present in case the need arose for their expertise, like Pt Shivkumar Sharma or Pt Hariprasad Chaurasia.

I would be after L-P to increase their price so that workload decreases, and I raised their remuneration for *Roop Ki Rani Choron Ka Raja* and doubled it for *Prem*, but Laxmi-ji told me that no producer should be turned back and refused to raise their fee outside!

The first film I did without L-P was *Loafer* with Anand-Milind, followed by *Judaai* with Nadeem-Shravan and *Pukar* with A.R. Rahman. Those were the first times I went out, because L-P was like home. I was so close to Laxmi-ji and I really felt very bad. But not only did those directors prefer those composers but there were some other well-known factors as well because of which I was forced to move away.

Before I left for the shoot of *Pukar*, I had gone to see Laxmi-ji in hospital, and I got scared seeing him like that because I had always seen him in full glory. But the day he passed away I could not make it as a particular sequence that needed my presence in Hyderabad was being shot. That has always been a great regret. When I came back and met Jaya ji, I broke down, and I have never had such a breakdown. Working with L-P had never been like a professional arrangement.

Few know that both of them had had a serious rift even at the time of *Woh 7 Din* in the early 1980s. Some of the BGM for that film was done by Laxmi-ji. I went to Tirupati and took a vow that if they come together again, I would shave my head, and I did!

Let me tell you an interesting anecdote. "Kaate Nahin Kat-Te" was actually made for a film that top South director K. Bhagyaraj was planning with my brother Anil Kapoor. He wanted a rhythm-based song, like whipping, and though that film never happened, Laxmi-ji had made the tune and the thought remained with me. When we made *Mr India*, Laxmi-ji made Javed (Akhtar) saab hear the tune and there and then, the lyricist instantly recited the words, "*Kaate nahin kat-te yeh din yeh raat kehni thi tumse yeh dil ki baat*." The song became so popular that I would carry a cassette of it to parties, as there would be great demand for it.

As for the iconic "Hawa Hawaii" from *Mr India*, Kavita rendered it with so much gusto, which is what elevated the song to that level. Yes, it was to be dubbed by Asha Bhosle, but we all felt that Kavita's voice went very well with Sridevi's, so we retained her.'

K. Vishwanath, Phalke Laureate

'Laxmikant-Pyarelal were a director's dream! I have never seen any composers so amicable, flexible and approachable, without the slightest superiority complex and very, very cooperative! During my Hindi debut, *Sargam*, I felt as if I was working on a Telugu film—the atmosphere was so comfortable.

Their songs for my films are all memorable. We worked on *Sur-Sangam*, *Sanjog* and *Eeshwar* as well. They chose the main voices, like Rafi saab in *Sargam* or Nitin Mukesh in *Eeshwar*.

Laxmi-ji had told me that when they were signed for *Milan*, the Hindi remake of *Mooga Manusulu*, they were aware of the excellence of K.V. Mahadevan's score and wanted to ensure that their music was as popular. So when I offered them *Sargam*, the remake of my *Siri Siri Muvva*, another Mahadevan score, they were initially a shade apprehensive about the same thing. But they did it again! *Sargam* was a brilliant score!

For *Sur-Sangam*, we worked with Pt Rajan-Sajan Misra. The brothers sang many different *raags* during the many sittings we had with them. From these, Laxmikant-Pyarelal selected the suitable ones and composed the tunes. Rajan ji sang all the songs, with Sajan ji rendering some of the alaaps. But like Shankar-Jaikishan, the Misra brothers always take joint credit for their work.

Yes, the music was not appreciated then, but today, connoissseurs swear by the melodies. I think the heavy classical element was not appreciated. That happens in regional music too! This time, eminent classical musicians like Pt Ravi Shankar and Pt Hariprasad Chaurasia had told me it would be a very challenging job to remake *Sankarabharanam*, which championed the cause of Indian classical music, in Hindi. But we went ahead with it.

Pt Ravi Shankar himself and also Naushad saab were among those I considered for scoring the music. But I chose L-P because their range is terrific. Over the years, they have proved they can handle any kind of subject and according to me, their work was superlative! Once again, my original composer in *Sankarabharanam* was K.V. Mahadevan. This time, they could match him only in the calibre, not in popularity!

I have a good ear for melody, but I am not trained in music

and cannot differentiate between *raags*. My permanent composer Mahadevan ji has composed such great songs in all my films that I have come to be associated with great music! And in Hindi films, L-P did the same!'

Ketan Desai

'My father (Manmohan Desai) wanted me to learn all aspects of filmmaking, so I would go for every sitting of Laxmikant-Pyarelal's *Coolie*, which I was the producer of, and also an assistant director. After our sitting, my father and I discussed everything with him and I gave my honest feedback. Dad would be very frank with Laxmi-ji, and he would also keep my preferences in mind, but the final decision was always his.

At the time of *Deewana Mastana*, the L-P hangover was still there, and I told my director David Dhawan that I wanted to do one more film with them. David, who had been working with others, loved the idea of doing something different. Laxmi-ji too was delighted, and said, "Now Man ji is not there, and you have given me cause for worry! I have to work 10 times harder for you!" For me, it was like coming back home.

I realize that around that time, Raj Kapoor's sons and Manoj Kumar had also returned to L-P. Laxmi-ji asked David ji what genre he wanted, and when he was told that David ji wanted my father's genre, Laxmi-ji's reply was that it would be like home ground for him!

And every song he gave me became popular—"Mummy Mummy", "Hungama Ho Gaya", "Head Ya Tail" and "Tere Bina Dil". Two of these songs were made on the spot! One day, I was describing to Laxmi-ji how I tried to cajole my mom to let me eat non-vegetarian food, saying, "Mummy, mummy, let me eat it outside the house, please! Daddy, please tell her!" Laxmi-ji told me to sit, ruminated for a few seconds and came up with the hit tune for Govinda, "O mummy mummy, o daddy daddy"!

On another occasion, I was present at his last sitting of the day and he had this habit of playing a closing note on the harmonium before he closed its bellows. I liked those notes and told him so. He looked at me strangely, and the next day, he called me over and said, "I have made a song for you", and belted out, "Tere Bina Dil Lagta Nahin" based on that closing note!

We normally met in the morning at 11:15 a.m., and he would discuss casual matters for the first 15 minutes. He would then eat his first paan and had told me that without it, he could not work. One day, I asked him to give a paan to me as well. He looked at me and said, "Do you know what is in it? It's not your cup of tea! If you eat it, I challenge you that you will not reach my gate!" When I insisted, he gave me just a pinch of what was inside the paan, and I collapsed and threw up after just walking down 10 steps.

As for Pyare-ji, he was God's gift to India! He is beyond the deepest meaning of the word "genius"! I am among the very few who knew that, at one time, he was to collaborate on an album with John Williams, one of the biggest names in BGM and the man behind scores for *Star Wars* and *Harry Potter*.

I have sat next to Pyare-ji while recording an 80-piece orchestra with 30 violins, and he would call one violinist out of them by name and ask him why he had made a mistake! In his veins runs musicnot blood— he is something else. He knows the art of BGM to perfection, and would make a mark on where there should be a blank space to accentuate the earlier music as well. And at his level, he would still listen to musicians and improve his music!

Pyare-ji would always ask my dad and choreographer what was planned in the visuals of a song and arrange the song accordingly. Like in the hit song "John Jani Janardhan" in *Naseeb*, he timed the words "*De dana dan*" to match with action hero Dharmendra's visuals and the accordion, Raj Kapoor's favourite instrument, when Raj saab was to be in the frame!

Laxmi-ji would call me Ketan babu. Dad started working with him in *Roti* (1974) and I was so interested in music that I was learning the piano as I wanted to be a music director. Dad would organize music sittings for me in the evening so that I could attend their music sittings after school. Sometimes, a director and composer match just clicks, and Laxmi-ji somehow knew what my dad or any other filmmaker wanted, as he would study their temperaments! He would know who wanted poetry, who wanted something unusual or something commercial.

Laxmi-ji and Pyare-ji knew my father from the time of *Chhalia* and *Bluff Master* when they were assisting Kalyanji-Anandji. You can quote me: the phrase "*Dum dum diga diga*" in the *Chhalia* chartbuster came from Laxmi-ji! My father had noticed their talent then and had told them they would work together. And years later, Laxmi-ji met my father at a function and reminded him. Incidentally, the last film my father had announced as our return to them was *Dum Dum Diga Diga* with Anil Kapoor and Salman Khan.

And Laxmi-ji would be very quick. In fact, many a time, my father would like something he had come up with, but it was Laxmi-ji who would ask for another sitting because he thought he could do even better! And I must immensely respect Laxmi-ji for one thing: if Pyare-ji came in after a song was finalized and found some shortcoming in the song even at that stage, Laxmi-ji would never go ahead with the song.

And my dad too would agree—only when both of them and my dad were on the same page would the song be recorded! Pyare-ji had a deep understanding of tunes. Between the two of them, the tuning was fantastic—Pyare-ji would often play his BGM pieces to Laxmi-ji and he would also sometimes suggest changes. And with us, the tunes came first, but they did compose a song whenever (Anand) Bakshi ji said that he had some fantastic lines.

There is a very funny story about the song Laxmi-ji sang for us, "Gore Nahin Hum Kaale Sahi" in *Desh Premee*. He had requested my father that he wanted to sing, and my father said, "Would you ask Rafi to compose a song? So let him sing and you only compose." Even Pyare-ji told Laxmi-ji the same thing. But Laxmi-ji was adamant as he had a great desire to sing. He told Pyare-ji, "Pancham (R.D. Burman) sings too!" Daddy explained that Pancham had a good voice and was a singer as well! But Laxmi-ji still went ahead.

The credits of *Desh Premee* mentioned *two* singers named Laxmikant—the second was Laxmikant Karpe! He was my father's assistant and recited and wrote the Hyderabadi portions in Kishore's "Khatoon Ki Khidmat Mein"!

My father, however, considered Rafi saab to be like his guru, and could not see beyond Rafi saab. So, he wanted a clone when *Coolie* was being planned. He told Laxmi-ji, "Find a voice like his from anywhere!" Laxmi-ji asked him how we could get that range or that scale in anyone. My father just replied, "We will train him!" Laxmi-ji pleaded with me to save him, but I could not help as my father's mind was made up. So, Laxmi-ji managed to trace Shabbir Kumar and got him.

Short of officially adopting him, Rafi saab too considered my father like a son, and I remember Amitabh Bachchan freaked out when my father called him to record "Chal Mere Bhai" live with Rafi saab. "How can I sing with him? I have grown up on his songs. I thought you were taking my voice-track!" he had objected when my father told him. But things became easy because even Rafi saab turned out to be Amit ji's fan!

After *Coolie*, dad became a bit upset with Laxmi-ji as he could not devote enough time to him, and told him, "Laxmi-ji, let me go elsewhere. The moment you have more time, I will come back." But when that happened, and he signed L-P for *Dum Dum Diga Diga*, my father passed away. And then I made *Deewana Mastana* with them.'

Kiran Shantaram

'V. Shantaram Productions was known to work with stalwarts like Vasant Desai, C. Ramachandra and Ramlal. When the subject of *Jal Bin Machhli Nritya Bin Bijli* was decided around 1969, my father Anna (V. Shantaram), family members and I discussed who should score music for the dance musical and we all came to a consensus—Laxmikant-Pyarelal.

Anna called them for a meeting and they were delighted. L-P were very busy, so one of the pre-conditions was that on the day they did our music, the whole day had to be ours. They agreed, and Anna told them the film's story and explained the song situations.

Also very happy was Lata didi, who told my father, "These two are very good, and for them, such an opportunity would be excellent. For your banner too, they will bring in a newness and freshness in the music." I think that didi also recommended Majrooh saab's name for the lyrics.

All the sittings for the songs were done here at Rajkamal Studios in my father's presence, but some rehearsals had to be done at Laxmi-ji's sitting room at Parle, and for that only I would go. So I formed my independent bond with both of them.

The first song to be recorded was the title song, "Unnki Pyaas Mere Man Se Na Nikli". Anna had imported the Stereophonic Sound recording machine, which is still there in our studio, and it had six tracks, a big thing then. He and our in-house recording whiz Mangesh Desai wanted the music in Stereophonic Sound, a first then for Hindi cinema. When L-P heard this, both of them, especially Pyare-bhai, were totally thrilled!

The first Stereo recording in a Hindi film became an event. All the big names in the industry led by Yash Chopra, and, I think, Raj Kapoor, were present. L-P showed us how a large orchestra should be used—they had up to 80 violins, and with six tracks it was a difficult job, but they did it!

For the final mixing, the stereo division of the instruments—Pyare-bhai and Mangesh in that order deserve the magnificent credit for the fantastic result. I say, hat's off to them! When the then-recording engineer at HMV, which marketed our album, first heard it, he went mad!

All the songs were made in not just a friendly, but a fun atmosphere. Both Laxmi-ji and Pyare-bhai would arrive at 9:30 a.m. and we would be together for almost 12 hours, sharing meals, and calling for snacks in the evening from a nearby iconic restaurant, Ladoo Samrat. These wonderful sittings made my father rave about them and exclaim, "There's no one like them!" And these sittings went on, with breaks, for a period of seven or eight months.

One unforgettable memory was of the song "Kajraa Lagaake" that L-P made in the reverse way! As the heroine, Sandhya ji had composed the dance first, and they composed the music according to her steps and movements and Majrooh saab wrote the lyrics to it!

My only musical contribution was the finalization of "Taaron Mein Sajke" sung by Mukesh ji. I simply loved the tune. Pyare-bhai told my father, "This one's been selected by Kiran!"and Anna beamed with pride at my musical ear!

Incidentally, while I was dropping Pyare-bhai home one night, we were listening in my car to the music from *For A Few Dollars More*. I told Pyare-bhai I would like something along those lines and he composed a variation and put it in "Taaron Mein Sajke"!

I am still moved by their memories and their music—what a body of work they have, and how nice they both were. My father also recorded the background score in Stereo, and the only reason why the film was not made in that way was that at that time, he would have had to go abroad for processing it. Like for *Sholay*, Mangesh went with R.D. Burman to London. And for Laxmikant-Pyarelal's *Kranti*, he went to Sony Corporation Studios in Japan. I do not think Pyare-bhai went with him though.

Anna also asked them to score the Hindi version of *Pinjra* later, but he then replaced them with the original Marathi hit's composer Ram Kadam. I think that at that time, they had so many commitments that they could not have given my father the exclusive time they had given on *Jal Bin Machhli Nritya Bin Bijli*, but the sweet memories remain.'

Pravesh Sippy

'L-P's music had a definite bigness and Indianness blended with a symphonic feel. As a youngster, I learnt and absorbed this. Apart from my father N.N. Sippy's films as producer (*Haar Jeet, Sargam, Ghazab* and *Meri Jung*), we distributed most of Subhash Ghai's other films besides *Meri Jung*, and most of them had their music. Pay heed to the orchestration of "Ding Dong O Baby Sing Song" or "Nindiya Se Jaagi Bahaar" from *Hero*, and, it is easy to understand what made them overtake giants like Shankar-Jaikishan! I would be with Subhash ji all the time, and in the case of *Sargam, Ghazab* and *Meri Jung*, I would go for the sittings too.'

Rajkumar Kohli

'Way back in 1965, I was planning a musical film with seven to eight songs and wanted to work with new people. Who better than Laxmikant-Pyarelal, all of whose songs had become hits? So I signed them for *Lootera*. And every song was a hit. I knew I will get what I want from them. When I had an understanding with them, why should I even think of working with others, even if they may be good? The variety of singers was often decided by me, which included Pakistani singer Reshma's selection in *Pati Patni Aur Tawaif* (1990). Reshma came down and stayed with me—she had already sung for them in *Hero*.

There is one classic song from *Jaani Dushmun* (1979—Rafi saab's "Chalo Ri Doli Uthaao Kahaar", that comes in parts all through the film. It was linked to the story and I kept filming such a song in my mind throughout the entire film, for every time a doli (a bride's palanquin in procession) was shown, the bride disappears! I knew the kind of lyrics I wanted, the shot divisions. Then, after the last sequence was filmed, we actually recorded the song with Rafi and it synched perfectly. Also, when I recorded Mukesh-Lata's "Dheere Dheere Bol Koi Sun Na Le" (*Gora Aur Kala*), my crew did not like it. They said it was like someone singing while in a toilet! So after it became a chartbuster, I asked them again what they now thought of it! They saluted my judgment! But I think that the audience likes anything good, and they certainly do not think a song is good merely because it is from my film or V. Shantaram's, from a specific composer, singer and so on.

With *Nagin* (1976), it was not intentional that all the four songs began with variations of the same word—"Tere Sang Pyar Main", "Tere Mere Yaarane Ho", "Tera Mera Mera Tera" and "Tere Ishq Ka Mujhpe". Forty-five years later, I realize that such a thing has happened. I know that most of L-P's songs are being re-created now, and that is because they have given the maximum hits. So they alter L-P's music somewhat, change the singers and present it as a new song, because they are proven hits that have been loved by the people.'

Ravi Tandon

'When I signed Laxmikant-Pyarelal for *Anhonee*, they were already famous and I was working with lyricist Verma Malik in my directorial debut *Balidan*. So I suggested we take him. Laxmi-ji could have insisted on a big name, but he told me, "Get the songs written, I will tune them." Incidentally, when I produced my next film, *Apne Rang Hazaar* (1975), Anjaan, who stayed in my building, expressed a wish to work with me. Laxmi-ji again told me the same thing: get the words, and he would make the music for them. The first song he composed for my second production was "Ganga Mein Dooba Na Jamuna Mein Dooba"— what a composition it is! I have heard hundreds of their songs, but two songs that elicit repeated cries of exultation in my mind are "Ek Pyar Ka Naghma Hai" (*Shor*) and this song.

In between, after *Anhonee* became a hit, I was signed by their loyal producer Premji to direct *Majboor* (1974), which had lyrics by Anand Bakshi, and also for *Nirmaan* by producer Deenanath Shastri, with Majrooh. The latter producer, who also stayed in my building, was erratic and nothing would please him, and he dropped me midway. I do not know how the film was completed and I had almost nothing to do with its music.

As for Premji, he had an excellent tuning with them, and most of the music of *Majboor* and the film we did later—*Jawaab* (1985) was done by him. I myself had no knowledge about music, but sometime in the 1980s, I met their assistant Aadesh Shrivastava at a party, and he told me, "Do you know that Laxmi-Pyare have a theka (a beat), that they call the 'Ravi Tandon theka'?" I asked Pyare-bhai about this later, and he smiled. Both of them had sensed my taste in music.

Once, I was shooting at Mehboob Studios when Laxmi-ji came there in his car (in those days their recordings would be at Famous, Tardeo). He wanted to make me listen to a song he had made, "Dekha Phoolon Ko Kaanton Pe Sote Huye", the hit from *Majboor*. The number one composer had made the effort to meet and make me listen to a new composition he had made for my film!

There is also an interesting memory I have about the song that is now a cult favourite: "Hungama Ho Gaya" from *Anhonee*. In those days, there was only one discotheque in Mumbai— Blow-Up at Mumbai's 5-star Hotel Taj Mahal, which was India's first nightclub. I had gone there and decided that I wanted that kind of disco effect in the song, so I took my cinematographer Ramchandra, my choreographer P.L. Raj, Laxmikant, Pyarelal and Verma Malik there.

I salute and doff a hat to all of them, and to Asha (Bhosle) ji, Bindu ji and my editors Waman Bhosle and Guru Dutt for the result! As a song, almost five decades have passed and it sounds as fresh as ever, and it was used again in 2014 in *Queen*!'

Satish Kaushik

'Icons are the only words that encapsulate Laxmikant and Pyarelal. *Parasmani, Lootera*—from the beginning, they gave terrific variety. Like the entire country, I too was crazy about their songs, and I was lucky to come into films as a profession. My first film as an actor, *Woh 7 Din*, had their music.

As associate director to Shekhar Kapur, I was a part of all the music sittings of *Mr India* and I was utterly fascinated by everything. The atmosphere was *kamaal ka* (beyond description) and a complete learning process.

There would be the filmmakers, Laxmi-ji, his musicians, the singers and in the last sitting, wherein the orchestral graph was decided, Pyare-ji as well. And there would be no hurry, though there would be so many filmmakers waiting outside, like in a doctor's waiting-room, patiently waiting their turn. Yes, whenever we were waiting outside Laxmi-ji's music room, we too have waited as long as two hours!

Their music had an Indian thaat, [44] but when I came to know Pyare-ji in person, I found that he is almost a Beethoven in his knowledge of Western music as well, and although it would have meant an incalculable loss to our film music, he would have been a thousand-fold more famous outside India!

While some songs would need two or three sittings, Laxmi-ji was generally very fast and the tune would come out after a

---

[44] A heptatonic—seven pitches per octave—parent scale in Hindustani music to which many *raags* can belong. There are 10 basic *thaats*—Bilawal, Kalyan, Khamaj, Bhairav, Poorvi, Marwa, Kafi, Asavari, Bhairavi and Todi.

few minutes of rumination. Then he would write the song in his own handwriting in a thick notebook that was like a Bible to him. Later, at the recording, Pyare-ji would write the notations in detail for every instrument. Nowadays, in the electronic era, such meticulousness is not needed as you can feed in the music you have written or made.

It was from them that I learnt, for the first time, terms and words of relevance like intro music, 1st music, 2nd music, crescendo, obligato, theme music and so on. I learnt the mathematics of music there—how the exact number of words and the correct ones had to come in.

Laxmi-Pyare never did a song just as a job. Sur, taal, brilliant use of the violins and the *dholak*, so much thought went into every single aspect. When "Kaate Nahi Kat-te" was made, Laxmi-ji rattled off the tune we had approved and told Javed (Akhtar) saab that he wanted staccato words in the mukhda, but at its end would be a soft, "I love you". Great lyricists like Anand Baskhi saab and him were very quick on the uptake.

In my *Roop Ki Rani Choron Ka Raja* for the song "Romeo Naam Mera", I suggested that L-P make a tune inspired by the *lezim*, a folk dance from Maharashtra named after a small musical instrument of that name, which was in the form of cymbals. And we also recorded the first rap song ever in Hindi cinema. I was exposed to rap in London, and came back and suggested that we make something like that. And Laxmi-Pyare were game, so we called in Suneeta Rao and Bali Brahmbhatt, whom I had already contacted in London.

I had a personal equation with both of them. Laxmi-ji's son Tinku (Hrishikesh) was my assistant in the two films. With Laxmi-ji, every evening at his house was like a party, while Pyare-ji was reserved. But I was among the few who spent late nights with him at his house. Their warmth and humility after so much work, success and their iconic position was incredible.'

Subhash Ghai

'I have been a film music buff since I can remember, with various favourite composers from Naushad to Madan Mohan, S.D. Burman and Shankar-Jaikishan. When I was training as an actor at the Film & Television Institute of India (FTII), Pune, I heard a song, "Hansta Hua Noorani Chehera", and I came to know it was from a small film called *Parasmani* and composed by two newcomers named Laxmikant-Pyarelal.

Aur meri zubaan se yeh shubh shabd nikal gaye—"*Yeh bahut bade banenge* (And the auspicious words slipped out, that these two will become big)" But from their names, I thought they must be hailing from some village!

Then, a few days later, I heard "Woh Jab Yaad Aaye" from the same film, and I laid a bet with my colleagues that they would soon outshine Shankar-Jaikishan, who had started becoming a bit predictable. When the music of *Dosti* came out, I even bought a gramophone and the *Dosti* record, though I could barely afford such things then!

And guess what? The first role I signed after I left FTII was a small one in *Taqdeer*, produced by Rajshri Productions in 1967. And they were the film's music directors. There was a song filmed on Farida Jalal, "Aaiye Bahaar Ko Hum Baant Le", and I was a part of that song too, strumming a guitar. I flipped over Rafi saab's "Jab Jab Bahaar Aayi" and most of the other songs, which were hits even though the film flopped.

When I turned filmmaker, the producer of my third film, *Gautam Govinda*, had worked with them earlier and had signed them, and Laxmi-ji met me enthusiastically, as I was then known as the director of the super-hit *Kalicharan*. The first song we recorded was "Ek Rut Aaye Ek Rut Jaaye", and Pyare-bhai also loved my narration of the visuals—the sun shining over arid land, the poverty and the effects of famine. It was one of Anand Bakshi's most beautifully written songs and Pyare-bhai's atmospheric orchestration to a superb tune by Laxmi-ji earned Laxmi-Pyare and me a call from none other than Raj Kapoor. It was nothing less than an Oscar for me!

And yet, people said that I was a good director but had no music sense, so I thought my next film should be a musical. It was *Karz* with a pop singer as a hero. Obviously, I should have signed R.D. Burman for it, but I was impressed by their range and told L-P to accept the challenge that I was giving them. And how beautifully they scored!

Pyare-bhai had made different musical pieces for the theme, which was the first to be recorded. He liked the fifth one he offered, but I preferred the third, which is the famous one now. I don't know music, but I react to it, and after the theme music became cult, Pyare-bhai admitted that I had made the correct choice!

The saga of Laxmikant-Pyarelal is the story of two emperors, each unrivalled in his own right. Only they could have given a Western colour to a ghazal-like composition in "Dard-e-Dil Dard-e-Jigar", in which they used a drum instead of a dholak! And they decided to use Mohammed Rafi's voice in a score that had Kishore Kumar singing all other songs. The complex tune had all the three verses structured differently, and hat's off to Laxmikant for treating the song that way.

After our *Krodhi* flopped badly—but the music did not—I told them that my next film, *Hero*, would be made without stars, and that the music had to be a hit or we would die! And again, look at the terrific music with which they came up!

The standout song from *Hero* today is "Lambi Judaai", and I was keen that Reshma, from Pakistan, should sing this litany of separation: we had heard her at Raj Kapoor's party. Laxmi-ji told me that such artistes rarely sing film songs, as their scale and tone are different. He told me that folk singers are like lions we can use only occasionally!

When I still insisted, and Reshma agreed to sing, Laxmi-ji told me that we should get the song written first from Anand

Bakshi according to the situation, and that he would compose it in her style, not in the L-P way, so that she would be comfortable! On the day Reshma was recording, I entered the recording studio to find Pyare-bhai rehearsing with nine musicians. I thought more would come, as L-P's normal orchestra would be around 100-strong, but he told me that Reshma would sing in her free, open way and the orchestration should make her voice stand out, not intimidate her.

Such was the visionary greatness of these two composers. I remember that I had penned the thematic lines for *Karma* in my script, "*Har karam apna karenge ae watan tere liye / Dil diya hai jaan bhi denge ae watan tere liye*". I gave Laxmi-ji the lines and was leaving his sitting room, as many producers were waiting, when he called me back. He had composed the tune you hear now, a tune he made in less than five minutes but lives on 35 years down!

Pyare-bhai asked me what kind of orchestration I had thought of for the same song, and my answer was, "It should be like Delhi's Vividh Bharati music!" And so the theme music was made by him in that fashion!

Our understanding and affection was so complete and wonderful that you can just see the progression of our music—*Ram Lakhan*, *Saudagar*, *Khal Nayak*. I can write a 500-page book on these magicians who met so many challenges successfully!

"Choli Ke Peeche", the much-maligned song from *Khal Nayak*, around which an artificial controversy was created, was another example of their brilliance. Bakshi ji asked me what kind of a song I wanted, and my reply was that it should be the kind of raunchy song classically found in North Indian folk, if need be with abuses, as my male lead is a villain.

I was going to Mount Abu to hunt for locations and I saw a small kid on the way playing an attractive tune on his iktara (a single-stringed instrument). I recorded it, tipped the boy, and played it to Laxmi-ji. He liked it and modified the tune, and we added the refrain *"kuk-kuk-kuk-kuk"*.

Later, Bakshi ji called me up and said, "I have written the mukhda." When he recited the words, *"Choli ke peeche kya hai"*, I said I did not want such words and hung up! He rang up again and said, 'Listen to the next two lines at least—*"Choli mein dil hai mera, chunari mein dil hai mera, yeh dil main doongi mere yaar ko, pyar ko."*

The lines were good, and no one found the song objectionable. Alka Yagnik and Ila Arun recorded it, Saroj Khan choreographed it for Madhuri Dixit and Neena Gupta and the song was out.

It was then that social workers descended on us and said that we were spoiling our children! They tried to bring a stay on the song, but the courts refused! The *Indian Express* called it a classic piece of Indian cinema, and today, "Choli Ke Peeche" is a part of every dancing class and even children sing it!

So that was Laxmikant-Pyarelal, both excellent at all aspects of music. But when work increased, they devised a smart working system where Laxmi-ji would look after making tunes for producers while Pyare-bhai looked after BGM and song orchestration.'

21

THEIR MUSICIANS

Amar Haldipur

'With Laxmi-Pyare, it was never a naukri (job)! The word for them was "obsessed", like Laxmi-ji would tell Pyare-ji, "*Kal ka gaana jamaa dete hain, Pyare* (Let's record a solid song tomorrow, Pyare)." I was a musician with them right from 1966. Laxmikant-Pyarelal exposed everyone to how work in music should be done. L-P's musical phrasing was crystal clear and nuanced—where should Lata ji sing a harkat and where the weight on a syllable should be put, were clear mandates. The music as well as their brief told Lata ji exactly what they wanted, whether they wanted it as *e-x-a-c-t-l-y* or maybe *e-x-x-a-c-t-t-l-y*! Many people may know the spelling of a word, but only a few can pronounce it perfectly. This attention to nuances was so detailed and very precise, and was always seen in the way they got results from all singers. Pyare-bhai had this temperament—not just singers but even musicians could not do anything they wished, like they could with other composers—it had to be the L-P way, but blended with the musician's own creativity.

So Pyare-bhai would extract something from within you… "*Accha hai, yeh expression accha hai* (Its good, this expression is good)," he would tell a musician. This blend is what Pyare looked for, and it was like, "Hari ji (Pt Hariprasad Chaurasia), I am throwing you the ball, but it's up to you how to hit it. I will not tell you to use a straight cut." We were doing "Hum Banjaron Ki Baat", the super-hit from *Dharam-Veer*. Pyare-bhai told me what he wanted from me in musical language. That is why he wanted his regular names at recordings as players—Hari ji, Shiv ji (Pt Shivkumar Sharma), even me, all the time. Whether we played on the song or not, greeting us when he entered boosted his confidence psychologically.

While they were teaching Lata bai the song, they would tell her the minutiae at each point. Most other music directors would sing the song in totality and the singer would catch whatever he or she wanted and sing. But with L-P, it was strict detailing—"This is the dinner I want now, and at exactly 10 p.m., I want this sweet dish, and at 10:30, I want coffee!" That is why L-P's songs were always different, distinctive and unique.

I have observed that Lata ji is the only singer whose song reflects the music director so clearly that I can see him. The reason is very clear: Lata never puts her own expression into any song—that's her special point. She never sings from herself, but always from what is given to her by the composer. That is why her songs always sound fresh. Many singers do not absorb a song, they just sing it.

The mood had to be followed strictly in L-P's music. And *application*, more than knowledge, was important. That is where Pyarelal went beyond being a mere arranger—he was like a mother to his songs, teaching the compositions manners, imbibing culture into them. See the orchestration that creates the atmosphere of midnight and the judicious gentle use of the period pipes in "Man Kyoon Behka" (*Utsav*). I have seen such detailing genius only in one more composer—Sonik, of Sonik-Omi, who earlier arranged music for Madan Mohan.

I was working throughout with so many composers, from sittings to recordings, as a very interested observer. It is said that you can't teach anyone, you can only correct him. Pyare-bhai was unequalled at this—a complex person with his genius coming in from probably a previous birth.

I have worked with Pyare-bhai for 33 years, and he never composed music at home. In 30 minutes in the studio, he would make the theme music of a song. This is what I want to emphathize: some people make music, but Pyare-bhai just expressed himself. It is just how Dilip Kumar's glance or Rishi Kapoor's raised eyebrow can speak volumes in place of even 10 lines of dialogues by others.

And when Pyare-bhai composed a tune, it was inwards, reflective, ghazal-like: "Yeh Dil Tum Bin" (*Izzat*), "Tum Gagan Ke Chandrama Ho" (*Sati Savitri*) or "Yeh Jo Chilman Hai" (*Mehboob Ki Mehndi*) are by Pyare-bhai. Laxmi-ji had a more open style, like "Yoon Besabab Jahaan Mein" (*Mehandi Rang Layegi*). With Pyare, it was more about the detailing of the intricate musical phrases, whereas with Laxmi-ji, it was more about gaayaki (vocal expertise).

As for Laxmi-ji, he too would never come prepared, but was always worked-up. "I want to do something today!" was his credo. I have seen just three other composers like him— Madan ji, Shankar ji and Usha Khanna. Put the words in front of them, and there were dozens of tunes ready in as many minutes. These are not composers, but people who *express*, as I said! When you interpreted the same thing differently, a different tune would emerge. Laxmi-ji had a fire within him. He wanted to do something special every day. That fire was there in early Shankar-Jaikishan, but after they became successful, their attitude became a tad mechanical. With Laxmi-Pyare, it was never a naukri (job)! The word for them was "obsession".

Both of them never referred to any song as *hamara gaana*, but as *apna gaana*, suggesting a sense of belonging. One morning, I recorded a song for *Shahenshah*, my own film as composer, and in the same afternoon I was playing the violin for them, and Amitabh Bachchan was surprised to see me there. But they both told him, "He is like our baccha (our son)." They never looked on me as a potential rival. They nurtured me like parents do.

When they had their unfortunate fight in the '90s, Laxmi-ji called me up the next day and asked me to come at noon. He said he wanted me to arrange a song. I was shocked, but I told him that if I did that, I would have to first tell Pyare. And he immediately said, "Of course, tell him I told you. He will not forbid you." And that's what happened. Pyare-bhai told me, "Do it well. I will like it if you do it." I arranged two songs, but told Laxmi-ji that we should stop. And Laxmi-ji replied, "Just wait till tomorrow. There is an urgent song. Pyare will have cooled down by then, and I will go and get him!" That was their bond!

If you observe film music, there is only one composer entity that has given the industry a line of singers, and not just discovered or introduced them but made them successful. And the way they treated musicians—Do you know that at any recording, where if there were 45 to 50 musicians in the morning, they would swell to 90 by evening? Any musician who had no work for a few days would be cordially invited by Laxmikant to meet Pyare-bhai and sit in the orchestra. This trait was there in Shankar-Jaikishan as well, but to a very limited extent. But the L-P recording was like a fair, an event.

If any other recording was cancelled and Pyare-bhai came to know, he would call the musicians from there—even if he already had 40 violins, he would summon 15 more. Grandeur was L-P— they loved their work! Other music directors would have four or five musicians in the woodwinds section, L-P would have 35 to 40! There was an abundance of sitar—as many as eight! Guitar, banjo, rabab, mandolin, santoor—there was no end! At least 100 families' households ran because of Laxmikant-Pyarelal—no one else has done it. And L-P never made anyone feel they were doing any favours. They would say instead, "*Hamein chahiye aap log.* (We need you.)" Out of work composers and arrangers—Prabhakar Jog and Srinivas Khale from Marathi films, Dattaram, who had worked with S-J, Jai Kumar Parte from Kalyanji-Anandji's team, Master Sonik himself, Basu from R.D. Burman's team—who would play cello at every recording—and even Babloo Chakravorty, all worked with us.

Including me, there would be 30 to 35 music directors playing at L-P's recordings, including Viju Shah, Anil Mohile, Arun Paudwal, Sameer Sen, Kishore Sharma and others!

And L-P were so fastidious that they would wait for even a month for a specific musician. I remember getting a call from Amitabh Bachchan himself when I was doing my own song in a studio, because Pyare-bhai wanted only me for an important part of the *Khuda Gawah* background score that was being recorded—it was Amit ji's own production. And for the same film's song "Tu Na Ja Mere Badshah", Pyare-bhai told me that he did not want my violin to sound like a typical violin but something with a Pashto ang (feel). He was very specific: "I want Afghanistan, not Arabia, Lebanon or Egypt."

For Rafi saab's "Dard-E-Dil" (*Karz*), Pyare-bhai postponed the recording by three hours because I was delayed at a Pancham recording. My solo violin was there, and there was not enough space to stand next to Rafi saab, so an extra microphone was arranged! All the violin solos in L-P's songs have always been mine, except for in "Ek Pyar Ka Naghma Hai" (*Shor*), which was played by Jerry Fernandes.

With any other music director, a violin was a violin, but not with these geniuses. In innumerable cases, a trumpet would be played like a shehnai and vice-versa. Gorakh, Pyare-bhai's brother, would play guitar pieces to the notes of a *sarod*, and the reverse too would happen. Working with them was not easy in that sense.

Laxmi-ji also had that rare art of listening and talking to a producer who had come to meet him, while keeping a sharp ear on the song being recorded for someone else at the same time. He was obsessed with work.

L-P knew exactly what to take from every singer or musician, and what an artiste could give them, otherwise they would not call that person. Yet Pyare-bhai even changed the prelude of "Choli

Ke Peeche" (*Khal Nayak*) and would change any other song if the musician could not play what they wanted, or was uncomfortable doing it, and there was no one better in his eyes for that piece.

So many people became arrangers because of Pyare-bhai. Many musicians do not encourage anyone standing next to them when they are writing music. With Pyare-bhai, it was the reverse: stand next to him and learn whatever you can. And yet, at learning music himself, even now, Pyare-bhai is like a small boy. He humbly asks the youngest musicians whose work he likes how they wrote their music, and he goes back home, opens his music books and sees how they had done the chord progressions!

I will also tell you about their unique bond, that I have never seen in any other duo: Laxmi-ji would not only make most of the tunes but also look at the business angles, like producers, budgets and studios. (Anand) Bakshi ji would largely deal with him, and even the musicians that Pyare-bhai wanted would be told to come by Ramanand, Laxmi-ji's right hand.

At work, if Pyare-bhai knew just one bar of Laxmi's tune, after the characters, situation and filmmakers were discussed, he needed nothing more. He would know exactly where Laxmi-ji would musically go after that. I remember an incident—Laxmi-ji had composed the mukhda of the title song of *Sajan*—"Sajan Sajan Pukaroon Galiyon Mein". But he was stuck at the antara and told Pyare-bhai. Within minutes, Pyare-bhai composed the antara and asked Laxmi-ji, "How is it?" And Laxmi-ji raved about it.

I have seen the other side too: Pyarelal composing some music for a song or a background score, and Laxmi-ji would spontaneously come up with a piece of melody and ask Pyare to fit it in if possible. Pyare-bhai would do it, no questions asked. There are endless music pieces composed by Pyare-bhai for a background score, from which Laxmi-ji would remember the chhand (metre) and make a tune for a song! I wish I could remember a few offhand, but you watch their films and you will know.

And the Punjab they brought in—also because of Bakshi ji—was something no Punjabi composer could give. That was a different colour completely. "Likhnewale Ne Likh Daale" (*Arpan*), "Main Jat Yamla" (*Pratiggya*), "Bindiya Chamkegi" (*Do Raaste*)... *kya baat hai!* But here again, if they did take lock stock and barrel from Punjabi folk, they would break the song down and make an original.

I would like to shed light on one unhappy aspect: that both Lata ji and Asha ji were severely upset with Laxmi-ji when he shifted to the younger singers in the late '80s and early '90s. But what could he do then with so much work pressure? The two sisters were frequently out on tours and there was no time to wait for weeks or months. Sadly, the brunt of this anger was borne only by Laxmi-ji, which was very unfair. As for Pyare-bhai, he knew only to focus on music. If he was watching television or a movie with you, he would be least bothered about what was happening but would focus only on the BGM, its pattern and how it went with the scene. One day, we were driving past a Ganpati visarjan (Lord Ganesh immersion) procession. He was least bothered about the traffic or what the people were doing. Instead, he asked me to listen to a phrase one of the musicians was playing.

Such a team will never return. Shankar-Jaikishan never worked as a pair. It was like a contract—two people working individually. L-P was a proper team that complemented each other.

At the end of the day, L-P were like the Gangotri, the origin of a limitlessly rich creative river that flowed everywhere. I have worked with so many composers, heard so many others, but at the end of the day, I come back to a L-P song and think, "*Man! They were something else!*" It's just like no matter how much you think a young singer has excelled, you still come back to Lata and Asha and realize that they are the best.

And let me tell you something about Kishore Kumar. What he has sung for them he has never sung outside. L-P always used Kishore differently. And the way Rafi saab has sung for L-P... My God!

Mukesh was the purest and most open-hearted soul among them all. What he sang for L-P is also far different from all his work under everyone else. He connected with the listener's heart, and you wept when he sang "Khushi Ki Woh Raat Aa Gayi" (*Dharti Kahe Pukar Ke*). That was his triumph, and theirs.'

Padma Vibhushan Pandit Hariprasad Chaurasia

'They had a single thought-process—to hook the world, and when they made songs like "Chahoonga Main Tujhe" (*Dosti*), the world was eating from the palm of their hands! Even today, their shows and songs are a rage.

Only when you have the right learning, your parents' and God's blessings and you work hard with so much interest and passion that you see the heights Laxmikant-Pyarelal reached. There are musicians, and then there are Laxmikant and Pyarelal. There are composers, and there are Laxmikant-Pyarelal.

There was a difference between what I got to play for others, and what I did for them. Every musician and observer will agree with me. The reasons were very simple: Both were excellent singers, composers and musicians. They had grasped and perfected Western and Indian music and the music of Maharashtra, where every musician is born with *Sa Re Ga Ma Pa Dha Ni* in his core being. Pyarelal's father taught so many eminent musicians. The hard work was exceptional, and so, were the blessings.

I got to learn so much from them both. Very often, as a flautist, I would sit in their orchestra and they would simply tell me, "*Kaam mat kijiye. payment leke jaiye.* (Don't work. Just take your payment and go.)" At such times, I would attend their rehearsals to just sit and learn from the fascinating things that were happening before me. We would also sit together and brainstorm for new things we could do, which was always their special interest.

They were both classically trained, but were so fabulous at *sugam sangeet* (light music). I too aspired to that, as our songs in films like *Silsila* and *Chandni* show.

Their favourite lyricist, Anand Bakshi, became our favourite as well when Pt Shiv Kumar Sharma and I joined to form the Shiv-Hari team in films. I never saw a team like Bakshi with L-P. Again, in the department of how important words are, there was so much to learn! When *Sur-Sangam* (1985) was being planned, I had suggested Pt Rajan Misra and Pt Sajan Misra as the voices to writer-director K. Vishwanath, with whom I had a great relationship. He loved them and suggested them to L-P.

Laxmikant-Pyarelal wanted pure classical music in the film, along the lines of *Baiju Bawra*'s "Aaj Gaawat Man Mero" or Vasant Desai's songs in *Jhanak Jhanak Payal Baaje*. Could they do it? Of course they could! And their bond was unequalled. *Miya biwi saath mein nahin rehte jitna yeh rahe.* (Couples do not remain together as long as they did.) Wah!'

Rajesh Roshan

'In the beginning, I had started making tunes, and my mother knew Anand Bakshi saab as he had also worked with my father, Roshan saab. I had done my formal classical training and she suggested that I assist a composer and learn the ropes. Bakshi saab told my mother that he could place me either with R.D. Burman saab or with Laxmikant-Pyarelal.

Though I was familiar with their work, I still consciously listened to both again and chose L-P, because *thoda apne type ka music lagaa* (the music seemed to suit to my taste). You must mention this point, because if you were told to write a book on one of two composers, you will freshly study their work before making a choice, even when you were familiar with the music of both!

When I joined L-P, I was 19 years old, and there would be

a line of producers at Laxmi-ji's music room—as many as 25 in a day!—and up to three songs daily would be finalized! Though I was first playing the khanjari (a small tambourine) and also percussion, I would also arrange for his tea, water, juice and paan. Laxmi-ji's advice to me was to keep making tunes, and I made so many and made him listen to them. But he never used them, the way other composers use tunes made by assistants, and I was too scared to ask him why!

Laxmi-ji had a small tape recorder in which he would store tunes approved by filmmakers to retrieve and work on them later. When the man assigned to look after all that started making a mess of it, he assigned me the job, and from then on, I took over, cued them and that became my fixed duty! I then had to be there at his sittings, as there would be a problem if I did not go any day.

I also started playing the daff (a tambourine drum) and from then on, only I would play it there. The solo daff in the chartbusting "Jhoot Bole Kauva Kaate" (*Bobby*) when Lata ji sings the words "*Main maayke nahin jaaongi*" is mine.

Pyare-ji thought it was shameful that the son of Roshan was playing just the daff and khanjari for them and made me learn the piano. He even refused to send me to his father Pt Ramprasad Sharma, because he tended to be too strict with his disciples! Yes, both of them had humongous respect for my father.

I also played the kabaas, a coconut-shaped instrument with beads, and the congo. Aboni, a Burmese musician, also gifted them a special instrument that he had made. As it resembled a congo, we called it "congi". While working on *Shor*, Manoj (Kumar) ji and I came close, and in my absence, he told Laxmi-ji and Pyare-bhai that he wanted to give me a break. Pyare-bhai immediately came to me, and said, "Train yourself, be prepared and keep tunes ready! Manoj ji and we will launch you together!" And I reflected, "*Kaise hain yeh log*? (*What kind of people are these?*)" Anyone else in their place would have convinced Manoj ji not to take me and instead choose to work with them. People like L-P are not from this world, I tell you!

After that, it was Mehmood saab who gave me a break in *Kunwara Baap* and soon I was in direct competition not just with L-P but also with Kalyanji-Anandji and R.D. Burman. I signed films with L.V. Prasad, Mohan Segal, Devar and Raj Khosla, all L-P's regulars. But my tuning with L-P never changed. When I had a tiff with a big-name producer, Laxmi-ji came to know of it and called me home. He asked me what happened, and his advice was, "The world works this way. But you should think only of business. Bear his abuses, but don't let him go to someone else!" Again, I wondered, "*Kya the yeh log? (What kind of people were these?)*"

I must confess that I tried to copy their style in my own way in *Jaag Utha Insan*, because they knew how to get the correct feel for any subject. I can challenge you, that not a single composer could make the complete orchestral structure for a song. Today, I do not need arrangers. I may use them many times, but I have learnt to be independent from Pyare-bhai.

And that personal equation remained. Laxmi-ji had bought a table-tennis table and would always play a couple of games with me after work was over. One day, he called me at 10 in the morning, and I came even without taking my bath. He was not a very good player, but if we played 100 games, I must have won less than a handful! I would often be his confidante for trivial complaints he had against something or someone, to which he would open up while drinking as I was driving him around in his car.

Pyare-bhai too would drop me on the way home in his car while returning from Laxmi-ji's music room. They were like my gurus, and I never dared cross that sacrosanct line. But if ever I was worried about something, Laxmi-ji would tell me, "*Tu darr mat, main idhar hi hoon.* (Don't worry. I am here for you.)"

Sameer Sen, *Musician and Composer*

'Most new singers would initially copy and follow Lata Mangeshkar and Mohammed Rafi, most new actors would copy Dilip Kumar and most new music directors would copy Laxmikant-Pyarelal in one or more ways! Like Shankar-Jaikishan, they were all-rounders. They considered S-J their gurus, and emulated the good things about them, but for my generation, L-P were the inspirations.

When L-P entered, they shook everyone, including S-J, putting in such hard work even in small films. Today I can safely say that in film music and orchestration, no one is as good as these two duos.

I have worked with L-P as a musician for 10 to 15 years, and I was one of their favourites, working on percussion, congo (called tumba here), dholak and bass guitar. It was in 1968–9 that my father, the late composer Shambhu Sen, took me to Pt Ramprasad Sharma, Pyare-bhai's legendary father, to learn staff notation for rhythm. I became his favourite pupil and he took me to Pyare-ji, who was so busy that he had no time to listen to me. But eventually he did.

My father had taught me to play Indian classical on the djembe, and Pyare-bhai even used this gift of mine for a sequence featuring Sanjay Kapoor and Tabu in *Prem*. It was thrilling beyond words to watch Pyare-bhai's symphony performance abroad some years ago, and after he concluded, the applause was never-ending and the conductor touched Pyare-bhai's feet.

And back home, just a few weeks back, I was called to perform for a Laxmikant-Pyarelal concert conducted by Pyare-bhai, who wanted me and only me as I had played the congo for the opening music of "Om Shanti Om" in *Karz*. My son, composer Sohail Sen, was invited to sing. This was the fourth generation of Sens associated with L-P: they were musicians with my grandfather, the late Jamal Sen, they had a great friendship with my dad, and now my son was singing their songs under Pyare-bhai's supervision.'

Vinay Mandke, *Musician and Singer*

'As a singer in two of their films, *Hum* for Rajinikanth, and a song in *Badi Bahen* (1993), what was obvious about L-P was the largeness of their music—over 10 sitars were used, all played by big names, in "Bada Dukh Deena" from *Ram Lakhan*.

I was called for their recordings with people like Kishore Sharma (who later formed the Mahesh-Kishore duo with Pyarebhai's brother Mahesh Sharma), Surinder Singh, Nirmal, Prakash Narvekar, Surendra Rao, Anil Sawant, Ramakant, Kishore Rathod and others. I have been playing for them since 1974. I would also sing some more for them, purely for the experience of singing with a huge orchestra, knowing that my song would be dubbed later by Amit Kumar or someone else!

And their songs would be difficult. They had gaayaki (singing nuances), so untrained singers would find it tough. And look at their range—they have not only made songs in every genre but made great songs in every genre. Laxmi-ji would often refer to Roshan saab's genius for his way of seamlessly coming back to the mukhda and to the antara, like in "Mehlon Ka Raja Mila" from *Anokhi Raat*, and he similarly adored the work of Madan Mohan, Chitragupta and others. He once sang the C. Ramachandra classic "Yeh Zindagi Ussi Ki Hai" in the styles of Naushad, Madan Mohan and O.P. Nayyar. The gist of what I am trying to say is that Laxmi-ji knew how to break and dissect a song into its components, and create something new. The lyrics in such cases can vary, but the important thing is what you make of such creations. So if L-P adapted a song from somewhere else, the intention was clear: to experiment and make something new that had their stamp but also resembled the original! The intention is to deliver something new, and with gaayaki.

For example, I was there when the mukhda of "Saudagar Sauda Kar" (*Saudagar*) was made. Laxmi-ji hummed out the tune to Pyare-bhai with some of the words, like "*Tu panchhi da da da...*" up to the end of the line and Pyare-bhai just continued with the next few lines. A classic was born!

The most moving thing was Laxmi-ji's confession to me was when he had no work at the end. He told me that when work was not coming, there was no point in living. He said, "*Aur creative aadmi ko to rehna hi nahin chahiye. Bas ho gaya ab* (A creative person should not even remain alive. I have lived enough)."

As for Pyare-bhai, there was limited contact with him, but I have seen his hands just fly over the piano when he was making the music for a song, and spellbound, I would just watch magic happening in front of me!'

22

THEIR RECORDING ENGINEERS

A.N. Tagore, *Recording engineer at Mehboob Studios*

'What was so special about Laxmikant and Pyarelal and L-P as a duo? Well, one important point is that in the hundreds of songs that have been recorded with me at Mehboob Studios, I have never seen Laxmikant ever lose his cool, no matter what. There was never any tension, no tempers, only work.

Also, the USP of their music was that *unhonein Indian music ko kaayam rakhte hue sabse accept karwaaya* (they stuck to Indian music and made it accepted by everyone). So though there was exceptional melody, it was liked by all classes of listeners. And Laxmikant and Pyarelal had an uncannily perfect system of working in harmony. In 30 years, there are three changes of generations and major changes in lifestyles, trends and tastes. And L-P bridged the generation gap by bringing the preferences of three generations of Indians to one common point! This immortal *khazana* is so large that generations to come will enjoy from it, as originals or as remixes! I was intimately connected with the duo from the time that I assisted recording wizard Robin Chaterjee, and have worked extensively with many other stalwarts too. Others had used Western orchestration all down the years, but the symphonic canvas that Pyare-bhai gave a purely Indian tune by way of arrangements was something unique and unmatched.'

D.O. Bhansali, *Legendary recording engineer at Famous Studios, Tardeo*[45]

'I remember how huge temple bells were actually brought into the studio for the live recording of the title song of *Satyam Shivam Sundaram* (1978). That is the reason the bells sounded so genuine! I think Shankar-Jaikishan, Laxmikant-Pyarelal and Madan Mohan have generated an encyclopedia from which today's music directors can do what I call smuggling. And I think that L-P lasted the longest probably because they were the only composers who had no arranger. Pyarelal was the only composer who arranged his own music.'

---

[45] In an interview with the author in 1997.

23

FAMILY PRIEST, FRIEND, FINANCIAL ADVISOR—AND FAN

Vallabh Joglekar, *Personal Assistant to Laxmikant*

'My father Aniruddh was a bhatji (priest) with the family. He performed the Vastu Shanti of Laxmi-ji's bungalow Parasmani in 1971. Though I was a graduate, after him, I too became a priest, but I could not continue for certain reasons, and Laxmi-ji asked me to become his personal assistant.

I hesitated because I felt that most such people in the film line had to tell lies. Laxmi-ji agreed that was needed so that people were not hurt! I said that I will not lie, but Laxmi-ji was free to abuse me and cajole them if someone felt hurt because of me! The commonest reason here was the excuse producers made about paying their dues, and I would tell them in such cases to clear the previous payments first if they wished to work with L-P again.

As I also knew Laxmi-ji's financial status, I told him that after so many years in this line, he needed a second source of income. He asked me what I meant, and then left it to me. At that time, satellite channels had come in and there were barely any editing studios. Laxmi-ji's son Hrishikesh and I started one in the bungalow, and initially we did well, until such studios began to mushroom. We then began to produce serials, but were duped by a partner from Delhi and had to back out.

Very few people are aware that the Indian Performing Rights Society copyright laws also apply to BGM. Payments are made to creators whenever their work is used or performed or re-recorded anywhere. My relationship with Pyarelal ji was good until one man in that organization lied about me and Pyarelal ji unfortunately believed him when he played dirty about his dues—this was long after Laxmi-ji was no more.

I was very close to Laxmi-ji all along, and still conduct *pujas* for his family. There are countless memories. Like on one Diwali day, he had suddenly left the party in his house to record a tune that had occurred to him—he was many pegs down! The next day, astonishingly, he remembered making something and taping it!

Or there was the time when he rushed out of his bath one morning, still wet, took the tumba and recorded a tune that had occurred to him with dummy words—"*Kajri ne kajra daala, dadada dadadada*"! I was an eyewitness to this! The tune went on to become the very popular Alka Yagnik-Vinod Rathod duet "Dil Lene Ki Rut Aayi" from Rajiv Kapoor's *Prem Granth*.

Very few outsiders realized that in his music room there was a picture of Lord Vishnu, and Laxmi-ji's position in that room would be such that he would be opposite that. Lord Krishna and Lord Vishnu were his favourites, and he would keep looking at that picture as he concentrated on making tunes with his fingers on his harmonium!

But the most unforgettable incident I must narrate is about an oldish man coming to meet Laxmi-ji one rainy night. Everyone had gone home, and Laxmi-ji too had just left the music room. The visitor asked in Marathi, "*Laxmi-ji aahet* (Is Laxmi there)? *Mee Dattaram* (I am Dattaram)! I have come from very far. Please call him." Midway from the music room to his house was the *puja* room, and Laxmi-ji was still there, as was his norm while going upstairs, when I gave him the message. Laxmi-ji told me, "Tell him to sit." Five minutes later, Laxmi-ji came and greeted him respectfully, and the man started weeping and hugged him. He told him that he was in a bad financial situation and narrated his problems. Calmly, Laxmi-ji told him, "Come for our recordings from tomorrow. Such things happen in life. Don't worry!" The man left, and the next day, I told Sudhir, Laxmi-ji's assistant, about this. And Sudhir said, "He is Dattaram, a famous man who was also Shankar-Jaikishan's assistant as well as composer. When Laxmi-ji and Pyare-bhai had gone to the senior duo for a chance to play for them, Dattaram had abused both of them and told them to get out!"

And Dattaram played for them for many years. For me, Laxmi-ji epitomized humanity.'

24

LAXMIKANT-PYARELAL: UNIVERSAL L-ONG P-LAY

This was no history book!

Let me explain. Technically, Laxmikant-Pyarelal stopped composing for movies in 1998 when Laxmikant passed away. What Pyarelal alone has done since, and is doing even today, is nothing less than remarkable, and bordering on the spectacular, which we will look at later. But since that is still happening, it cannot be called history.

But then, Laxmikant-Pyarelal are not history in terms of their music either, which is thriving, evergreen, loved and heard all over the world, every single hour: on radio, digital media, reality shows, stage programmes, in temples and even during festivals and celebrations.

Says Mukesh Desai, consultant at T-Series since 1996, the company that took off with the 1985 L-P hit *Pyar Jhukta Nahin*: 'There is not a day or hour when an L-P song is not heard anywhere. I hardly knew Laxmi-ji and Pyare-ji, though they had a long relationship with T-Series, and with Gulshan (Kumar)ji in particular. But to me, L-P represented melody at its musical best, updated to the needs of current times yet worked to the needs of the situations. Laxmikant and Pyarelal will go down in the annals of history as master magicians and the perfect blend of sur and taal.'

A twisted proof of this fact lies in the re-creations of their classics, which are very much 'current coin'—2019 alone saw three of their songs reappearing in a long list (see Appendix).

Another proof, even more remarkable, is the statement made in 2004 (and it is very likely to be the case today as well for obvious reasons) by the then-Indian Performing Rights Society (IPRS) director-general, Sanjay Tandon. On record, he has said that 'L-P were always among the Top Three royalty earners, alongside whichever were the top names of a particular period!'

IPRS royalties are given to the creators and rights holders of recorded music whenever their music is broadcasted or otherwise played, either in original format or reproduced vocally or instrumentally by original or fresh singers, at all public places, workplaces, and live or televised events and shows. It also covers usage in new films, shows and serials. Today, this also extends to the digital domain, like the use of the song 'Ae Phansa' (*Bobby*) during the credit titles of the 2018 ALTBalaji web series *Apharan—Sabka Katega*.

This book is thus the saga of a music duo that lives on, and will live on, as long as Hindi film music does.

And so, let us look at what the 'current coin' names have to say about the longest-ruling and most versatile composers in showbiz. Like Mukesh Desai, not all have been professionally or personally associated with them—and that is the beautiful part.

A.R. Rahman[46]

'"Choli Ke Peeche" from *Khal Nayak* influenced me as the most important anthem of the 1990s, which is the era being shown when "Ringa Ringa" appears in my *Slumdog Millionaire*. That was the reason why I chose not to compose a completely diverse song for this situation and also why I took the same singers—Alka Yagnik and Ila Arun. It was my ode to Laxmikant-Pyarelal, Subhash Ghai and the song's team.'

---

[46]During a post-Oscar interview with the author.

Anu Malik

'I think that it is impossible to discuss all of L-P's music, which is so immense in quality and quantity—but no history of film music can be complete without them. I grew up on the music of Shankar-Jaikishan, and on R.D. Burman's *Teesri Manzil* and *Hare Rama Hare Krishna*, but the music that made me sit up was that of *Bobby*. I think that few songs can surpass "Mujhe Kuch Kehna Hai" or "Hum Tum Ek Kamre Mein Band Ho" in all aspects of a film number. The antara of "Mujhe Kuch Kehna Hai" even influenced R.D. Burman in the antara of "Suno Kaho" in *Aap Ki Kasam*—listen to both songs back-to-back and you will know. Or take the sheer genius of Lata ji singing "Ae Phansa" and the cadences that rise and sway in the interludes. The second interlude, especially, was astounding. And I always wondered how L-P thought of it!

I remember asking Anand Bakshi ji what they were thinking when Lata ji was recording "Suno Sajana" (*Aaye Din Bahaar Ke*), and he simply replied, "Nothing! Only tears were rolling down my cheeks." That's how their songs affected you.

I recall watching Dev Anand's *Jaaneman* as a college student at Mumbai's Chandan cinema and I was blown by the construction of the title song, with its caressing notes and the long mukhda. When the antara returns to the mukhda, we call it a bridge, and making that is sometimes difficult for us composers. But L-P had made a bridge for the mukhda to come back to its own first line! After starting with the cooing notes of "Jaaneman Jaaneman" and going on to soar high with "*Phir bhi yeh naam honton pe na ho / Aisi koi subah nahin shaam nahin*", they effortlessly came back to the soft beginning.

Then there were the undulating notes of the song *Main Aaya Hoon* from *Amir Garib* with its soft prelude that began with Kishore Kumar's soothing words, "Ladies and gentlemen…"—and then came the loud trumpets! L-P just kept surprising me. And who could imagine Kishore Kumar singing a rousing qawwali like "Haal Kya Hai Dilon Ka" for Jeetendra in *Anokhi Ada*? But my friends and I would dance to that song! I came to know later that L-P had arranged for Kalyanji-Anandji's *Jab Jab Phool Khile* and for R.D. Burman's *Chhote Nawab* and *Bhoot Bangla*. They had seen it all, done it all, done so much for so many composers. And the variety was incredible.

I would go to see their recordings at Mehboob Recording Studios. I remember that they were recording a song for Raj Kapoor once, and midway, Manoj Kumar arrived and went up to meet them. Shortly, he left and Manmohan Desai came and went up! It was incredible how their work satisfied everyone and how they created completely different numbers even while one song was being recorded. Can you imagine anything as diverse as *Prem Rog*, *Kranti* and *Coolie*? At any one time, they would be making songs for Amitabh Bachchan, Jeetendra, Rishi Kapoor and so many diverse actors, scoring hits with all.

Both of them would justifiably take so much pride in their work. I recall the recording of *Hero* with 100 musicians, including the cream like Pt Shivkumar Sharma, Pt Hariprasad Chaurasia, Charanjit Singh and Pyare-bhai's brother Gorakh. Pyare-bhai stood conducting in the centre, and I saw the sheer pleasure on his face when the recording was over and there was resounding applause.

When I did my first film, I told my arranger, Naresh Sharma, who is Pyare-bhai's brother, that I would love to get a Pyare-bhai-like sound. And he told me that was impossible, but that he would try his best. No composer can deny what L-P have taught us through their work. We have to keep hearing such greats and then add our own creativity.

The level of orchestration also went up with them. Today there is so much attention on sound and production, but it all started with L-P. They picked it up from where Shankar-Jaikishan had left, observed them, and Pyare-bhai refined the balancing—look at the way the violin plays to echo the falling curtain in "Dard-E-Dil" (*Karz*). Pyare-bhai is not a normal human being—he is a GENIUS, in capital letters, and a world-class composer. He is at that level.

And what do I say about the ever-sweet Laxmi-ji? I listen to their songs from *Anita*, like "Gore Gore Chand Se Mukh Par", and I go mad. Whatever mukhda he made, the antaras were even more solid. Laxmi-ji would love to make everyone present listen to his tunes at the studio, singing with paan in his mouth! I recall him singing "Yeh Galiyan Yeh Chaubara" (*Prem Rog*) this way at Mehboob (Studios).

Led by Rajesh Roshan and Shiv-Hari, so many musicians who played for them later became music composers while L-P were still around. They even loved to encourage the musicians who worked with them.

My first major film *Poonam* was made by Harmesh Malhotra, who had always worked with them. When Manmohan Desai signed me for *Mard*, I went one morning to Laxmi-ji's house to seek his blessings. He was jogging at home and said, "Anu, mera aashirwad hai. Zabardast kaam karna. Tumko maloom hai na humne kaisa kaam kiya hai Manji ke liye? (My blessings are with you. Do a terrific job. You know the level of music we have given in Manmohan Desai's films?)" And I told him honestly, "Sir, you are scaring me!"

Laxmi-ji had loved my song "To Chalun" from *Border* and had told his daughter Rajeshwari: "How did I not think of such notes?" Later, Rajeshwari told me something that touched me deeply: that when he was ill in his last days, he would sing "To Chalun" (Can I take your leave?) to his wife Jaya ji and to her. We will never get such people again.

When I lost two Best Music awards for *Border*, he called up specially and asked if people were jealous of me or had lost their sense of music. I told him that his words were my biggest award. And again, *Border* was my first film with J.P. Dutta saab, who had only worked with them earlier, that too in five films. And the final incredible part is that Laxmi-ji and I share our birthday—both of us are born on 2 November!'

Ayushmann Khurrana

'Laxmikant-Pyarelal are legends. They started very young and I have been their huge fan as a singer and composer. When I signed *Dreamgirl*, I remembered their benchmark song "Kisi Shaayar ki Ghazal Dream Girl", one of their many classics that I love, from their film that was also titled *Dream Girl*.'

Himesh Reshammiya

'The prime standout quality in their songs was their unique, larger-than-life sound—the 70mm feel and grandeur. But that was also accompanied by their intense melodies. Laxmikant-Pyarelal understood completely the vision of the director. Take Subhash Ghai, Manoj Kumar...their films cannot be imagined without L-P, and without those songs, the films won't even be iconic. Shanker Jaikishan and L-P are unequalled in music. There are few music directors whose songs are liked by rural people and also have an urban appeal. L-P transcended all such barriers, and their universal appeal lasted for over 30 years. The most vital element for a composer out here is versatility, and objectively speaking, no one could outclass L-P in this regard. L-P took versatility to another level. There is no kind of film that they have not done, no genre of song that they have not touched with their highly individualized melody that remains a great inspiration for me. They were never typecast as music directors who could do only a specific kind of film.

They ruled the industry for so long because they changed with the times. They were a complete combination and always got their due, for every song was like an announcement of their supremacy! Their intro pieces could never be ignored, and for me, that strangely showed a leadership quality.

It was my prediction many years ago that though L-P had been sidelined for a few years after Laxmi-ji passed away, they are going to make a comeback even in the remix era. And the fact that they are leading in re-creations today proves that their melodies are timeless. The process has begun for the world to realize that L-P's music is as fresh and young as today!

I have always said that *main Laxmikant-Pyarelal ki roti khaata hoon* (I earn because of their music)! And I mean that. They are my source of inspiration and somewhere, my songs do try for that wholesome Indian flavour.

Also, on a personal level, my musician father Vipin Reshammiya, played for about 30 years for them. And Laxmi-Pyare were a big support for him all along.'

Karan Johar

'The first memory I have of L-P's music is when I accompanied my father (producer Yash Johar) as a kid to the shoot of *Dostana* (1980). Their duet "Dillagi Ne Di Hawaa" was being shot and I remember asking my father how Zeenat Aman's playback voice seemed to be like a man's. He explained that the song had been recorded by Kishore Kumar for Amitabh Bachchan, but Zeenat's lines had been dubbed by his composer Laxmikant. This was because her voice, Asha Bhosle, had not been available on the day of the recording and the song's shoot had been already fixed!

Later, of course, I was introduced to Laxmikant-Pyarelal, and attended many recordings for the three films they did for my father. *Dostana*, *Agneepath*, which released a decade later, and finally, *Gumrah*. And *Dostana* set our Dharma Productions banner rolling.

As a young man, I was amazed at the way they worked, and by Pyarelal's mastery over the orchestration. My father's friendship with them grew and soon, Laxmi-ji's son Hrishikesh and I became friends as our families would even go out of town together. Dad always had a great friendship with Laxmi-ji, but he got a bit upset when dad signed R.D. Burman after *Dostana* for our next film *Duniya*, because of the film's director Ramesh Talwar. Later, Bappi Lahiri came in as Prakash Mehra directed *Muqaddar Ka Faisla*. My father explained to Laxmi-ji that he gave full freedom to his directors to choose their teams. And so, when Mukul S. Anand wanted L-P for our *Agneepath*, they were back!

I personally loved the music of R.D. Burman as it resonated more with me, but I could understand why L-P's music had an edge over his: they were completely Indian in their approach and their songs connected with everyone as they had the aroma of our soil. And I adore so many L-P songs and have also used some in a medley in *Student of the Year*.

The biggest secret I would like to share here is that their mega-hit "Jumma Chumma De De" from *Hum* was originally composed to be a part of our *Agneepath* score! However, due to some reasons, our director Mukul S. Anand and my father decided not to use the song, and it went into *Hum*, Mukul's other film with Amitabh Bachchan.'

Neil Nitin Mukesh

'I was about six years old when I accompanied my dad (singer Nitin Mukesh) to Laxmi-ji's house for the sitting of the song "So Gaya Yeh Jahaan" from *Tezaab*. And yet, I remember the song and the meeting clearly. I remember a fair man, speaking and singing with a paan inside his mouth, always smiling and treating both my father and me with affection.

Equally graphically, I remember being at the recording of the same song, and Papa told me later that at the last moment, Pyare-ji had halted the recording midway because he had a fresh idea for an additional music interlude, which he composed there and then and recorded! When I watched the film, Papa showed me that part, and I realized how well that new music piece he had thought of fitted the mood and backdrop of the song that was filmed at night on the rain-soaked streets of Mumbai! I learnt that L-P would dramatize their compositions to make them unpredictable.

And "So Gaya Yeh Jahaan" was the song that instantly came to mind when I was producing my film *Bypass Road*. We got the re-created song ready and then decided to approach Papa to sing a part of his portion again. He very sportingly agreed, as the song is one of his top favourites!

Another distinct personal memory I have is of quietly playing the piano in a hotel lobby abroad one morning, during a concert tour in which we had accompanied L-P. I was in my teens then, loved to play the instrument, but would be scared in case someone came up and scolded me. Pyare uncle saw me and heard what I was playing. For almost an hour, we were sitting together there, and he was teaching me the importance of how chords are supposed to be played. I always go back to that memory, which was like a quick but comprehensive tutorial.

Their affection for Papa (Nitin Mukesh) drew me closer to them. Among the hundreds of their musical scores that I love, the *Karz* theme and my grandfather Mukesh ji's "Ek Pyar Ka Naghma Hai" (*Shor*) are my greatest favourites. They resonate so much with even today's youngsters.

With all the technology today, we still can't create the magic they did. We even over-compose! But L-P's melody remains supreme.'

Pankuj Parashar

'I was friends with (actor-filmmaker) Manoj Kumar's brother Rajeev Goswami, and that's how I first saw and met L-P when I would go to Manoj Kumar's house for their discussions and sittings. You can even say that a lot of the music of *Shor* and *Roti Kapada Aur Makaan* took birth in front of my eyes!

As a film director and ad filmmaker, I had a great equation

with composers Anand-Milind, and I remember we were all on a massive L-P trip then. If you hear the music of my first film, *Ab Aayega Mazaa*, in which Anand-Milind composed the popular "Raja Tere Raste Se Hat Jaaongi", you will understand what I mean!

The chance to work with L-P came with *Chaalbaaz*, which was produced by A. Purnachandra Rao, who had always worked with them. And there are interesting memories of that film.

Remo Fernandes, the pop singer from Goa, is a good friend of mine. I had loved a song he made, and I told Laxmi-ji that I wanted to use it. He said, "Okay, leave this tape with me and come tomorrow." The next day, he had done something incredible. He had dissected the song, changed it and the result was a song that still resembled Remo's tune and yet was 100 per cent Laxmikant-Pyarelal.

The song was "Tera Beemar Mera Dil".

For the next song, "Na Jaane Kahan Se Aayi Hai", also part-inspired by "Part-Time Lover", I told Laxmi-ji that I wanted a distinct and different sound. I made him hear what I had in mind and he told me that I better talk to Pyare-bhai. Rather hesitantly, I did, and Pyare-bhai called me that evening.

It was a meeting I will never forget, for it went on till 4 in the morning. He had acquired a Korg M1 keyboard that cost ₹1.25 lakh in the late 1980s! We ended up with him playing the chords with his left hand while I, as I knew some music, was doing the rhythm with my right hand!

When I called up Laxmi-ji the next morning, he told me, "You sit and make music with Pyare-bhai for a few nights. He is impressed and no one has ever made music in his house after Raj Kapoor!" We spent five nights and Pyare-bhai was a treasury of anecdotes of their career, including a day when Rafi saab was not getting a song from *Dosti* right and they were so disturbed that both of them did not eat dinner!

On the day of the recording, Pyare-bhai told me, "You go to Mehboob in the morning. For three hours, I am setting you loose there! Make whatever music you know."

By that time, I had bought a Passport Trax, the first Midi software connected to a keyboard, and had read magazines and knew a bit about programming. At 2.30, Pyare-bhai reached, he fixed everything within 15 minutes, telling the musicians what was good in what I had done and what was bakwaas (rubbish)! When Laxmi-ji arrived, he loved the new sound.

People tell me that the two films on which I worked with them, *Rajkumar* (1996) being the other one, are very different in sound, and probably that was because of my interest in music and electronic gadgets.

I must admit that the ideas for all the inspirations that I made them do came from me! "Payal Meri" from *Rajkumar*, which was adapted from a George Michael song, was another example, and obviously Laxmi-ji made changes to that as well, stating that Pyare-bhai "will throw you out if he comes to know what you have done!"

Its dummy words were written by Nitin Raikwar, who was a struggler then, and Laxmi-ji told me to keep the mukhda and take it to Bakshi saab, who, he said, will "throw you out if you tell him who has written it!" And so Bakshi saab wrote the song to the mukhda.

All in all, I think L-P were way ahead of Shankar-Jaikishan. *Kuch bhi kar sakte the!* (They could do anything!)'

Pritam[47]

'When I was a student of Sound Engineering in the Film & Television Institute of India, we were exposed only to some visiting foreign musicians and to the music of R.D. Burman, whom we all considered the best. When I came to Mumbai, started working on ad films and serials and reading film publications like *Screen*,

---

[47] As told to the author in 2003 and 2019.

I realized that film music had much more to it, and there were many equally significant or even bigger composers in terms of contributions. Among these many other names were Laxmikant-Pyarelal. As someone who has always approached even Indian music with a Western approach, and for whom classical mainly meant Western classical, I realized that L-P even approached Western music in an Indian manner! Their expertise in folk also really went very deep. So, it took some time for me to like that style. And yet what really attracted me to their songs was their utter simplicity. And of course, their huge variety, which was inspiring. The music of people like Laxmikant-Pyarelal and Kalyanji-Anandji was rich yet simple, and therefore easy to understand.'

Ranveer Singh[48]

'I was assisting Shaad Ali in those days. One day in 2006, I received a call from him, asking me to board a flight to Paris immediately as he was giving me a chance to face the camera. He was doing a Hindi song in Paris for the city festival. It was a special number composed by Pyarelal sir and sung by Sonu Nigam and Shreya Ghoshal. The video should be lying somewhere at YRF Studios. But you are telling me that this sofa I am sitting on used to be the very one on which Laxmikant-sir would sit? No wonder I am speaking so well today! I have grown up on their music.'

(Ranveer's wife Deepika Padukone, a close relative of Pyarelal, made her debut in *Om Shanti Om* in 2007, in which the song 'Dhoom Tana' had been arranged by him.)

---

[48]During an interview held at Mehboob Studios' erstwhile recording room.

Sanjay Leela Bhansali

'I have always been a huge fan of Laxmikant-Pyarelal. My first choice for *Hum Dil De Chuke Sanam* had been Laxmikant-Pyarelal, but the film was launched in 1998, when Laxmikant passed away. This was my second musical misadventure—I had wanted R.D. Burman for *Khamoshi—The Musical*, but he too was not around by the time that film was launched.'

Shaad Ali

According to a reliable source within Yash Raj Films, Ali's one-line brief to his composers Shankar-Ehsaan-Loy for the music of his Bunty Aur Babli (2005) was 'I want Laxmikant-Pyarelal in Benares!' The filmmaker admitted that he wanted the deeply folk-based melody for which L-P were always known.

'I have always been a huge fan of L-P's music, and they had straddled both the black-and-white and color eras, coming on right up to the 1990s. They have left an endless treasury of songs and sound behind.

I had the extraordinary fortune of working with Pyare-bhai on a song written by Gulzar saab and sung by Shreya Ghoshal with Sonu Nigam. We presented this song in Paris, and had spent two months on it: it took 15 to 20 days for the genius to mix it. He used a 150-piece orchestra. The song was presented on stage by Ranveer Singh—it was his debut of sorts years before his first film, and a French actress. I will cherish this experience forever.'

Shreya Ghoshal

'My first song for Pyare uncle was for the album *Pascal of Bollywood*, which I sang with Pascal Heni. It was an Indian, modern version of the French "La Vie En Rose". The album was arranged by Pyare uncle, who also taught me the musical part of the song. That's the first time I actually met him. Then I did a song for his album with Magnasound.

This song was recorded but never released—but what an amazing experience it was, where I realized what Pyare uncle really is! I would take a Walkman then with me to recordings for rehearsals, and it was the first time that a 90-minute cassette tape proved too short for the number of variations he gave me to sing, and all the new ideas he taught me. That's where you feel the magic of a legendary composer—that sincerity and the understanding of every line, the beauty of the Indian element in the unique tune, the harkatein, the weight on every word.

I rehearsed that song in Pyare uncle's home with a few musicians. I could sense the deep gratitude and respect of these loyal musicians, which account for almost half of those who are playing today, who owed their livelihoods and careers to Laxmi-ji and Pyare-ji.

Pyare uncle is very down-to-earth. His home is so humble. Having said that, I feel that a blessing like both of them must be a part of every singer's career and I feel so lucky to be a part of his music. His teaching me the song was itself like an entire course in playback singing! I have never met Laxmi-ji, but I think every singer should go at least once through this university of learning. I wish I could have worked with them, because I feel this song is one of the highlights of my entire career.

I always think how wonderfully Lata ji had sung individual words in their songs, and that makes you realize and understand what L-P were, because Lata ji's singing is so different in L-P's songs. For Lata ji's voice, these two were blessings: they were the game-changing composers for her! In turn, the Lata-L-P combination is a blessing to all music lovers.

I have been always exposed to the best of L-P. For me, one of the most important songs in my life is "Jeevan Dor Tumhi Sang Bandhi" (*Sati Savitri*) because that was the song that got me my first film, *Devdas*, in 2002! For my audition, Sanjay (Leela

Bhansali) sir had asked me to sing any Lata song, and I sang it. By chance, he had been singing the same song to himself that day! That coincidence clinched me my debut film.

But I do not take "Jeevan Dor Tumhi Sang Bandhi" as a typical L-P song. They made many songs to make a statement, for ruling the charts, but some were very personal, like "Jeevan Dor Tumhi Sang Bandhi". As a singer, I feel that the reason we find their songs completely different is because they took an extremely important stand on the sound of the words.

Today, there are many songs in which a singer finds herself getting stuck on some words because of their flow, but in their songs, you will always find that they gave the right kind of words for the singer to have a trouble-free enunciation. That, I think, was the key magic in their songs. They were a singer's dream composers, because so many singers have done their best work with them.

Their songs had a great blend of folk and classical, and that is why people could relate to them so much and they connected with most of India. The *mitti ki khushboo* (fragrance of the soil) was very evident. Most of their songs are so easily understood by the masses, and a lot of music directors tried to pick this quality up. I think that among today's composers there is a R.D. Burman school and an L-P school. The R.D. school of music is very influenced by the West, while the L-P school is completely rooted in India, in the Indian style of phrasing.

There are so many L-P songs I sing frequently, to myself, or on stage, like "Jaane Kyoon Log Mohabbat" (*Mehboob Ki Mehndi*), "Ankhiyon Ko Rehne De" (*Bobby*) and "Main Tere Ishq Mein" (*Loafer*), and when I sing them, I often can't control myself and start crying. When this happened once on the television show *Indian Idol*, everyone asked me why I was crying, and I said I could not pinpoint why. There is something about these songs that has this effect.

L-P have always been my mother's favourite composers and

she makes me sing "Jaane Kyoon Log Mohabbat" again and again! The art that both of them have created is timeless, and should be beyond politics! At the same time, they have done songs that were not really in their nature, like most of the songs of *Karz*. Here again, a favourite is Lata ji's "Aa Jaan-E-Jaan" (*Intaqam*)—as a composition, and for its arrangements, like the big brass section—I think they were the only composers who brought brass sections like that into film music.

When I select older songs to sing at concerts, I end up picking more of L-P's songs than anyone else's, because they are not just great and popular songs but they offer so many opportunities even for the musicians to shine. Their music is a supermarket, a joyride. When you listen to a L-P song, you listen to an entire package of emotions and entertainment.

I have heard tales of their friendship with Kalyanji-Anandji and the two Burmans, and the way they would meet and spend time together. They would make each other listen to their songs and complete the antaras of each other's compositions. That only means they were all very secure as composers! Can you imagine that happening today?'

Sivamani

'Whenever I play as a percussionist for today's composers, I compose the music pieces after seeing what the story needs, and asking for a rough feel of what they want. Then I create what comes spontaneously. But older music directors like Ilaiyaraaja, Laxmikant-Pyarelal and R.D. Burman would generally tell me what they wanted by playing it and I would add my own nuances and modulations. Working with them was like being under a huge banyan tree. Every master had his own style. There was so much to learn, brother.'[49]

---

[49]During a *Screen* interview with the author.

Sohail Sen

'They were probably the composers to whom all the musicians were very close—naturally, it was mutual affection. Pyare-ji would have a 100-piece orchestra, often calling for his favourite musicians, like my father Sameer Sen and so many others! He loved being in the comfort zone of his favourites, so that if someone was needed, he would be available immediately!

As a composer-to-be, these and other stories were told to me by my father as I was growing up. The bottom-line were his words: "If you want to do film music, listen to the songs of Laxmikant-Pyarelal. Only then will you know what film music is. You will know the kind of music that comes across as big inside a movie theatre, on the big screen."

In this era of electronics and digital music, it has thus always been my effort to keep at least a little bit of acoustics, like the violin section in the songs of my first film, *What's Your Raashee?* When I moved to *Khelein Hum Jee Jaan Sey*, I even used a live orchestra.

In *Gunday* (2014), if you listen to "Tune Maari Entriyaan", you will again get that L-P-like vibe. For the qawwali, "Mann Kunto Maula", which I recorded at Yash Raj Studios, my father was a part of setting the orchestra. When producer Aditya Chopra listened to the recorded song, he loved the sound, and asked me who was responsible. When I told him it was my father, he said, "I knew it! Today, both of you have brought the sound of Mehboob into Yash Raj Studios!"

Adi-sir has always been a huge fan of Laxmikant-Pyarelal's music, and what he meant by the "sound of Mehboob Studios" was obviously L-P's sound!

A few weeks back, my father told me that I had to perform at a live Laxmikant-Pyarelal show, where he too would be playing. Pyare-ji wanted me as he loves to encourage new talent and I had sung "Bala" for *Housefull 4* that had become a rage. For 10 days since that news, I was so nervous I could not sleep properly! I wanted to give my 100 per cent as I had to sing all the three popular Kishore Kumar songs from *Karz*: "Om Shanti Om", "Paise Yeh Paisa" and "Ek Hasina Thi". As a score, it is also among my personal favourites, as I grew up on that music.

We had rehearsals, and "Paisa Yeh Paisa" proved very tricky with its musical pattern and the male and female chorus overlapping the vocals. Also, whenever I perform on stage, there are seven or eight musicians, but here there was a live 50-piece orchestra! Afterwards, Pyare-ji hugged me and said that I was the highlight of the evening, and Laxmi-ji's daughter, Rajeshwari ji, was also in the audience and came up and congratulated me. The experience was surreal!'

Sonu Nigam[50]

'Mentioning the fabulous Pancham has become like a fashion statement today, while Pyare-bhai, as the surviving half of Laxmikant-Pyarelal, is so preoccupied with music that publicity means nothing to him. But L-P in fact had a decisive edge over Pancham—he was always second to L-P. From Raj Kapoor and V. Shantaram to Manoj Kumar and Subhash Ghai, the best filmmakers always went to L-P.

I made my debut with a song for a television serial composed by Usha Khanna and her arranger, Amar Haldipur, and they both coaxed me to meet L-P. "If you get to record for them, it will be like the ISI (Indian Standards Institution) mark on you and other music directors will accept you!" they said. I finally sang in a few films for L-P, and my big hit was "Hungama Ho Gaya" from *Deewana Mastana*.

Laxmi-ji's unique style of teaching a song stemmed from his classical orientation. Each antara would be differently structured

---

[50] As told to the author on Laxmikant's tenth death anniversary.

and the various subtle harkatein and murkiyaan would be tough to handle. As for Pyare-bhai, the musicians would be in awe of him. He would watch a movie and just write the background score on a paper pad!'

Sujoy Ghosh

'When I was growing up, I was exposed to the music of everyone—from Salil Chowdhury, Khayyam and Shankar-Jaikishan to Kalyanji-Anandji, R.D. Burman and, of course, Laxmikant-Pyarelal. So I had no particular favourite when I started listening to all the music directors.

I slowly veered towards R.D. Burman as my favourite, but I was equally fascinated by the music of Laxmikant-Pyarelal. Almost all the Jeetendra movies had their music, whether it was *Pyaasa Sawan*, *Judaai*, *Nishana* and so on. And they had started using Kishore Kumar for him, especially in the South-made films.

My turning-point was the day I heard a song on radio that I was absolutely sure it was R.D. Burman's—"Paisa Yeh Paisa" from *Karz*! But L-P were like that—they have an incredible portfolio.

There was some incredible interlude music in *Satyam Shivam Sundaram* and *Sargam* among others. *Shor* was such an amazing album, as also *Roti Kapada Aur Makaan* and *Bobby*. In melody lay L-P's strength, and that is why they were always more popular. And though I am a staunch Pancham fan, I dare say that L-P were probably that much more talented than him.'

Vishal Bhardwaj[51]

'I think it was L-P who began the practice of having prelude and interlude music that was remembered and became almost

---

[51]During an interview in 1996.

as popular as the song itself, though Shankar-Jaikishan had done it off and on before them!'

Wajid Khan (of Sajid-Wajid)

'The best of the best music directors have ruled for 10 to 15 years—but Laxmikant-Pyarelal ruled for 30! They were *chaumukha* (versatile) composers, capable of everything. They had their own identity and yet adapted to new things. Just when you thought they were becoming "typical" or stuck in a groove, they would come up with a score that would surprise, shock and shake. So many new composers came after them, but they still outclassed the others with their sheer body of work.

My father, table ace Ustad Sharafat Ali Khan, who played a lot for them, would often tell me to listen to a lot of old music as all those composers were very big teachers. In the 1970s, R.D. Burman came in like a cyclone, but L-P were still at the top, because they blended the commercial with the classic, the *raags*, taal and folk, so well. We can learn so much from them.

Theirs was larger-than-life music, which was an extraordinary mix of composition, lyrics, melody and rhythm, with layers that were very rare. During their reign, if you asked the question: "What is 70mm sound?", the answer would be: "L-P's music is 70mm sound!"

They would put their songs as the soul into the beautiful body—the film—to which the director gave birth! When I hear "Saanjh Dhale" from *Utsav*, or "Meri Qismat Mein Tu" from *Prem Rog*, I get goosebumps. And that was their biggest strength: Hindustani music was in their DNA, *ussi se unnki pehchan bani* (that became their identity), because their music caught the Indian pulse—it had mass-appeal, but with a classic touch.'

EPILOGUE

A full 22 years after Laxmikant passed away, Pyarelal continues to be immersed in music. Publicity about his activities means zilch to him. To repeat an old cliché, Laxmikant may be no more, but Pyarelal is no less.

In that sense, Pyarelal is, perhaps, the only surviving half of any Indian duo who has continued to contribute significantly to music—even internationally and at such a level—after his partner passed away. The heartening part is that he always feels and expresses (and what else is Pyarelal but solid expression) that it were as if Laxmikant is by his side even today.

In the first few years after Laxmikant's death, Pyarelal retired into a shell, though some big-name directors who had worked with the duo, including the late Yash Chopra and Mahesh Bhatt, had promised to work with him. The composer was going through some minor but disturbing health issues as well.

'We had lost ground after 1995 when Laxmi was still alive, and till about 2003 or so, I faced hard times emotionally and there were some problems with my knees,' admitted Pyarelal.

That was the time Pyarelal recorded over 40 songs for different albums that never came out due to reasons other than the musical content: one with Shreya Ghoshal for Magnasound, one with Adnan Sami, another album with multiple artistes and so on.

'But for me, every day was about waking up in the morning and working on music after my bath and prayers,' he went on. The values imbibed from his late and iconic father, Pt Ramprasad Sharma, ensured that the veteran reverentially touches the piano before hitting the first notes of the day. The maestro also has a roomful of books on all aspects and types of music that he frequently refers to for technical aspects of his work.

Among the earliest work Pyarelal did alone was the title song and theme music (billed as Pyarelal Ramparasad Sharma) for the television serial *Aryamaan—Brahmaand Ka Yodha* featuring Mukesh Khanna, who also produced this show in 2002. The duo had, incidentally, composed music for Mukesh's brother Ved Khanna's 1982 production *Insaan*.

Khanna had asked Pyarelal to compose a theme for the opening credits. In those days, ₹30,000 was paid for composing a theme on TV, but Khanna was so impressed with the result that he paid Pyarelal 10 times that figure! And so, it was clear that even through the disturbed times, his magnificent talent was intact.

Then finally began what the legend describes as a 'new chapter in my life.'

The composer, considered India's finest violinist, made his first unique experiment when he recorded three songs (with only a basic rhythm and percussion) with popular playback singers singing the chorus and instrumental portions of some famous L-P songs, while a fresh chorus sang the vocal portions!

His eyes were alight with the pure joy of an innovative creator as he told me, 'For "Ek Pyar Ka Naghma Hai" from *Shor*, I have also used choir voices as the strings section. I wanted to make an album of eight such numbers. Lata ji and Amit ji (Amitabh Bachchan) heard these songs and asked me how I could conceive something that had never been done before anywhere, but I am always thinking of how to come up with something new!'

In 2004 in Paris, Pyarelal had arranged an album of Indian film hits for leading French artiste Pascal Heni, called *Pascal of Bollywood*. The songs were neither restricted to Laxmikant-Pyarelal songs nor to Hindi films alone. The album began with the title song of Shankar-Jaikishan's *An Evening in Paris*. Heni, a diehard fan of Indian music, performed on all songs, some of which featured co-singers like Sadhana Sargam, Poornima, Jaspinder Narula, Shreya Ghoshal and Smriti Minocha. The last three, incidentally, had never worked under L-P!

In 2004 also, Pyarelal visited the Bharatiya Vidya Bhavan's London branch on invitation from its chief, John Moore, who wanted him to write eight lines of music. The composer wrote in Indian, Japanese, Malaysian and Arabic styles as well as Western music, and Moore had asked him, 'How did you write all this? This is real World Music!' Pyarelal's only reply was, 'If you don't like it, I will write something else!'

But the real answer to this feat lay in their film career, says Pyarelal, 'Shankar-Jaikishan were our main teachers and idols. But we picked up so much from studying the music of giant pioneers like Pt Dhaniram, Khemchand Prakash, Bulo C. Rani, O.P. Nayyar, Naushad, S.D. Burman and many others.'

In 2003, a British violinist named Candida had also visited Pyarelal and persuaded him to visit England's Trinity College of Music. From 2004 to 2007, Pyarelal had spent some months there every year, working and teaching (even the professors) at the Trinity College of Music in London, and associating with the London Philharmonic. 'But I also learnt from the musicians and students there!' stressed Pyarelal.

It was here that, when Pyarelal informed managing director David Welton (who had told him that 'Your music is like pure gold!') that Laxmikant and he had done the songs and BGM of 500 films, he told the composer in awe, 'Then you must be at least 300 years old!'

Pyarelal also taught the British musicians to play his music. 'The London Philharmonic Orchestra got used to playing Western classical music with an Indian folk music touch and pan-Asian influences. I introduced new drums and wrote to a 2-4 beat, when they were used to playing on the 5-4 beat. I also taught them to stop moving from side to side while playing!' smiled the composer.

'In 2007, I wrote a Quartet—a music piece to be played by four musicians—with demanding requirements in its writing,' he went on. 'It was published by German publishers Schott as *Indian*

Summer, but when it arrived in India, it was largely ignored by Furtado, Mumbai's music shop.'

However, the Symphony Orchestra of India (SOI), for whose previous avatar, the Bombay Symphonic Orchestra (BSO), Pyarelal had played as a teenager, presented the String Quartet in November 2014 at Mumbai's Prithvi Theatre. This was a venue built by Shashi Kapoor, with whom L-P had a long association as well. 'When the works of greats like Mozart and Beethoven were played alongside my work, I was speechless!' said the maestro proudly.

As of 2021, the 52-page score of *Indian Summer* is still available online for as low a sum as $29! And here is an excerpt from its online PR material, indicating how the world viewed Pyarelal and his work:

> For the first time, The Schott String Quartet Series features a collection of pieces that have been originally composed in a style unique to string quartet arrangements. Internationally-acclaimed Bollywood composer Pyarelal Sharma has provided music and songs for over 450 films. This set of string quartets, composed especially for Schott, is influenced by Indian film music, Indian folk, Arabic and light Indian classical music, thus combining the alluring sound of the East with the stability of a classic Western ensemble. Another new feature that this volume has brought to the series is a special bonus CD containing performances of these charming pieces by leading members of the London Philharmonic Orchestra.
> …The pieces are suitable for amateur musicians or school students and are ideal for public performance.

On 27 October 2007, Pyarelal also performed at the Royal Festival Hall with musicians from the Royal Philharmonia Orchestra and held several workshops too. In the same year, the Birmingham Quartet performed his music as well. Pyarelal shrugged when asked why such achievements had been kept under wraps back home. 'I only speak about them to anyone who asks me,' he replied.

And speaking of 2007, the music of Shah Rukh Khan's home production *Om Shanti Om* was released around the same time. Director Farah Khan and music directors Vishal-Shekhar approached Pyarelal to arrange their composition 'Dhoom Tana', which was to be filmed in retro fashion.

The request for a feel of the 1970s, one of the two decades L-P had fully ruled, and the promise to have a live and acoustic sound, led to the composer accepting the assignment. And while the tune was already made, Pyarelal obviously tweaked it as well to suit L-P's distinct style and sound.

The film, incidentally, was inspired by L-P's *Karz*, with its title derived from their chartbuster in the 1980 film. It also began with a good chunk of the original film's footage and even featured Pyarelal in the end-video credits.

A year earlier, Kumar Sanu had persuaded Pyarelal to arrange his own compositions in his debut production *Utthaan*. Among the singers, was again someone with whom L-P had never worked: Hemaa Sardesai.

In the same year, 2006, director Shaad Ali recorded a 10-minute song penned by Gulzar and sung by Sonu Nigam and Shreya Ghoshal for a Paris Festival. The song was staged live by Ranveer Singh and a French actress in a performance directed by Ali. The concert had other songs of Laxmikant-Pyarelal performed live as well. Singh made his film debut four years later!

For many years, the maestro also had a dream of decades—to compose a symphony—which was realized in 2008. It was Lata Mangeshkar, said the composer, who had first inspired him to fulfil his dream by asking him once why he had never thought of composing a symphony.

'Composing a symphony is not easy at all,' stated the composer. Associates watching Pyarelal direct the live symphony later (the videos are available online) were moved to tears when the musicians there, led by the conductor, touched Pyarelal's feet when it concluded. It was, indeed, an unforgettable moment for Indian music and an Indian musician.

About creating the symphony, Pyarelal elaborated, 'A symphony can only be visualized in the mind. What can be played is the melody. For 11 months, every single day from 11 to 2:30 in the day and 5 to 8 in the evening, I worked on it.'

Pyarelal's magnificently comprehensive knowledge of the various components of music helped him. 'In a symphony, you have strings, comprising violin, viola, cello, etc.,' he rattled off. 'Woodwinds include piccolo, oboe, flute, tenor flute, bass flute, English horn, clarinet, E-flat clarinet, bassoon and others, and in brass, there is piccolo trumpet, tenor piccolo trumpet, horn trombone, bass trombone, tuba, bass tuba and more. Then there is percussion with many drums like tympany, bass drum, castanet, tambourine and others.'

In 2008, Pyarelal flew to Los Angeles to register his symphony on 16 March. The certificate has a place of pride in his living room, for any symphony is approved only after stringent evaluation in a series of steps that take months. 'The symphony will remain in their museum,' exulted the composer with due pride.

Titled *Om Shivam in A-Minor*, it has elements from film music too, the composer noted. Pyarelal has also incorporated Indian classical elements, including the dadra and keherwa taals, and has two simultaneous beats playing in it. 'Indian classical music is unequalled, though Western classical music is almost mathematically precise,' he explained with a smile.

'An official letter about my first symphony tells me, "Your music is pure." Because a key requirement for any symphony is that nothing in it should sound like any existing piece of music,' the composer told me. He added that his Symphony was also performed by the SOI at Prithvi Theatre on the day *Indian Summer* was presented there.

On 15 March 2012 in Dubai, Pyarelal conceived another unique experiment in front of a 5000-strong live audience including world musicians. Indian and Western musicians joined forces for a

World Music performance called *Absolute India* composed and arranged by Pyarelal and conducted by Kristjan Jarvi, Permanent Guest Conductor of the London Philharmonic Orchestra. 'It was in a 12-tone scale of original music that can eventually form the language of a new harmonious amalgam of Indian and Western music,' Pyarelal stated.

'We also called it *Beyond Bollywood* and had over 20 artistes and musicians from the US and other countries and 22 Indian greats including Dr L. Subramaniam, Pt Shivkumar Sharma, Pt Hariprasad Chaurasia and Zakir Husain,' said the composer. 'I wrote music pieces for each of the Indian and Western specialists—those who played the violin, oboe, flute and so on. I also told some of the greats that they should perform their own music solo as well, so that they should not feel that I am intruding into their creative space.'

Pyarelal had the idea of Indian as well as Western musicians playing together on what is composed, written and conducted. Kavita Krishnamurthi Subramaniam, Amit Kumar, Sonu Nigam and others sang 10 of their hit songs as well. Composer Jatin Pandit of Jatin-Lalit insisted on singing L-P's 'Tere Pyar Ne Mujhe Gham Diya', originally sung by Mohammed Rafi in *Chhaila Babu* (1967).

Of course, back home for years now, Pyarelal has not only held regular music workshops in Mumbai, Pune and Indore, but is also busy doing at least two Laxmikant-Pyarelal concerts, which he personally conducts, every year. Their music continues to grow and attain higher immortal levels with the passage of time. A fan group on Facebook has among the highest number of fans for such groups on composers, and for Pyarelal, the sky is obviously not the limit.

As he concludes, 'From my father Pt Ramprasad Sharma and my guru Anthony Gonsalves to the master composers we observed, I have absorbed so much of music. But the more I learn, the more I realize that there is no end to musical knowledge.' And we are sure Laxmikant, in a far-off world, agrees with his partner. Because Laxmikant-Pyarelal together simply mean the finest there can be in Hindi film music.

Appendix 1

LAXMIKANT-PYARELAL FILMOGRAPHY

1963–1969

1. Parasmani
2. Harishchandra Taramati
3. Sati Savitri
4. Sant Gyaneshwar
5. Aaya Toofan
6. Dosti
7. Hum Sab Ustad Hain
8. Mr X in Bombay
9. Shriman Funtoosh
10. Lootera
11. Mera Dost
12. Boxer
13. Duniya Nachegi*
14. Pyar Kiye Jaa
15. Sau Saal Baad
16. Naag Mandir
17. Laadla
18. Dillagi
19. Daku Mangal Singh
20. Mere Lal
21. Chhota Bhai
22. Dillagi
23. Chhailla Baboo (I)
24. Aasra
25. Aaye Din Bahaar Ke
26. Milan
27. Anita

28. Milan Ki Raat
29. Jaal
30. Farz
31. Shagird
32. Taqdeer
33. Spy In Rome
34. Night In London
35. Patthar Ke Sanam
36. Mere Hamdam Mere Dost
37. Baharon Ki Manzil
38. Raja Aur Runk
39. Sadhu Aur Shaitan
40. Madhavi
41. Wapas
42. Jeene Ki Raah
43. Dharti Kahe Pukar Ke
44. Aansoo Ban Gaye Phool
45. Intaqam (I)
46. Meri Bhabhi
47. Aaya Sawan Jhoom Ke
48. Sajan
49. Anjanna
50. Jigri Dost
51. Do Raaste
52. Pyasi Sham
53. Shart

1970s

54. Pushpanjali
55. Himmat
56. Jawab (I)
57. Humjoli
58. Khilona
59. Maa Aur Mamta
60. Devi
61. Bachpan
62. Abhinetri

Appendix 1

63. *Suhana Safar*
64. *Satyakam*
65. *Jeevan Mrityu*
66. *Sharafat*
67. *Mastana*
68. *Do Bhai*
69. *Man Ki Aankhen*
70. *Darpan*
71. *Aan Milo Sajana*
72. *Lagan*
73. *Jal Bin Machhli Nritya Bin Bijli*
74. *Mehboob Ki Mehndi*
75. *Haathi Mere Saathi*
76. *Mera Gaon Mera Desh*
77. *Haseeno Ka Devta*
78. *Manmandir*
79. *Aap Aye Bahaar Ayee*
80. *Bikhre Moti*
81. *Chahat*
82. *Uphaar*
83. *Piya Ka Ghar*
84. *Banphool*
85. *Dushmun*
86. *Shor*
87. *Raja Jani*
88. *Gaon Hamara Shehar Tumhara*
89. *Raaste Ka Patthar*
90. *Gora Aur Kala*
91. *Buniyaad*
92. *Subah-O-Sham*
93. *Jeet*
94. *Ek Nazar*
95. *Mom Ki Gudia*
96. *Ek Bechara*
97. *Dastaan*
98. *Wafaa*
99. *Haar Jeet*

100. Roop Tera Mastana
101. Shaadi Ke Baad
102. Woh Din Yaad Karo
103. Loafer
104. Daag
105. Gaai Aur Gori
106. Anokhi Ada
107. Sweekar
108. Anhonee
109. Gaddaar
110. Gehri Chaal
111. Kucche Dhaage
112. Keemat
113. Jalte Badan
114. Bobby
115. Nirdosh
116. JwarBhata
117. Suraj Aur Chanda
118. Insaf (I)
119. Manchali
120. Badla
121. Dost
122. Naya Din Nayi Raat
123. Imtihan
124. Amir Garib
125. Roti
126. Roti Kapada Aur Makaan
127. Bidaai
128. Majboor (I)
129. Prem Shastra
130. Pocketmaar
131. Shaandaar
132. Barkha Bahar
133. Paise Ki Gudiya
134. Nirmaan
135. The Cheat
136. Kahani Hum Sab Ki

Appendix 1

137. Pagli
138. Duniya Ka Mela
139. Geetaa Mera Naam
140. Vaada Tera Vaada*
141. Jurm Aur Saza
142. Dulhan
143. Ponga Pandit
144. Aakhri Dao
145. Pratiggya
146. Aakraman
147. Apne Rang Hazaar
148. Chaitali
149. Dafaa No 302
150. Prem Kahani
151. Anari
152. Lafange
153. Zinda Dil
154. Mere Sajana
155. Free Love
156. Sewak
157. Zindagi Aur Toofan
158. Nagin
159. Dus Numbri
160. Charas
161. Suntan
162. Jaaneman
163. Aap Beati
164. Maa
165. Naatak
166. Koi Jeeta Koi Haara
167. Prayaschit*
168. Ooparwala Jaane*
169. Anurodh
170. Dharam-Veer
171. Chacha Bhatija
172. Chhaila Babu (II)
173. Dildaar

174. Chor Sipahee
175. Amar Akbar Anthony
176. Parvarish
177. Dream Girl
178. Imaan Dharam
179. Jagriti
180. Aaj Ka Mahatma
181. Do Ladkiyan
182. Thief Of Baghdad
183. Chhota Baap
184. Tinku
185. Aashiq Hoon Baharon Ka
186. Aadha Din Aadhi Raat
187. Do Ladkiyan
188. Kali Raat*
189. Kachcha Chor*
190. Apnapan
191. Satyam Shivam Sundaram
192. Main Tulsi Tere Aangan Ki
193. BadalteyRishety
194. Dil Aur Deewaar
195. Phool Khile Hain Gulshan Gulshan
196. Palkon Ki Chhaon Mein
197. Sauda
198. Kaala Aadmi
199. Phaansi
200. Amar Shakti
201. Aahutee
202. Naach Uthe Sansaar
203. Sawan Ke Geet*
204. Daku Aur Jawan
205. Gautam Govinda
206. Maan Apmaan
207. Amar Deep
208. Kartavya
209. Jaani Dushman
210. Chakravyuha

211. *Magroor*
212. *Prem Bandhan*
213. *Yuvraaj*
214. *Sargam*
215. *Suhaag*
216. *Muqabla*
217. *Prem Vivah*
218. *Lok Parlok*
219. *Dil Kaa Heera*

1980–89

220. *Aasha*
221. *Jyoti Bane Jwala*
222. *Karz*
223. *Judaai*
224. *Dostana*
225. *Maang Bharo Sajna*
226. *Nishana*
227. *Be-reham*
228. *Ram Balram*
229. *Zaalim*
230. *Chunaoti*
231. *Choron Ki Baraat*
232. *Bandish*
233. *Yaari Dushmani*
234. *Kali Ghata*
235. *Ganga Aur Suraj*
236. *Patthar Se Takkar**
237. *Do Premee*
238. *Hum Paanch*
239. *Kranti*
240. *Aas Paas*
241. *Krodhi*
242. *Ladies Tailor*
243. *Waqt Ki Deewar*
244. *Ek Aur Ek Gyarah*
245. *Khoon Aur Paani*

246. Khuda Kasam
247. Sharda
248. Meri Awaaz Suno
249. Pyaasa Sawan
250. Ek Hi Bhool
251. Gehrayee
252. Naseeb
253. Ek Duuje Ke Liye
254. Fiffty Fiffty
255. Kala Pani*
256. Mastan Dada
257. Raaste Pyar Ke
258. Apna Bana Lo
259. Jeevan Dhaara
260. Vakil Baboo
261. Rajput
262. Teesri Aankh
263. Ghazab
264. Badle Ki Aag
265. Desh Premee
266. Main Intaquam Loonga
267. Insaan
268. Mehandi Rang Layegi
269. Farz Aur Kanoon
270. Baghawat
271. Prem Rog
272. Teri Maang Sitaron Se Bhar Doon
273. Samraat
274. Deedaar-E-Yaar
275. Jeeo Aur Jeene Do
276. Taaqat
277. Do Disayen*
278. Zara Si Zindagi
279. Arpan
280. Prem Tapasya
281. Avtaar
282. Andhaa Kanoon

Appendix 1

283. *Mujhe Insaaf Chahiye*
284. *Jaanwar*
285. *Bekaraar*
286. *Woh 7 Din*
287. *Coolie*
288. *Hero*
289. *Baazi*
290. *Jeene Nahi Doonga*
291. *Mera Dost Mera Dushmun*
292. *Pakhandee*
293. *Ghar Ek Mandir*
294. *Yeh Ishq Nahin Aasaan*
295. *Akalmand*
296. *Zakhmi Sher*
297. *Asha Jyoti*
298. *Inquilab*
299. *Sharaara*
300. *All-Rounder*
301. *Mera Faisla*
302. *John Jani Janardhan*
303. *Ek Nai Paheli*
304. *Tadap (Pyaase Honth)**
305. *Maang Sajaa Do Meri**
306. *Uddhaar**
307. *Pyar Jhukta Nahin*
308. *Sarfarosh*
309. *Do Dilon Ki Dastan*
310. *Ghulami*
311. *Utsav*
312. *Sur-Sangam*
313. *Meri Jung*
314. *Mera Ghar Mere Bacche*
315. *Jawaab (II)*
316. *Dekha Pyar Tumhara*
317. *Sanjog*
318. *Teri Meherbaniyan*
319. *Yadon Ki Kasam*

320. Jaanoo
321. Bayen Hath Ka Khel*
322. Mera Jawaab
323. Love 86
324. Naseeb Apna Apna
325. Qatl
326. Aakhree Raasta
327. Aag Aur Shola
328. Swarag Se Sunder
329. Triveni
330. Aap Ke Sath
331. Kali Basti
332. Kala Dhanda Goray Log
333. Swati
334. Amrit
335. Pyar Kiya Hai Pyar Karenge
336. Karma
337. Naam
338. Sadaa Suhagan
339. Nache Mayuri**
340. Nagina
341. Mazloom
342. Asli Naqli
343. Dosti Dushmani
344. Aisa Pyar Kahan
345. Hukumat
346. Mr India
347. Sindoor
348. Kudrat Ka Kanoon
349. Insaaf (II)
350. Loha
351. Sansar
352. Parivaar
353. Watan Ke Rakhwale
354. Insaaf Kaun Karega?
355. Jawab Hum Denge
356. Uttar Dakshin

357. Mard Ki Zabaan
358. Insaf Ki Pukar
359. Anjaam
360. Jaan Hatheli Pe
361. Khazana*
362. Mera Karam Mera Dharam
363. Aulad
364. Nazrana
365. Madadgaar
366. Patthar Dil
367. Pyar Ka Mandir
368. Charanon Ki Saugandh
369. Bad Aur Badnaam
370. Ram Avtar
371. Khatron Ke Khiladi
372. Shoorveer
373. Pyar Mohabbat
374. Ganga Tere Desh Mein
375. Qatil
376. Mar Mitenge
377. Agnee
378. Intaqaam (II)
379. Janam Janam
380. Tezaab
381. Dayavan
382. Biwi Ho To Aisi
383. Hamara Khandaan
384. Ram Lakhan
385. Eeshwar
386. Chaalbaaz
387. Suryaa
388. Elaan-E-Jung
389. Gharana
390. Dost Garibon Ka
391. Oonch Neech Beech
392. Santosh
393. Do Waqt Ki Roti*

394. Kasam Suhag Ki
395. Hathyar
396. Yateem
397. Batwara
398. Bees Saal Baad
399. Do Qaidi
400. Sachai Ki Taaqat
401. Shehzaade
402. Bade Ghar Ki Beti
403. Parayaa Ghar
404. Main Tera Dushman
405. Brashtachaar
406. Nigahen
407. Pati Parmeshwar
408. Shararat*

1990–99

409. Izzatdaar
410. Sher Dil
411. Humse Na Takrana
412. Veeru Dada
413. Pyar Ka Karz
414. Sheshnaag
415. Amiri Garibi
416. Saki Haatimtai
417. Majboor (II)
418. Pratibandh
419. Agneepath
420. Pati Patni Aur Tawaif
421. Kroadh
422. Azaad Desh Ke Ghulam
423. Qayamat Ki Raat
424. Aaj Ka Inteqaam*
425. Naag Nagin
426. Atishbaaz
427. Amba
428. Jamai Raja

429. Jeevan Ek Sungharsh
430. Engineer No. 1*
431. Hum
432. Akayla
433. Ajooba
434. Saudagar
435. Dhun*
436. Narsimha
437. Prahaar
438. Paap Ki Aandhi
439. Mast Kalandar
440. Ranbhoomi
441. Banjaran
442. Do Matwale
443. Kanoon Ki Zanjeer*
444. Qurbani Rang Laayegi
445. Deshwasi
446. Khoon Ka Karz
447. Pyar Ka Devta
448. Pyar Hua Chori Chori
449. Shankara
450. Benaam Badshah
451. Paap Ki Aandhi
452. Khilaaf
453. Lakshmanrekha
454. Sapnon Ka Mandir
455. Sahebzaade
456. Khuda Gawah
457. Prem Deewane
458. Heer Ranjha
459. Humlaa
460. Angaar
461. Humshakal
462. Badi Behen
463. Apradhi
464. Swarg Se Pyara Ghar Hamara*
465. Rishta Ho To Aisa*

466. Dil Hi To Hai
467. Yugandhar
468. Kshatriya**
469. Aashik Aawara
470. Tirangaa
471. Roop Ki Rani Choron Ka Raja
472. Chahoonga Main Tujhe
473. Bedardi
474. Dil Hai Betaab
475. Khal Nayak
476. Gumrah
477. Chauraha
478. Tejaswini
479. Mohabbat Ki Arzoo
480. Insaaf Apne Lahoo Se
481. Dilbar
482. Prem
483. Trimurti
484. Aag Ka Darya*
485. Parakrami*
486. Aatank
487. Prem Granth
488. Paappi Devataa
489. Rajkumar
490. Aurat Aurat Aurat
491. Mohabbat Ki Aag*
492. Kaun Rokega Mujhe?
493. Bhairavi
494. Deewana Mastana
495. Mahaanta
496. Maha Yuddh
497. Barsaat Ki Raat
498. Jai Hind—The Pride

2000

499. *Yun Hi Chup Chup**/**

2004

500. *Mere Biwi Ka Jawab Nahin***

REGIONAL FILMS

Bengali

501. *Agamikal* (1983)

Marathi

502. *Bala Jo Jo Re* (1993)

Telugu

503. *Majnu* (1987)
504. *Neti Siddhartha* (1990) (dubbed as *Aur Ek Dharmatma* in Hindi)

Tamil

505. *Uyire Unakkaga* (1986)
506. *Mangai Oru Gangai* (1987) (dubbed as *Charan Dada* in Hindi)
507. *Ragasiya Police* (1995) (dubbed as *Insaniyat Ki Jung* in Hindi)

Malayalam

508. *Jeevitha Samaram* (1971) (dubbed version of *Jeevan Mrityu*)
509. *Upaharam* (1972) (dubbed version of *Uphaar*)
510. *Poonilamazha* (1997)

---

*Films that did not release at all or could not release pan-India. Some of these films were only released on video but not as audio albums.

**Films that featured other music directors as well.

Appendix 2

THE VOICES AND LYRICISTS OF LAXMIKANT-PYARELAL

A record number of voices, not all of them playback singers or even film singers, entered the recording studios of Laxmikant-Pyarelal. L-P's overwhelming favourites were Lata Mangeshkar (over 700 in a total of almost 2,900 Hindi songs) and Mohammed Rafi (around 400), both of whom sang more for them than for any other composers. Asha Bhosle (over 400), Kishore Kumar (a documented 399), and Mukesh in that quantitative order, ranked next among the legends, with a significant quantum for Mahendra Kapoor, Manna Dey, Suman Kalyanpur and Usha Mangeshkar.

Among younger singers, Alka Yagnik and Kavita Krishnamurthi Subramaniam, and Mohammed Aziz (who began singing for them in 1986!) led the roster in the female and male segments. Mohammed Aziz clocked up over 200 songs in 12 years, showing the preference L-P had for Rafi sound-alikes. Significant contributions came from Anuradha Paudwal, Amit Kumar, Nitin Mukesh, Shailendra Singh, Suresh Wadkar, Shabbir Kumar, Manhar Udhas and S.P. Balasubramaniam from the South.

L-P scored music for regional films as well, and many singers, SPB apart, sang only for those films, like Sujatha Mohan, Mano and Swarnalatha. Among them were singers who also collaborated on their Hindi film songs, like Yesudas and S. Janaki. Top Marathi playback singer Jaywant Kulkarni also came in for a Hindi film.

A standout feature of L-P's music was their tendency to get actors to come in as well, for anything from dialogue interpolations (Leena Chandavarkar, Jeetendra, Johny Lever, Asrani et al) to full-fledged songs (Mehmood, Amitabh Bachchan and Hema Malini).

Lyricists Anand Bakshi and Pradeep also came in to sing, besides

Appendix 2

Laxmikant himself, their assistant Aadesh Shrivastava, Rajeshwari Laxmikant, Kanal Pyarelal and filmmaker Subhash Ghai. Senior composer-singers C. Ramachandra (as Chitalkar) and Hemant Kumar also came in, as did legendary writer-director Prayag Raj and choreographer (uncredited) P.L. Raj.

Overseas singers like Reshma, Runa Laila, Mehdi Hasan and Salim Prem Ragi, NRI pop singer Bali Brahmbhatt, other pop singers like Usha Uthup, Ajit Singh and Suneeta Rao also came in, and among the odd names were filmmaker Mehul Kumar's relative Hussain Bloch, Rani Mukerji's mother Krishna Mukerji and Manmohan Desai's assistant Laxmikant Karpe.

Indian classical, folk, devotional, qawwali and ghazal specialists also found opportunities with them. Pt Rajan Misra and Pt Sajan Misra, Shobha Gurtu, Gurdas Mann, Narendra Chanchal, Ila Arun, Iqbal Sabri and popular non-film artistes Pankaj Udhas, Talat Aziz, Roopkumar Rathod and Anup Jalota featured in their songs.

Child artistes did not have a major role in their songs, but among those who recorded as children for them were Sulakshana Pandit, the above mentioned Rajeshwari and Kanal and also Baby Tabassum and Master Raju.

A point to note is that many singers were introduced by them, and more significantly, singers who had made their debuts with other composers got their career breakthroughs with a L-P film or song.

To sum up, 72 female voices and 105 male voices figured in their music, including in the dubbed Hindi versions of some of their South films. A few voices were recorded within the film and not for the soundtracks, while with some, the films never saw the light of day.

The singers listed below in **bold** are those who sang from fair to extensive songs for them.

Female Singers

1. Aarti Mukherjee*
2. Alisha Chinoy
3. **Alka Yagnik**
4. Annapurna*
5. Annette*
6. Anupama Deshpande

7. **Anuradha Paudwal**
8. Aruna Irani*
9. **Asha Bhosle**
10. B. Vasantha*
11. Baby Tabassum*
12. Chandrani Mukherjee
13. Chitra*
14. Dilraj Kaur
15. Hema Malini*
16. **Hemlata**
17. Ila Arun
18. Ila Desai*
19. Jayashree Shivram
20. Kanal Sharma*
21. Kaumudi Munshi*
22. **Kavita Krishnamurthi Subramaniam**
23. Krishna Mukerji*
24. **Lata Mangeshkar**
25. Laxmi Shankar*
26. Leena Chandavarkar*
27. Meena Patki*
28. Minoo Purshottam
29. Noorjahan*
30. P. Susheela*
31. Padmini Kolhapure Sharma*
32. Parveen Sultana*
33. Poornima (a.k.a Sushma Shrestha)
34. Preeti Uttam*
35. Priya Mayekar*
36. Purnima*
37. Raakhee*
38. Rajeshwari Laxmikant
39. Ranu Mukherjee
40. Reema Dasgupta*
41. Reshma
42. Runa Laila
43. S. Janaki

Appendix 2

7. Amrish Puri*
8. Anand Bakshi
9. Anand Kumar
10. Anil Kapoor
11. Anup Jalota
12. Anwar
13. Arun Bakshi
14. Asrani*
15. Aziz Nazan*
16. Bali Brahmbhatt*
17. Bharat*
18. Birbal*
19. Chandru Atma*
20. Chitalkar (C. Ramachandra)*
21. Gurdas Mann*
22. Hariharan
23. Hemant Kumar
24. Hussain Bloch*
25. I.S. Johar*
26. Iqbal Sabri*
27. Jackie Shroff*
28. Jagjit Singh
29. Jani Babu
30. Jaspal Singh
31. Jaaved Jafferi*
32. Jaywant Kulkarni*
33. Jeetendra*
34. Johny Lever*
35. Johnny Whiskey
36. Jolly Mukherjee
37. Kamal Haasan*
38. Kamlesh Awasthi
39. **Kishore Kumar**
40. Kumar Sanu
41. Laxmikant
42. Laxmikant Karpe*
43. **Mahendra Kapoor**

81. Sonu Nigam
82. Subir Sen**
83. Subhash Ghai*
84. **Sudesh Bhosle**
85. Sukhwant
86. **Sukhwinder Singh**
87. **Suresh Wadkar**
88. Talat Aziz
89. Talat Mahmood*
90. **Udit Narayan**
91. V. Shrivastava*
92. Vijay Benedict*
93. Vinay Mandke
94. Vinod Mehra*
95. **Vinod Rathod**
96. Vinod Sharma
97. Vivek Verma*
98. Wasi Raza*
99. Yesudas
100. Zahid Nazan*
101. Dinesh Babu (Tamil only)
102. Ponnusamy (Tamil only)*
103. Mano (Tamil only)*
104. M.G. Sreekumar (Malayalam only)*
105. K. P. Brahmanandan (Malayalam only)*

Lyricists

The word 'lyricist' is a broad term, for it includes poets who came in for specific songs or films, or whose poetry, already written, was tuned and recorded for a film, with or without modifications. L-P, once again, worked with a spectrum of such writers, and their 'oldest' writer was Sufi titan Amir Khusrau (born in 1253!), whose song, 'Chhap Tilak Sab Chhini', was recorded for *Main Tulsi Tere Aangan Ki*. Among their work were also adaptations in part from the classic verses of Mir Taqi Mir, Meerabai and Kavi Surdas. But since most of those lyrics were freshly written and original, the songs were credited to those lyricists. Scriptwriters Govind Moonis, Jainendra Jain, Prayag Raj, Sarshar Sailani

44. S.P. Shailaja*
45. Sadhana Sargam
46. Sagarika Mukherjee*
47. Salma Agha
48. Sapna Mukherjee
49. Sarika Kapoor*
50. Shamshad Begum
51. Shivangi Kolhapure Kapoor
52. Shobha Gurtu*
53. Shobha Joshi
54. Shyama Chittar / Hemmady
55. Sonali Bajpayee
56. Sudha Malhotra
57. Sulakshana Pandit
58. **Suman Kalyanpur**
59. Suneeta Rao*
60. Usha Khanna*
61. **Usha Mangeshkar**
62. Usha Timothy
63. Usha Uthup
64. Uttara Kelkar
65. Vandana Shastri*
66. Vani Jairam*
67. Vijayta Pandit **
68. Zeenat Aman*
69. Padmini Roy (dubbed Hindi version)*
70. Padma (Tamil only)*
71. Swarnalatha (Tamil only)*
72. Sujatha Mohan (Malayalam only)*

Male Singers

1. Abhijeet
2. Aadesh Shrivastava*
3. Afzal Sabri*
4. Ajit Singh*
5. **Amit Kumar**
6. Amitabh Bachchan

44. Mahesh Kumar
45. Majid Irfan Qawwal*
46. Mangal Dhillon*
47. Mangal Singh*
48. **Manhar Udhas**
49. **Manna Dey**
50. Master Raju*
51. Mehboob Chavan*
52. Mehdi Haasan*
53. Mehmood
54. **Mohammed Aziz**
55. **Mohammed Rafi**
56. **Mukesh**
57. Mukri*
58. Mukul Agarwal*
59. Nalin Dave*
60. Narendra Chanchal
61. **Nitin Mukesh**
62. P.L. Raj*
63. Pankaj Mitra*
64. Pankaj Udhas
65. Pradeep*
66. Prayag Raj*
67. Pt Rajan Misra*
68. Pt Sajan Misra*
69. Rajendranath*
70. Rishi Kapoor
71. Roopesh Kumar*
72. Roopkumar Rathod
73. **S. P. Balasubramaniam**
74. Sachin*
75. Saeed Sabri*
76. Salim Prem Ragi*
77. **Shabbir Kumar**
78. **Shailendra Singh**
79. Shashi Kapoor
80. Shatrughan Sinha

and K.K. Singh and non-film writers like a professor, Pt Vasant Deo, and writer and producer Mangesh Kulkarni also came in, while in regional films, the biggest names included Vaali and Vairumuthu from the South, Jagdish Khebudkar in Marathi and Gauri Prasanna Majumdar in Bengali.

A total of 84 writers (including in regional cinema and its dubbed Hindi versions) form the L-P catalogue, led obviously by Anand Bakshi with over 300 released soundtracks, making the team Hindi cinema's most repeated combination. Majrooh Sultanpuri, Rajendra Krishan, Verma Malik, Anjaan. Sahir Ludhianvi, Asad Bhopali, Indeevar, Sameer, S.H. Bihari and Santosh Anand had significant contributions, with decent scores for Farukh Kaiser, Javed Akhtar, Hasrat Jaipuri and Hasan Kamal. Also, like in singers, some lyricists worked with them in films that were not completed. Lyricists in **bold** did fair to extensive work with them.

1. Ameer Meenai*
2. Amir Khusrau*
3. Amir Qazalbash*
4. Amit Khanna*
5. **Anand Bakshi**
6. **Anjaan**
7. Arzoo Lucknowi*
8. **Asad Bhopali***
9. Attam Prakash Shukla*
10. Aziz Quaisi*
11. Bharat Vyas
12. Col. Dwarkanath*
13. Dev Kohli
14. Dr Hariram Acharya*
15. Dr Mohan Pradeep*
16. Dr Rahi Masoom Reza*
17. **Farukh Kaiser**
18. Govind Moonis*
19. Gulshan Bawra
20. Gulzar
21. **Hasan Kamal**
22. **Hasrat Jaipuri**
23. **Indeevar**

24. Jainendra Jain
25. **Javed Akhtar**
26. Jigar Moradabadi*
27. K.K. Singh*
28. K.K. Verma*
29. Kafeel Azar
30. Kaifi Azmi
31. Khursheed Hillauri*
32. Kulwant Jani
33. **Majrooh Sultanpuri**
34. Mangesh Kulkarni*
35. Manoj Kumar
36. Maya Govind
37. Mumtaz Rashid*
38. Naqsh Lyallpuri*
39. Neeraj*
40. Nida Fazli
41. Pradeep*
42. Prayag Raj
43. Prem Dhawan**
44. Prem Pandit*
45. Pt Narendra Sharma
46. Pt Ram Bhardwaj
47. Pt Vasant Deo
48. Qamar Jalalabadi* **
49. Raja Mehdi Ali Khan
50. **Rajendra Krishan**
51. Rajesh Malik
52. Rajkavi Inderjit Singh 'Tulsi'
53. Ram Avtar Tyagi*
54. Rani Malik
55. **S.H. Bihari**
56. **Sahir Ludhianvi**
57. Salauddin Parvez*
58. **Sameer**
59. **Santosh Anand**
60. Sarshar Sailani*

Appendix 2

61. Satya Prakash*
62. Shahenshah*
63. Shahryar**
64. Shakeel Badayuni*
65. Shivkumar Saroj*
66. Sudarshan Faakir*
67. Tabish Ramani*
68. Taj Bhopali*
69. Vitthalbhai Patel
70. Yogesh*

Lyricists in Regional Films and in Their Dubbed Hindi Versions

71. Gauri Prasanna Majumdar (Bengali)*
72. Jagdish Khebudkar (Marathi)*
73. Veturi Sundararama Murthy (Telugu)*
74. Dasari Narayana Rao (Telugu)*
75. Metha (Tamil)*
76. Pulamaipithan (Tamil)*
77. M.G. Vallaban (Tamil)
78. Muthulingam (Tamil)
79. Valli (Tamil)
80. Vairamuthu (Tamil)*
81. Gireesh Puthenchery (Malayalam)*
82. P. Bhaskaran (Malayalam)
83. Brij Bihari (Dubbed Hindi version, *Aur Ek Dharmatma*, of Telugu film *Niti Siddharth*)*
84. B.R. Tripathi (Dubbed Hindi version, *Charan Dada*, of Tamil film *Mangai Oru Gangai*)*

Note: Indeevar also wrote lyrics for *Aur Ek Dharmatma* and also for *Insaniyat Ki Jung*, the dubbed version of the Tamil film *Ragasiya Police*. Sameer penned a Hindi song in the Malayalam film *Poonilamazha*.

---

*One film or one song only with L-P.
**Recorded a song but film was never completed.

Appendix 3

PROMINENT AWARDS AND SALES TROPHIES WON BY LAXMIKANT-PYARELAL

AWARDS

I. Filmfare*

1. *Dosti* (1964)
2. *Milan* (1967)
3. *Jeene Ki Raah* (1969)
4. *Amar Akbar Anthony* (1977)
5. *Satyam Shivan Sundaram* (1978)
6. *Sargam* (1979)
7. *Karz* (1980)

II. Sur-Singar Samsad Awards For Best Classical Film Song of The Year

1. 'Painjaniya Chhanke Ram' (*Wapas*) Lyrics: Majrooh Sultanpuri Singer: Mohammed Rafi / 1968
2. 'Pag Padam' (*Nache Mayuri*) Lyrics: Anand Bakshi Singer: S. Janaki / 1986
   (As per convention in those days, all songs were credited to the film's composers, and so L-P accepted the award. This song had been composed by S.P. Balasubramaniam as a part of his background score in the film. In fact, it had been composed as the title-track of the film's original version, *Mayuri* released in 1985.)

---

*For 1986 and 1987 when L-P had a very good chance, the Filmfare awards were not declared at all.

3. 'Bada Dukh Deena' (*Ram Lakhan*) Lyrics: Anand Bakshi Singer: Lata Mangeshkar / 1989

III. Screen

Best Background Music: *Prem* (1995)

IV. Star & Style-Lux Awards

1. *Nagina* (1986–1987)
2. *Tezaab* (1987–1988)

V. Special Award—Society for Prevention of Cruelty to Animals (SPCA)

1971: 'Nafrat Ki Duniya' / *Haathi Mere Saathi* Co-winners: Anand Bakshi, Mohammed Rafi & Producer Sandow M.M.A. Chinappa Devar

AWARDS WON BY SINGERS FOR SONGS COMPOSED BY LAXMIKANT-PYARELAL

1. Mohammed Rafi

'Chahoonga Main Tujhe' / *Dosti* / Filmfare / 1964
'Painjaniya Chhanke Ram' / *Wapas* / Sur-Singar Samsad / 1968
'Nafrat Ki Duniya' / *Haathi Mere Saathi* / SPCA / 1971

2. Lata Mangeshkar

'Aap Mujhe Acche Lagne Lage' / *Jeene Ki Raah* / Filmfare / 1969
'Bada Dukh Deena' / *Ram Lakhan* / Sur-Singar Samsad / 1989

3. Narendra Chanchal

'Beshak Mandir Masjid' / *Bobby* / Filmfare / 1973

4. Mahendra Kapoor

'Aur Nahin Bas Aur Nahin' / Roti *Kapada Aur Makaan* / Filmfare / 1974

5. S.P. Balasubramaniam

'Tere Mere Beech Mein' / *Ek Duuje Ke Liye* / National Best Playback Singer / 1981

6. Anuradha Paudwal

'Mere Man Baaja Mirdang' / *Utsav* / Filmfare / 1985

7. Alka Yagnik

'Ek Do Teen Char' / *Tezaab* / Filmfare / 1988

8. Alka Yagnik & Ila Arun

'Choli Ke Peeche Kya Hai' / *Khal Nayak* / Filmfare / 1993

AWARDS WON BY LYRICISTS FOR SONGS COMPOSED BY LAXMIKANT-PYARELAL

1. Majrooh Sultanpuri

'Chahoonga Main Tujhe' / *Dosti* / Filmfare / 1964
'Painjaniya Chhanke Raam' / *Wapas* / Sur-Singar Samsad / 1968

2. Anand Bakshi

'Nafrat Ki Duniya' / *Haathi Mere Saathi* / Spca Special Award / 1971
'Aadmi Musafir Hai' / *Apnapan* / Filmfare / 1978
'Tere Mere Beech Mein' / *Ek Duuje Ke Liye* / Filmfare / 1981
'Bada Dukh Deena' / *Ram Lakhan* / Sur-Singar Samsad / 1989

3. Santosh Anand

'Main Na Bhoolunga' / *Roti Kapada Aur Makaan* / Filmfare / 1974
'Mohabbat Hai Kya Cheez' / *Prem Rog* / Filmfare / 1982

4. Pt Vasant Deo

'Man Kyoon Behka' / *Utsav* / Filmfare / 1985

PROMINENT EXTRAORDINARY SALES DISCS FOR RECORDS, CASSETTES AND CDs

1. *Haathi Mere Saathi* (HMV* Silver Disc—first such Sales Disc awarded in India)
2. *Bobby* (HMV Gold Disc—a first in India, with sales ranking among

Appendix 3

the Top 10 albums of all time *worldwide*—Source: Economic Times, 1974)

3. *Roti Kapada Aur Makaan* (HMV Gold Disc)
4. *Dharam-Veer* (Polydor** Gold Disc)
5. *Amar Akbar Anthony* (Polydor Gold Disc)
6. *Satyam Shivam Sundaram* (First HMV pre-release Gold Disc, followed by first-ever Platinum Disc)
7. *Sargam* (HMV Gold Disc)
8. *Jaani Dushman* (HMV Gold Disc)
9. *Aasha* (HMV Gold Disc)
10. *Karz* (HMV Gold Disc)
11. *Dostana* (Polydor Gold Disc)
12. *Kranti* (HMV Platinum Disc)
13. *Hero* (HMV Platinum Disc)
14. *Coolie* (Music India** Gold Disc)
15. *Pyar Jhukta Nahin* (T-Series Platinum Disc)
16. *Karma* (HMV Gold Disc)
17. *Naam* (HMV Gold Disc)
18. *Mr India* (T-Series Platinum Disc)
19. *Ram Lakhan* (HMV 'Quadruple Platinum' Disc)

No sales discs were officially announced for *Tezaab* (T-Series), *Hum & Saudagar* (HMV) and *Khal Nayak* (Tips), all of which reported extraordinary sales.

Tips have stated that *Khal Nayak* remains their highest-selling album, and T-Series has included both *Pyar Jhukta Nahin* and *Tezaab* among their 12 all-time top sellers.

---

*HMV is now known as Saregama.
**Polydor, later called Music India, is now known as Universal Music.

Appendix 4

LAXMIKANT-PYARELAL'S *BINACA GEETMALA* TOPPERS

With 11 winners out of 27 in the Annual No. 1 song from 1967-1993 in *Binaca Geetmala*, India's oldest and—until the television era—only countdown show, Laxmikant-Pyarelal are miles ahead of any other composer—senior, contemporary or junior.

The *Binaca Geetmala*'s annual list of toppers had 32 songs divided over two weeks. In L-P's tenure, there were 1,008 such melodies, and the duo amassed an incredible score of 250, almost a quarter of the total, single-handedly! Legendary radio host Ameen Sayani has always convincingly answered all accusations of favouritism on the show, even outside the L-P ambit, and has negated every charge with aptly demonstrated material and data that was a part of the decision-making process.

Here are those Laxmikant-Pyarelal songs that made it to the 'Year's No. 1' lists, with notes wherever relevant, in parenthesis.

1. 1967: 'Saawan Ka Mahina'/*Milan* Lyrics: Anand Bakshi; Singers: Mukesh & Lata Mangeshkar
2. 1968: 'Dil Vil Pyar Vyar'/*Shagird* Lyrics: Majrooh Sultanpuri; Singer: Lata Mangeshkar* (Late 1967 release)
3. 1969: 'Kaise Rahoon Chup'/*Intaqam* Lyrics: Rajendra Krishan; Singer: Lata Mangeshkar
4. 1970: 'Bindiya Chamkegi'/*Do Raaste* Lyrics: Anand Bakshi; Singer: Lata Mangeshkar (Late 1969 release)
5. 1975: 'Mehangai Maar Gayi'/*Roti Kapada Aur Makaan* Lyrics: Verma Malik; Singers: Lata Mangeshkar, Mukesh, Jani Babu & Narendra Chanchal (Late 1974 release)
('Haye Haye Yeh Majboori' from *Roti Kapada Aur Makaan* at No. 2)

6. 1980: 'Dafli Wale Dafli Bajaa'/*Sargam* Lyrics: Anand Bakshi; Singers: Lata Mangeshkar & Mohammed Rafi (Late 1979 release) ('Om Shanti Om' From *Karz* at No. 2 and 'Sheesha Ho Ya Dil Ho' from *Aasha* at no.3— both were 1980 releases)
7. 1984: 'Tu Mera Jaanu Hai'/*Hero* Lyrics: Anand Bakshi; Singers: Manhar Udhas & Anuradha Paudwal (Late 1983 release)
8. 1986: 'Yashoda Ka Nandlala'/*Sanjog* Lyrics: Anjaan; Singer: Lata Mangeshkar (Late 1985 release)
   ('Duniya Mein Kitna Gham Hai' from *Amrit* at No. 2 and 'Ae Sanam Tere Liye' from *Karma* at No. 3—both were 1986 releases)
9. 1987: 'Chitthi Aayi Hai'/*Naam* Lyrics: Anand Bakshi; Singer: Pankaj Udhas
   (Late 1986 release)
10. 1989: 'My Name Is Lakhan'/*Ram Lakhan* Lyrics: Anand Bakshi; Singers: Mohammed Aziz, Nitin Mukesh & Anuradha Paudwal
11. 1993: 'Choli Ke Peeche'/*Khal Nayak* Lyrics: Anand Bakshi; Singers: Alka Yagnik & Ila Arun (Tips**)
    (This song also topped the first three television countdowns that began in 1993: *Philips Top Ten* on Zee TV, *Superhit Muqabla* on Doordarshan and *BPL Oye* on Channel [V])

---

*Introductory couplet by Mohammed Rafi was there only within the film
**All other Top songs were on HMV (Saregama)

Appendix 5

AN EXTENSIVE ASSOCIATION WITH DADASAHEB PHALKE LAUREATES

Anil Kapoor has stated that Laxmikant-Pyarelal fully deserve to be conferred India's highest award in cinema—the Dadasaheb Phalke Award. This is presented annually to one pan-Indian recipient at the National Film Awards ceremony by the Directorate of Film Festivals, an organization set up by the Ministry of Information and Broadcasting. The conferee is honored for making an outstanding contribution to the growth and development of Indian cinema.

While we hope that dream of his and millions of fans comes true, an interesting part of their sustained success was that Laxmikant-Pyarelal were associated with or scored music for the maximum number of legends who have been conferred the Phalke!

No composer across the country comes close to L-P's remarkable score among Phalke laureates, yet again demonstrating the sweeping excellence and unimaginably broad span of their music.

Here we present the associations in the chronological order of the winners.

Prithviraj Kapoor

He acted in *Harishchandra Taramati* and *Lootera*, and the classic song 'Jagat Ke Roshni Ke Liye' was filmed on him in the former film, though there was no lip-sync.

P. Jairaj

Ten films as a character artiste, including all three of Jairaj's releases—*Kranti, Khoon Aur Paani* and *Fiffty Fiffty*—in 1981

Naushad

Both Laxmikant and Pyarelal worked as musicians with this veteran Phalke laureate composer.

Durga Khote

From 1969 to 1980, she acted in 12 films of theirs as character artiste, including her milestone roles in *Jeene Ki Raah*, *Bobby*, *Bidaai* and *Karz*. The popular song 'Acche Samay Pe Tum Aaye' was filmed on her without lip-sync in *Bidaai*.

V. Shantaram

Jal Bin Machhli Nritya Bin Bijli in 1971, **which has India's first film soundtrack in Stereophonic Sound**, was produced, directed and edited by V. Shantaram.

Raj Kapoor

Bobby, *Satyam Shivam Sundaram* and *Prem Rog* saw Raj Kapoor as producer-director-editor. He played the title-role in *Vakil Baboo* and acted as himself in a cameo in *Naseeb*. **Bobby won the first-ever HMV Gold Disc and *Satyam Shivam Sundaram* the first HMV pre-release Gold Disc followed by the first-ever HMV Platinum Disc.** However, no L-P song was lip-synched by him.

Ashok Kumar

From 1968 to 1992, Ashok Kumar featured in 35 films of L-P as a top-billed character artiste, including his home production *Aansoo Ban Gaye Phool*, in which he was the protagonist. He enacted their compositions in a few films with Kishore Kumar, Manna Dey, Mahendra Kapoor and Anup Jalota as his playback voices.

Lata Mangeshkar

From 1963 to 1996, **at an estimated 712 released songs (with many more unreleased), this is the most frequent singer-composer combination ever in Indian cinema.** Under their music direction, the songstress sang songs of all genres for actresses from Nirupa Roy to Divya Bharati.

Akkineni Nageswara Rao

He was the producer of *Prem Tapasya* (1983).

Majrooh Sultanpuri

Between 1964 and 1996, **he wrote songs for over 35 L-P films**, including *Jal Bin Machhli Nritya Bin Bijli*, India's first film soundtrack in Stereo, *Dosti* and *Wapas*, for both of which L-P and Majrooh both won awards. In most cases, the music was a bigger hit than the movie. He was their most frequent songwriter after Anand Bakshi.

Dilip Kumar

Dastaan, Kranti, Karma (in which Dilip Kumar also sang himself), *Izzatdaar, Saudagar* and *Aag Ka Darya* saw Dilip Kumar associate with the composers, with L-P composing music for five of his 13 releases between 1981 and 1998. Mohammed Rafi, Mahendra Kapoor, Mohammed Aziz, Shabbir Kumar and Sukhwinder Singh also sang for him.

Pradeep

In *Harishchandra Taramati* (1963) he was both the lyricist and a singer.

B.R. Chopra

Dastaan (1972) was produced and directed by B.R. Chopra.

Hrishikesh Mukherjee

Hrishikesh Mukherjee directed *Satyakam* (1970), which he calls his career-best film, and *Chaitali* (1975) as director. He also edited *Mere Hamdam Mere Dost, Pyasi Sham* and *Coolie*.

Asha Bhosle

Between 1963 and 1996, Asha Bhosle **recorded over 400 L-P songs** pictured on myriad artistes from Mala Sinha and Nanda to Shilpa Shirodkar.

Yash Chopra

Daag (1973) **launched the banner of Yash Raj Films.** He was the film's producer-director and co-wrote the screenplay.

Dev Anand

He worked with L-P in 1974 in *Amir Garib*, *Prem Shastra* and his production *Jaaneman* in 1976. Kishore Kumar, Mohammed Rafi and Anand Kumar C. were his singers.

Manna Dey

Between 1964 and 1991, Manna Dey **recorded over 65 songs** for artistes from Ashok Kumar to Jeetendra and Shatrughan Sinha and—minus lip-sync and in the background—Nana Patekar.

V.K. Murthy

V.K. Murthy was the cinematographer of L-P's *Chhota* Bhai (1966) and *Dream Girl* (1977).

D. Rama Naidu

D. Rama Naidu produced four films with L-P: *Dildaar*, *Dil Aur Deewar*, *Bandish* and *Jeevan Ek Sangharsh*.

K. Balachander

K. Balachander was director-writer of the blockbuster *Ek Duuje Ke Liye* as well as of *Zara Si Zindagi* and *Ek Nai Paheli*.

Pran

Between 1967 and 1999, Pran featured in 46 films of L-P, including *Lakshmanrekha* (1991) that he himself co-produced, and which was directed by his son Sunil Sikand. His other films included his playing the *Shaitan* in *Sadhu Aur Shaitan* (1968) and a dual role in *Insaf* (1974). Mohammed Rafi, Mahendra Kapoor, Manna Dey and Kishore Kumar were the voices L-P used for him.

Gulzar

Palkon Ki Chhaon Mein (also as scriptwriter), *Gehrayee* and *Ghulami* saw Gulzar work with L-P as a lyricist, but he also wrote the dialogues for *Shagird*, *Mehboob Ki Mehndi* and *Zara Si Zindagi*. L-P had been signed to score his directorial *Meeraa* but backed out as Lata Mangeshkar refused to sing for the film.

Shashi Kapoor

Between 1966 and 1991, **Shashi Kapoor acted in 33 of L-P's films**, including *Satyam Shivam Sundaram* (1978), *Suhaag* (1979) and *Vakil Baboo* (1982) where he recorded dialogues for songs, and *Utsav* (1985) as a producer too. He produced and directed *Ajooba* (1991). Mohammed Rafi, Mukesh, Mahendra Kapoor, Manna Dey, Kishore Kumar, Kumar, Nitin Mukesh, Kamlesh Awasthi, Shailendra Singh, Mohammed Aziz and Shashi Kapoor himself were his wide assortment of playback voices.

Manoj Kumar

Shor, Roti Kapada Aur Makaan and *Kranti* as writer-producer-director-editor and actor; *Jai Hind—The Pride* as writer-producer-director and editor; and *Kranti*. In *Kranti, Santosh* and *Jai Hind—The Pride* he also featured as lyricist. Manoj Kumar had a deep personal bond with L-P in a long association from 1967 to 1999. Manoj Kumar also presented *Deshwasi*, in which he had a cameo, while *Anita, Patthar Ke Sanam, Sajan, Dus Numbri* and *Santosh* also featured him in the lead. *Mujhe Insaaf Chahiye* saw him in a cameo as well. Mohammed Rafi, Mukesh, Mahendra Kapoor and Nitin Mukesh were his playback voices.

K. Vishwanath

K. Vishwanath wrote and directed *Sargam, Sur-Sangam, Sanjog* and *Eeshwar* in a decade-long association with L-P.

Vinod Khanna

Between 1970 and 1993, **Vinod Khanna starred in 31 films of L-P**, including *The Cheat* (1974), which was his home production. His playback voices were Mohammed Rafi, Mukesh, Mahendra Kapoor, Kishore Kumar, Manhar Udhas, Sudesh Bhonsle, Shailendra Singh, Mohammed Aziz and Amit Kumar

Amitabh Bachchan

Twenty-one films in the lead, including home production *Khuda Gawah*, in which he also recited the theme, make up Amitabh Bachchan's work with L-P. He also had cameos in *Dost* and *Kroadh* and was the narrator in *Ghulami* and *Batwara*. He also sang in *Naseeb* and recited a famous passage in *Amar Akbar Anthony*. His other playback singers were Mohammed Rafi, Mukesh, Mahendra Kapoor, Kishore Kumar, Amit Kumar, Sudesh Bhosle, Anwar, Shabbir Kumar, Mohammed Aziz, Laxmikant himself and Prayag Raj.

Rajinikanth

Besides his Hindi debut in *Andhaa Kaanoon*, L-P did Rajinikanth's triple role film *John Jani Janardhan*, *Chaalbaaz*, *Hum* and six more films. S.P. Balasubramaniam, Shailendra Singh, Mohammed Aziz, Suresh Wadkar, Hariharan, Vinay Mandke, Laxmikant himself, Manhar and Sudesh Bhosle sang for him.

Appendix 6

THE BIGGIES THAT NEVER MADE IT

Like everyone else, Laxmikant-Pyarelal had their share of shelved films, but with the way they worked and their prolific output, the quantum was mind-boggling.

We begin with the exquisite *Rajmata*, which we have mentioned earlier. We would love to hear the song rendered by Lata Mangeshkar for this bi-lingual Nutan-Sunil Dutt-Parikshat Sahni film.

A song I missed was Lata's four-language song recorded by R.K. Nayyar for his later-shelved directorial *Yeh Jo Mohabbat Hai*—Laxmikant had even invited me for the recording! But I had another scheduled commitment and never imagined that this Sanjay Dutt-Madhuri Dixit launched in the early 1990s would never see the light of day! Many years later, Sadhana, Nayyar's wife, admitted that she did have that song, but it was on a spool that was used in those days!

Mohammed Rafi's song from J.P. Dutta's first launched film, *Sarhad*, still exists with the filmmaker. The Sahir-written song for the shelved Vinod Khanna-Naseeruddin Shah-Mithun Chakraborty-Bindiya Goswami film was announced with a full-page spread in *Screen* when it was recorded.

Another film that could not be made was J.P. Dutta's *Bandhua* featuring Amitabh Bachchan.

The duo was to do Manoj Kumar's *Naya Bharat* with an impossible cast on which there are many surmises. This film was to be made after *Roti Kapada Aur Makaan* and starred, at least, Manoj Kumar, Rajesh Khanna, Amitabh Bachchan and Zeenat Aman. Other possible names thrown up then included one or more of Shashi Kapoor, Rishi Kapoor, Shatrughan Sinha, Hema Malini and Moushumi Chaterjee, in addition to some of the earlier names, that is!

Manmohan Desai, after *Dharam-Veer*, had made a Diwali 1977

announcement of *Ghazab* featuring the entire cast of that film (Dharmendra, Jeetendra, Zeenat Aman and Neetu Singh) along with Amitabh Bachchan, Rishi Kapoor, Hema Malini and Parveen Babi. Later, another producer announced another *Ghazab* with the director, featuring Bachchan, Khanna, Rishi and Randhir Kapoor and Zeenat Aman. Both films were still-born. And L-P did have a different *Ghazab*, a South remake, in 1982!

Then there was Manmohan Desai's freedom saga *Sarfarosh* featuring Amitabh Bachchan, Rishi Kapoor and Parveen Babi. L-P later did Jeetendra's home production of that name in 1985!

Desai had been assigned to make *Bajirao Mastani* with Rajesh Khanna and Hema Malini, which was the actor's home production in 70mm. It was to be produced by Khanna's maternal uncle K.K. Talwar.

A Subhash Desai production, to be directed by Surendra Mohan, was *Khuda Gawah* featuring Bachchan, Rishi Kapoor, Parveen Babi and Bengal's Uttam Kumar and Supriya Chowdhury—it was to be a cowboy Western in genre. It had nothing to do with L-P's 1992 release of that name, which was Bachchan's home production.

Prayag Raj was to direct *Ram Krishna Hari* with Shammi Kapoor, Shashi Kapoor and Randhir Kapoor.

70mm was a passing infatuation after *Sholay* and L-P got more such films than anyone else. *Time Bomb* (later called *Lajawab*) featuring Dharmendra and Hema Malini was to be directed by Pramod Chakravorty. O.P. Ralhan's *Samson and Delilah* was to be made with the same pair. Chakravorty was to make at least one more film with Dharmendra and L-P.

Speaking of *Sholay*, Ramesh Sippy had announced *Ram Ki Seeta Shyam Ki Geeta*, which never took off. Proposals, and not proper projects, were indeed endemic in the 1970s and 1980s!

Sippy then took on *Zameen* in the late '80s. The film was to star Vinod Khanna, Rajinikanth, Sridevi, Sanjay Dutt, Madhuri Dixit and Sujata Mehta. A song was recorded by Alisha Chinoy for Dixit, and the crooner made the unforgivably pompous blunder of saying in an interview, 'The song is okay, but it is for some actress called Madhuri Dixit or something.' This was obviously just before the release of *Tezaab* and she never got to sing for Dixit ever again!

This film's producer, Suresh Malhotra, a tycoon then, also launched the unique *Time Machine*, to be directed by Shekhar Kapur after *Mr India*, with Naseeruddin Shah and Rekha playing Aamir Khan's parents. Raveena Tandon was the leading lady and Vijay Anand the scientist who invents the machine. A song by Udit Narayan was also recorded. Reportedly 75 per cent of the film was shot before funds ran dry and then Kapur went to the U.S.

Dharmendra and Shakti Samanta were to work on *Mahaguru*, the latter's return to crime after multiple socials. Madan Mohla, a staunch loyalist, had also announced *Paapi Devta* with Dharmendra and Zeenat Aman—with Hema Malini in a cameo! Dulal Guha was the director.

Jeetendra, Hema Malini and Amitbah Bachchan were to do the social-issue film *Paani*, directed by Dulal Guha and produced by Jeetendra's brother Prasanna Kapoor.

There is also a poster announcement that *Ek Do Teen Char* (produced by Hema Malini's secretary I.K. Bahl) featuring Dev Anand, Dharmendra, Shashi Kapoor, Rishi Kapoor, Hema Malini, Raakhee, Praveen Babi and Tina Munim was to have their music. Whether L-P's name was announced before R.D. Burman's or later, is now in the realm of conjecture. Vijay Anand was to direct the film.

After the success of the Hollywood disaster film *The Towering Inferno*, Ramesh Meer, a special effects expert even then, decided to make a film in the same mould in 70mm: *Aag Aur Angaarey*. Sanjeev Kumar, Jeetendra, Vinod Khanna, Sulakshana Pandit, Parveen Babi and Zarina Wahab were to star in the film.

Jeetendra, Hema Malini and Sulakshana Pandit were to also star in a film produced by recording whiz Mangesh Desai. However, wiser counsel must have prevailed and the latter dropped the idea of dabbling in filmmaking.

Shashi Kapoor was to star in an Arjun Hingorani presentation, *New York New York*. This film was also still-born. With Hema Malini and Feroz Khan, he was to do *Zindaan* for director Ashok Roy.

Raj Khosla was to direct the 70mm *Nawab Aur Sharab* announced by Amarjeet, Dev Anand's right-hand man. Sunil Dutt, Sanjeev Kumar and Zeenat Aman were to co-star in the film. It was later titled *Nawab Aur Shabab* after the Emergency was declared in 1975 and the authorities found the word *sharab* (alcohol) objectionable. The film was never made.

Raj Khosla was also to direct Mushir-Riaz's *Tijori* featuring Dev Anand.

Shammi Kapoor was pitted to direct *Aaghaaz Aur Anjaam* as a Mohan Kumar presentation. The 70mm film was to star Dharmendra, Shashi Kapoor and Zeenat Aman and was a Diwali 1973 announcement. Later, the senior Kapoor backed out on creative differences and Kumar stepped in as a director. But the film did not take off.

Mohan Kumar had also announced *Aakhri Jaam* with Rishi Kapoor and Rameshwari sometime later. He was to also direct *Aasmaan* with Dharmendra, Hema Malini, Amitabh Bachchan and Rekha.

Deb Mukerji, today's director Ayan Mukerji's father, was to direct the multi-star *Dehati* featuring Shammi Kapoor, Jeetendra and his brother Joy Mukerji.

But the cake was taken by Ramanand Sagar, who was to make the 70mm mammoth film *Yogeshwar Krishna*. Rajendra Kumar (as Yudhishtir), Dharmendra (Arjun), Shashi Kapoor (Krishna), Dara Singh (Bhim), Vinod Khanna (Karna), Hema Malini (Draupadi), Sulakshana Pandit (Rukmini), Amjad Khan (Duryodhan) and Tamanna were to star in the film!

R.K. Nayyar was the man who truly made awe-inspiring announcements with them: *Krishna—The Hindu Story* was the biggest of them. This was to be the first of a series of mythological movies, and it had Rishi Kapoor as Lord Krishna!

At various points before this, Nayyar, in the 1970s, had announced *Gurkha Jung Bahadur* with Rajesh Khanna, and another film with Rishi Kapoor.

Subhash Ghai was another filmmaker who had announced a musical, *Sangeet*, with Kamal Haasan and Jaya Prada in 1982, and the Amitabh Bachchan film *Devaa* later, whose recorded song by Alka Yagnik, Ila Arun and Mohammed Aziz was played during Yagnik's *sangeet* ceremony before her wedding.

A couple of years later, Kamal Haasan and Jaya Prada were also to reprise their roles in the Hindi remake of the 1983 Telugu classic *Sagara Sangamam* directed by K. Vishwanath.

At different times, mostly in the 1970s, there were announcements of films to be directed by Mahesh Bhatt with L-P's music, mostly starring Vinod Khanna. None took off. In the 1980s, after *Naam*, producer-actor

Kumar Gaurav and director Mahesh Bhatt were to make *Naraaz* starring Raakhee, Kumar Gaurav, Madhuri Dixit and Naseeruddin Shah.

Finally, here is Kader Khan's recorded quote in *Screen*: 'I announced my production *Jaahil* in *Screen* with a full-page spread and just these words: 'Kader Khan presents *Jaahil*. Starring Amitabh Bachchan Music Laxmikant-Pyarelal'. All my territories were sold overnight! But we could not finally make the film because of Bachchan saab's illness.'

Sanjay Khan had announced a mega-budget film named *Sur-Zameen* with a cast led by Vinod Khanna. This film even had a song recording by Reshma, who had sung 'Lambi Judaai' for the duo. It did not go beyond the announcement stage.

An interesting film that never took off was *Karishma*, which was a remake of *The Reincarnation of Peter Proud*, and it was to be directed by Sunil Sikand, Pran's son, as his debut. Shashi Kapoor, Amitabh Bachchan, Sharmila Tagore and Parveen Babi were to be in the cast. And we say it is interesting because this Hollywood story soon inspired the cult Subhash Ghai film *Karz*.

Appendix 7

THE GARDENERS OF TALENT

Apart from making actors take to the microphone for everything from the interpolation or recitation of a few words to proper singing (see Appendix 2), Laxmikant-Pyarelal have had a major role in introducing new talent. Equally importantly, they have made it their business to give the career-defining breakthrough songs to so many artistes who were actually discovered by other composers.

I. Prominent Singers Introduced by Laxmikant-Pyarelal

1. **Sulakshana Pandit** (as child singer): *Taqdeer* (1967)
2. **Usha Uthup:** *Devi* (1970)
3. **Shailendra Singh:** *Bobby* (1973)
4. **Narendra Chanchal:** *Bobby* (1973)
5. **Talat Aziz:** *Aurat Aurat Aurat* (**First film song recorded in 1980**)
6. **Kavita Krishnamurthi Subramaniam:**
   As dubbing artiste: *Chacha Bhatija* (1977)
   As original singer: *Maang Bharo Sajana* (1980)
7. **S.P. Balasubramaniam** (in Hindi films): *Ek Duuje Ke Liye* (1981)
8. **Abhijeet:** *Mujhe Insaf Chahiye* (1983—**First released film and song**)
9. **Reshma (in Hindi films):** *Hero* (1983)
10. **Sukhwinder Singh:**
    A few lines: *Naam* (1986)
    As singer: *Karma* (1986)
11. **Roopkumar Rathod:** *Angaar* (1992)
12. **Bali Brahmbhatt:** *Roop Ki Rani Choron Ka Raja* (1993)

II. Prominent Singers Whose Career Breakthroughs Were with Laxmikant-Pyarelal

1. **Nitin Mukesh:** *Kranti** (1981) Introduced by Shanker-Jaikishan in 1970.

2. **Suresh Wadkar**: *Prem Rog** (1982) Introduced by Jaidev in 1978
3. **Shabbir Kumar**: *Coolie* (1983) Introduced by Usha Khanna in 1981.
4. **Anuradha Paudwal**: *Hero** (1983) Introduced by Kalyanji-Anandji in 1976.
5. **Manhar Udhas**: *Hero** (1983) Introduced by Kalyanji-Anandji in 1969.
6. **Mohammed Aziz**: In 1986 with 16 films of Laxmikant-Pyarelal, beginning with *Love '86*, followed by *Aakhree Raasta, Amrit, Karma, Nagina* and others. Introduced by Sapan-Jagmohan in 1983.
7. **Pankaj Udhas**: *Naam** (1986) Introduced by Usha Khanna in 1969.
8. **Alisha Chinai**: *Mr India* (1987) Introduced by Bappi Lahiri in 1985.
9. **Alka Yagnik**: *Tezaab** (1988) Introduced by Kalyanji-Anandji in 1981.
10. **Sudesh Bhosle**: *Hum** (1991) Introduced by R.D. Burman in 1988.
11. **Ila Arun**: *Khal Nayak** (1993) Introduced by Anu Malik, but with first release by Bappi Lahiri in 1985.

---

*These breakthrough numbers, however, were not their first recorded songs with Laxmikant-Pyarelal.

Appendix 8

WHEN LAXMIKANT-PYARELAL ENTERED HOME GROUND

Professionally, Laxmikant-Pyarelal reached a new high by doing films that were productions/unofficial productions/home productions/directorial ventures of many stars. Here is a list of such films.

A. Nageshwara Rao

The matinee idol of Telugu cinema never acted in Hindi films but produced the Jeetendra-Rekha-Reena Roy film *Prem Tapasya* (1983).

Amitabh Bachchan

Khuda Gawah (1992) was his home production officially produced by Manoj Desai and Nazir Ahmed.

Anil Kapoor, Sanjay Kapoor & Sridevi

Not only was Anil Kapoor the co-producer with brother Boney Kapoor for Sanjay Kapoor's launch-pad *Prem* (1995), but his *Woh 7 Din* (1983), *Mr India* (1987) and *Roop Ki Rani Choron Ka Raja* (1993) were also his family's productions. The last mentioned featured Sridevi after her marriage to Boney Kapoor and was her home production too!

Ashok Kumar & Anoop Kumar

Aansoo Ban Gaye Phool (1969) was Ashok Kumar's home production, which he presented, though it was officially produced by his actor-brother Anoop Kumar.

Asrani

The actor-comedian directed *Dil Hi To Hai* (1993).

Chetan Anand

The filmmaker, a one-time actor, directed and co-wrote *Jaaneman* (1976), the remake of his own film *Taxi Driver*.

Chiranjeevi

The South icon's Hindi debut *Pratibandh* (1990), was also his home production, produced by brother Allu Aravind.

Coca-Cola

The comedian, real name Kamal Raj Bhasin, produced the delayed film that was released under a new name—*Kaun Rokega Mujhe?*

Dev Anand

Dev Anand produced *Jaaneman* (1976) as a part of his banner Navketan's silver jubilee offerings, and his right-hand man Amarjeet produced *Prem Shastra* (1974).

Dharmendra & Sunny Deol

Pratiggya (1975) was his home production, officially co-produced by actor-brother Kanwar Ajit (Singh) and brother-in-law Bikram Singh. Bikram Singh also produced *Yateem* (1989). Dharmendra's brother-in-law S.J.S. Punchhe turned producer with *Satyakam* (1970). His brother-in-law Ranjit Virk officially produced *Krodhi* (1981). Their home production *Yamla Pagla Deewana* had its title derived from their Laxmikant-Pyarelal hit from *Pratiggya* and the song was re-created in it with L-P duly and prominently credited.

Feroz Khan

Feroz Khan produced, directed, edited and starred in *Dayavan* (1988).

Hema Malini

Hema Malini's mother Jaya Chakravarti and secretary I.K. Bahl produced *Dream Girl* (1977), in which Hema also sang a song. Her brother R.J. Chakravarti produced *Sharara* (1984), while her aunt R. Renuka produced *Do Disayen* (1983).

Jalal Agha

Along with Dhoondy, the comedian and character actor co-directed *Aadha Din Aadhi Raat* (1977) featuring Vinod Khanna and Shabana Azmi.

Jaymala

The actress, who was married to trade analyst and director B.K. Adarsh, produced and played the lead in *Spy In Rome* (1968).

Jeetendra

Jeetendra's brother Prasanna Kapur officially produced *Humjoli* (1970), *Jyoti Bane Jwala* (1980), *Pyaasa Sawan* (1981), *Deedaar-E-Yaar* (1982), *Sarfarosh* (1985) and *Aag Aur Shola* (1986).

Joy Mukerji

The actor directed his brother Shomu Mukerji's *Chhaila Babu* (1977). Incidentally, Shomu had married actress Tanuja and later produced and directed *Fiffty Fiffty* (1981).

Kumar Gaurav

The actor was billed as the producer of his father Rajendra Kumar's production to launch him—*Naam* (1986).

Manoj Kumar & Kunal Goswami

Mnaoj Kumar was writer-producer-director-editor in *Shor* (1972), *Roti Kapada Aur Makaan* (1974) and also *Kranti* (1981) and *Jai Hind—The Pride* (1999), in both of which he also wrote some lyrics. He acted in all films except the last.

Mehmood

Sadhu Aur Shaitan (1968) was his home production.

N.A. Ansari

The filmmaker-character actor produced and directed *Jurm Aur Saza* (1974) featuring Nanda and Vinod Mehra.

Nana Patekar

Nana Patekar directed, co-scripted and starred in *Prahaar* (1991).

Nanda

Veteran director Ravi Tandon revealed that *Nazrana* (1987), which he directed, was actress Nanda's home production, officially co-produced by her brother C.V.K. Shastry.

Nishi Kohli

The actress produced *Bees Saal Baad* (1989) and penned the story of *Badle Ki Aag* (1982). She had married filmmaker Rajkumar Kohli and presented most of his films with L-P.

Pran

The legendary actor co-produced *Lakshman Rekha* (1991) directed by his son Sunil Sikand.

Prem Chopra

Prem Chopra's brother Kailash Chopra co-produced *Lagan* (1971) with some South producers. Chopra was the male protagonist in it.

Raakhee

Raakhee's secretary Yusuf Hasan produced her film *Pagli* (1974). Later, her brother Shibranjan Majumdar co-produced *Taaqat* (1982), in which she also sang a song.

Raj Kapoor

Raj Kapoor produced, directed and edited *Bobby* (1973), *Satyam Shivam Sundaram* (1978) and *Prem Rog* (1982).

Rajan Sippy

Small-time actor Rajan Sippy produced *Shoor-Veer* (1988) and *Shehzaade* (1989), a multi-star film.

Rajeev Goswami

Manoj Kumar's actor brother acted in, produced, directed and edited *Deshwasi* (1991).

Rajendra Kumar

Besides backing *Naam*, Rajendra Kumar's other home production was *Gaon Hamara Shehar Tumhara* (1972) directed and officially produced by his brother Naresh Kumar.

Rajesh Khanna

Rajesh Khanna's maternal uncle K.K. Talwar co-produced his home productions *Roti* (1974) and *Aashiq Hoon Baharon Ka* (1977). His secretary Yusuf Hasan produced *Chakravyuha* (1979). In his initial hysteria days, Khanna also invested in H.S. Rawail's *Mehboob Ki Mehndi* (1971).

Randhir, Rishi & Rajiv Kapoor

The three brothers jointly produced *Prem Granth* (1996) in which Rishi acted as the hero. It was directed and edited by Rajiv Kapoor.

Reena Roy

Reena Roy's brother Raja Roy and secretary Desai produced *Muqabla* (1979). Raja Roy later produced *Takrao*, which remained incomplete, but Reena had quit the film after her marriage and Hema Malini had come in.

Sachin

Sachin directed, co-scripted and sang in *Prem Deewane* (1992).

Sadhana

Intaqam (1969) was Sadhana's home production directed by R.K. Nayyar, her husband. Sadhana also took official credit as director of her film *Geetaa Mera Naam* (1974) though her husband had ghost-directed it. Later, the couple made *Qatl* (1986) and *Pati Parmeshwar* (1989) with other heroines.

Sanjay Khan

Kala Dhanda Goray Log (1986) was directed by Sanjay Khan from his own story. He also starred as one of the three heroes in the film.

Sanjeev Kumar

Nakul Jariwala, Sanjeev Kumar's brother, co-produced the action drama *Do Waqt Ki Roti* (1988) featuring Sanjeev Kumar and Feroz Khan. The delayed film released in some parts of India three years after Sanjeev had passed away.

Satish Kaushik

The actor turned director made *Roop Ki Rani Choron Ka Raja* (1993) and *Prem* (1996). Before that, he was also associate director on *Mr India* (1987).

Shashi Kapoor

Besides recording dialogues in L-P's songs in three films, *Satyam Shivam Sundaram* (1978), *Suhaag* (1979) and *Vakil Baboo* (1982), Shashi Kapoor produced *Utsav* (1985) and produced and directed *Ajooba* (1991).

Shekhar Kapur

The actor-turned-director helmed *Mr India* (1987).

Soodesh Kumar

The character artiste produced *Manmandir* (1971), *Badaltey Rishtey* (1978) and *Jaan Hatheli Pe* (1987).

Som Dutt

Sunil Dutt's actor-brother produced *Yaari Dushmani* (1980) starring his brother.

Subhash Ghai

Subhash Ghai was an actor until he found his métier as a writer and filmmaker. He acted in L-P's *Taqdeer* (1967) and *Naatak* (1976) and then wrote, produced or/and directed a chain of films with them—*Gautam Govinda* (1979), *Karz* (1980), *Krodhi* (1981), *Hero* (1983), *Meri Jung* (1985), *Karma* (1986), *Ram Lakhan* (1989), *Saudagar* (1991), *Khal Nayak* (1993) and *Trimurti* (1995). He also wrote the story of *Yaari Dushmani*

(1980) and presented *Uttar Dakshin* (1987) from his own story, and *Prem Deewane* (1992).

Sunil Dutt

Sunil Dutt directed *Daku Aur Jawan* (1979) in which he co-starred with Vinod Khanna.

V. Shantaram & Sandhya

Sandhya starred in husband V. Shantaram's (also an erstwhile hero) film *Jal Bin Machhli Nritya Bin Bijli* (1971).

Vijay Anand

Also an actor, including in L-P's *Main Tulsi Tere Aangan Ki* (1978), Vijay Anand directed, edited and wrote *Ram Balram* (1980) and *Rajput* (1982).

Vinod Khanna

Vinod Khanna's home production *The Cheat* (1974) was officially co-produced by his brother Pramod Khanna, who recently played his role in *Dabangg 3*.

Appendix 9

A FEW MISSES AND THE LONGEST BONDS

For all their sweeping canvas of work, Laxmikant-Pyarelal did miss out on some huge names in the industry that were active in their times. Among those giants were producers S.S. Vasan of Gemini Productions, Gulshan Rai of Trimurti Films and Nasir Husain of Nasir Husain Films besides director Prakash Mehra.

And here are their longest bonds, first in number of films done together, and then in the number of years, possibly with lesser films.

Number of Films

T. Rama Rao—20 (1979-1990) 11 Years
K. Bapaiah—13 (1977-1991) 15 Years
Harmesh Malhotra—12 (1973-1992) 20 Years
J. Om Prakash—12 (1966-1988) 23 Years
K.C. Bokadia in various capacities—12 (1980-1994) 15 Years
Rajkumar Kohli—11 (1966-1990) 25 Years
L.V. Prasad—10 (1967-1986) 20 Years
Raj Khosla—10 (1967-1984) 18 Years
Subhash Ghai—10 (1979-1995) 17 Years
Manmohan Desai—9 (1974-1983) 10 Years
Mohan Kumar—9 (1969-1990) 22 Years
Dasari Narayana Rao—8 (1980-1987) 8 Years including a Telugu film

Number of Years

28 Years Manoj Kumar—4 official and some unofficial! (1972-1999)
27 Years Kalpataru a.k.a. K. Parvez—7 (1967-1993)
27 Years Madan Mohla—6 (1966-1992)
27 Years Premji—7 (1970-1996)

Appendix 9

25 Years Rajkumar Kohli—11 (1966-1990)
23 Years J. Om Prakash—12 (1966-1988)
22 Years Mohan Kumar—9 (1969-1990)
21 Years Mohan Segal—6 (1969-1989)
21 Years Surinder Kapoor—7 (1975-1995)
20 Years L.V. Prasad—10 (1967-1986)
20 Years Harmesh Malhotra—12 (1973-1992)
19 Years Dulal Guha—7 (1969-1987)
19 Years Satyen Bose—7 (1964-1982)
18 Years Raj Khosla—10 (1967-1984)

Appendix 10

THE RE-CREATED SONGS OF LAXMIKANT-PYARELAL

Laxmikant-Pyarelal happen to be leaders also in the deluge of re-created/re-used songs in our films, a dubious trend that started insidiously in the last two decades and has grown. Here is a list, as of 2020, of L-P classics re-used *in movies alone*.

1. 'Aa Jaan-E-Jaan' (*Intaqam* / 1969) in *Hello Darling* (2008)
2. 'Aaj Mausam Beimaan' (*Loafer* / 1973) The Mohammed Rafi original was used as it is in *Monsoon Wedding* (2001)
3. 'Aaj Phir Tumpe' (*Dayavan* / 1988) in *Hate Story 2* (2014)
4. 'Bhoot Raja Baahar Aaja' (*Chacha Bhatija* / 1977) in *Housefull 4* (2019)
5. 'Chahe Meri Jaan Tu Le Le' (*Dayavan* / 1988) in *Marjaavaan* (2019)
6. 'Dard-E-Dil' (*Karz* / 1980) in *Aap Kaa Suroor* (2007 / A recitation)
7. 'Ek Do Teen Char' (*Tezaab* / 1988) in *Baaghi 2* (2018)
8. 'Ek Hasina Thi' (*Karz* / 1980) in *Karzzzz* (the earlier film's 2008 remake)
9. Flute riff from *Hero* (1983) in *Gang Of Ghosts* (2013)
10. Flute riff from *Hero* (1983) in *Heropanti* (2014)
11. 'Hawa Hawaii' (*Mr India* / 1987) in *Shaitan* (2011)
12. 'Hawa Hawaii' (*Mr India* / 1987) in *Tumhari Sulu* (2017) (Incorporated the original sung by Kavita Krishnamurthi Subramaniam)
13. 'Hum Tum Ek Kamre' (*Bobby* / 1973) in *Hum Tum* (2004) (Recorded again in the voice of original singer Shailendra Singh as a solo)
14. 'Hungama Ho Gaya' (*Anhonee* / 1973) in *Queen* (2014) (Incorporated the original voice of Asha Bhosle)
15. 'Kaate Nahin Kat-Te' (*Mr India* / 1987) in *Sooper Se Ooper* (2013)

16. 'Main Jat Yamla' (*Pratiggya*/1975) in *Yamla Pagla Deewana* (2011)
17. 'Main Shaayar To Nahin' (*Bobby*/1973) in *Saawariya* (2007/A recitation)
18. 'My Name Is Lakhan' (*Ram Lakhan*/1989) in *Gangs Of Wasseypur* (2012)
19. 'Na Jaane Kahan Se' (*Chaalbaaz*/1989) in *I Me Aur Main* (2013)
20. 'O Meri Mehbooba' (*Dharam-Veer*/1977) in *Fukrey Returns* (2017) (Incorporated a part of the Mohammed Rafi original)
21. 'O Meri Mehbooba' (*Dharam-Veer*/1977) in *Yamla Pagla Deewana Phir Se* (2018)
22. 'Paisa Yeh Paisa' (*Karz*/1980) in *Total Dhamaal* (2019)
23. Prelude Music of 'Haye Haye Yeh Majboori' (*Roti Kapada Aur Makaan*/1974) in *Kaminey* (2009)
24. Prelude Music of 'Haye Haye Yeh Majboori' (*Roti Kapada Aur Makaan*/1974) in *Love Aaj Kal* (2009)
25. 'Ruk Janna Nahin' (*Imtihan*/1974) in *Soundtrack* (2011)
26. 'So Gaya Yeh Jahaan' (*Tezaab*/1988) in *Bypass Road* (2019) (Nitin Mukesh re-recorded his own portion)
27. 'So Gaya Yeh Jahaan' (*Tezaab*/1988) in *Nautanki Saala!* (2013) (The original was used with a faster beat)
28. 'Taiyab Ali' (*Amar Akbar Anthony*/1977) in *Once Upon A Time in Mumbaai Dobaara* (2015)
29. 'Tera Beemar Mera Dil' (*Chaalbaaz*/1989) in *Pagalpanti* (2019)
30. 'Yeh Jeevan Hai' (*Piya Ka Ghar*/1972) in *Soundtrack* (2011)

BIBLIOGRAPHY

Binaca Geetmala, audio excerpts, courtesy Ameen Sayani and Rajil Sayani.

LP Discography by Aditya Pant

Gulzar Bolar, 'The Incredible Men Behind the Hits and Splits of Laxmi-Pyare', *Showtime*, April 1992.

Interviews by Rajiv Vijayakar of Laxmikant-Pyarelal and Pyarelal in *G magazine, Screen, Rediff.com, bollywoodhungama.com, Deccan Herald* and *India West (USA)*.

Interviews by Rajiv Vijayakar of A.R. Rahman, K. Vishwanath, Mohan Segal, J. Om Prakash, Raj Khosla, Manoj Kumar, Subhash Ghai, Ameen Sayani, Shammi Kapoor, Sadhana Nayyar, Manna Dey, Mahendra Kapoor, Lata Mangeshkar, Hasrat Jaipuri, D.O. Bhansali, Majrooh Sultanpuri, S.P. Balasubramaniam, Kavita Krishnamurthi Subramaniam, Alka Yagnik, Shabbir Kumar, Suresh Wadkar, Sukhwinder Singh, Pankaj Udhas, Talat Aziz, Roopkumar Rathod, Sameer, Vishal Bhardwaj, Himesh Reshammiya, Sanjay Tandon, Sivamani, Sonu Nigam, and some others for *Screen, Mid-Day, India West (USA), Deccan Herald, Rediff. com, bollywoodhungama.com* and *G Magazine*.

Pyarelal Interview by Dr Shekhar. Available at https://groups.google.com/g/rec.music.indian.misc/c/_OQz_zOf9rw/m/pgSL4VigArcJ?pli=1. Accessed on 10 September 2021.

Rajiv Vijayakar, 'LP Record: Parts I & II', *Junior G*, Chitralekha Publications.

Rajiv Vijayakar, 'Shor' and 'Roti Kapada Aur Makaan', from '100 Greatest Films of All Time', *Stardust Special Issue*, Magna Publications.

ACKNOWLEDGEMENTS

A labour of love like this cannot be written without the involvement of the labour of love of many, many others.

So many wonderful people helped me in writing this book on my favourite composers. During the process I realized, to my unending delight, that I was actually penning an account of Hindi cinema's most complete, comprehensive and—dare I say—brilliant composers.

To start with, it felt surreal to enter the portals of a renovated Parasmani, Laxmikant Shantaram Kudalkar's bungalow, 21 years after his passing, and meeting his wife Jaya and daughter Rajeshwari. Long conversations and phone discussions followed. The two were forthrightness epitomized, and they introduced me to Jaya ji's sisters, Dr Priti Galvankar and the legendary actress Bindu. Bindu ji broke down more than once—clearly, the memories of her brother-in-law remain unalloyed by time as they are too proximal, too personal.

Pyarelal Ramprasad Sharma is someone with whom I was always in touch, but he met me often for the book itself, telling me every time that it was his pleasure to talk to *me*! Can you imagine the greatest violinist in the country saying that?

Of special importance were the men and women closest to Laxmikant-Pyarelal, or L-P as they are known, who took out endless time for me—Jeetendra, Anil Kapoor, Jackie Shroff, K. Vishwanath (whom I had met in the '90s, but one call was all it took), Kiran Shantaram, Rajkumar Kohli, Ravi Tandon, Subhash Ghai, Boney Kapoor, Amit Khanna, Pankuj Parashar, Satish Kaushik, Ketan Manmohan Desai and L-P's dearest admirers and colleagues, Amar Haldipur and Rajesh Roshan. Emotions suffused their memories.

Singers Nitin Mukesh, Manhar Udhas, Pankaj Udhas, Shailendra Singh, Talat Aziz, Sudesh Bhosle, Roopkumar Rathod, Shabbir Kumar, Anuradha Paudwal, Alka Yagnik, Kavita Krishnamurthi Subramaniam and even the late Narendra Chanchal (whose phone number I had found on the Internet and had called on a whim, but who obliged my questions and spoke at length on the duo) have all made this book much more special.

And what a phenomenal contribution the iconic Pt Hariprasad Chaurasia has made! The man truly has no equal.

An important mention would be of Madhuri Dixit-Nene, one of those rare individuals who has never forgotten that, on her way up the superstardom ladder, Laxmikant-Pyarelal had made a major contribution. In this self-centred era, the down-to-earth actress made time to speak with me on the phone for over 20 minutes rather than just anwer my questions impersonally over an email.

Two giants who made surprisingly monumental insights were Anu Malik and—very personally and emotionally—Shreya Ghoshal.

A truly revelatory contribution was made by my friend, the musician, musicologist and researcher, Dr Deepak Raja. In easy-to-understand musical terms, he gave a dazzling insight into the seemingly magical quality of L-P's compositions. And he has never met the duo!

Last, but not the least, I must thank Rudra Narayan Sharma for nurturing this book like his own, and to the Rupa Publications team with N.N. Anjasi, who did the copy-editing, and Amrita Chakravorty, for the fabulous cover design. Last but not the least, my gratitude for Mrs Jaya Laxmikant and Anil Bohra for the cover photograph.